AN URBAN
STRATEGY
FOR LATIN
AMERICA

AN URBAN STRATEGY FOR LATIN AMERICA

roger s. greenway

BAKER BOOK HOUSE
Grand Rapids, Michigan

TO EDNA

My wife and true companion

in faith, labor, and purpose

FOREWORD

"Ought to" books in the field of mission methods and philosophy are numerous; "how to" books are rare. Rarer still are the books that deal realistically with a strategy for urban missions. The history of the twentieth century is the story of man moving to the cities. The history of missions through the ages is basically a story of frustration on the part of people who tried to "find and fold" the wandering sheep in the urban jungle.

This book flows from the converging of many timely factors. One, it speaks of evangelization in Latin America at the "fullness of times." The restrictions of former years began to thaw with the work of the political liberators; the glacier was reduced greatly by the influence of liberal journalists and educators; concern for the man with the hoe and the declaration of human dignity proclaimed by both Marxist and Christian thinkers changed the pace from glacial slowness to a flood of demands for change and life on better terms than the masses had known before. In addition, Vatican II gathered up these and other currents and projected the Roman Catholic world into a new day of openness. Under the leadership of enlightened members of the Catholic clergy the movement toward spiritual life is becoming a "river in spate."

Another factor that adds to the value of this book is a sound conversion theology. Roger Greenway combines the best of a Calvinist theological inheritance with the "church growth-verdict theology" of the McGavran-Fuller emphasis. He brings realistic experience in church planting in Mexico City, and combines it with two years of diligent study and research in total mission history—in classical missionary literature and in current books and periodicals. He combines, thus, the best of practice with the best of academic theory and research.

All of this combines in an excellent book which can give realistic help to those who see the cities as today's opportunity and seek ways in which to capitalize on it.

CALVIN GUY
Professor of Missions
Southwestern Baptist Theological Seminary
Fort Worth, Texas

CONTENTS

PART III

Christian Roles and Responsibilities
in Latin American Cities

PART IV

Urban Strategy Tested in a Latin American City

INTRODUCTION

"Christian missionaries should be strategists," said the great preacher F. B. Meyer, "expending their strength where populations teem and rivers of world-wide influence have their rise."[1] With this idea in mind, I have prepared the following chapters in the hope that they will contribute toward a better understanding of the church's task in Latin American cities and the kind of strategy which will bring multitudes into the fold of Jesus Christ.

Among the ancient Egyptians, the hieroglyph representing the city was a circle with a cross in it. The circle stood for the wall or moat surrounding the city, and the cross represented the streets which led to the central market or forum, or temple. There was symmetry in those ancient cities, plus a neatness and order which no longer exist today.[2] A hieroglyph of the modern city would show a jumble of circles and crossroads, with highways extending from the city in every direction, and the mark of confusion could hardly be omitted. But the circle with a cross in it, analogically, represents the ultimate goal of the church's mission: the unification of urban life around the pivotal center of Christianity.

The purpose of this study is to explain and demonstrate the opportunity provided by modern urbanization for the spread of the gospel in Latin America. With special reference to Mexico

---

1. Cited in Fred E. Edwards, *The Role of the Faith Mission: A Brazilian Case Study* (South Pasadena, Calif.: William Carey Library, 1971), p. v.
2. Martin E. Marty, *Babylon by Choice: New Environment for Mission* (New York: Friendship Press, 1965), p. 56.

City, which is assumed to be typical of many other urban centers, it will be shown that certain sectors of the city population can be discipled and churches planted in great number during the present period of rapid urbanization.

What hope is there that Latin America will be converted to evangelical Christianity? Bright hope now gleams, and modern urbanization is part of the reason. God controls history and works through it to accomplish His redemptive purposes, and in this light the growth of cities should be viewed. What is happening is His doing, and this includes the confusing processes of urbanization. The Christian duty is to understand and accept the new urban environment of Christian missions, and move forward in the confidence that great things lie ahead.

"Conversion is a slow process," wrote the Spanish philosopher Miguel de Unamuno. "While it appears to erupt suddenly it is actually like the butterfly when it breaks the cocoon or the chick when it cracks the shell: an inner process has preceded it."[3] God has been at work a long time in Latin America. It is not as in parts of Asia or Africa where men can be found who never heard the name of Jesus. Confused, strangely syncretized, and tragically devoid of Biblical teaching; nevertheless, something of Christian knowledge has filtered through. Shaken free by urbaniza-

---

3. *Miguel de Unamuno: Diario Intimo* (Madrid: Alianza Editorial, 1970), p. 174. Translation mine.

tion from fetters of traditional religion, who can say that the time for conversion now has not come?

Men concerned with urban missions are a strange fraternity. They know, on the one hand, that the contemporary city itself is in a fight for survival. Whether it can meet the challenge of change and remain a fit place for human life is still an open question.[4] At the same time, they view the city as one of God's greatest gifts to mankind, as the place, to quote Mumford, where the "magnification of all the dimensions of life" occurs.[5] Therefore they strive together in the task of creating a good city, frightening as the task at times is, because human life and society—in both their beauty and their ugliness—are sacred commodities.

And all the while, these men concerned with city missions remember the Apocalyptic vision which passed from the ancient prophets to the apostle John and which has kept Christian hope alive through twenty centuries. It is the vision of the new Jerusalem, where all human failures at last will be erased, and the cities of men will become the City of God. It is a hope that makes all the present unpleasantries worthwhile; for then, with Jacques Ellul:

---

4. Vincent J. Giese, *Revolution in the City* (Notre Dame, Ind.: Fides Publishers, 1961), pp. vii-viii.
5. Lewis Mumford, *The City in History: Its Origins, Its Transformations, and Its Prospects* (New York: Harcourt, Brace & World, Harbinger Books, 1961), p. 576.

The detestable, gangrenous suburb I have to walk through, the workers' shacks with their peeling paint and permanent layers of dirt, the tool sheds sinking into the sewers and streams that reek of washings and toilets, and the corrugated iron that constitutes man's choicest building material—all are gone, transformed into a wall of pure gold, a new enclosure for the city, pierced by the river of living water, as by an eternal crystal.[6]

6. *The Meaning of the City* (Grand Rapids: Eerdmans Publishing Co., 1970), p. 209.

PART I

MODERN URBANIZATION
IN LATIN AMERICA

1

HISTORICAL ROOTS OF URBANIZATION

When the Spanish conquerors arrived in the sixteenth century they found flourishing urban civilizations in various parts of Middle and South America. The splendor of some of these urban centers evoked the conquerors' amazement. Bernal Díaz del Castillo, an officer in the army of Cortes which entered the city of Tenochtitlán (Mexico City) in 1519, wrote the following description of what the Spaniards saw as they approached the Aztecs' island capital:

> And when we saw all those cities and villages built in the water, and other great towns on dry land, that that [sic] straight and level causeway leading to Mexico, we were astounded. These great towns and *cues* and buildings rising from the water, all made of stone, seemed like an enchanted vision from the tale of Amadis. Indeed, some of our soldiers asked whether it was not all a dream. It is not surprising therefore that I should write in this vein. It was all so wonderful that I do not know how to describe this first glimpse of things never heard of, seen or dreamed of before.[1]

Little did Díaz and his fellow soldiers realize that the great city before them, with its high pyramid-temples, sprawling markets, rich palaces, and gleaming white houses, was actually the product of a long history of growth and development, and that the earliest

---

1. *The Conquest of New Spain,* trans. J. M. Cohen, Harmondsworth, Eng: Penguin Books, 1963), p. 214. Díaz explains that *cues* were temples, very high, and located throughout the cities and towns of Mexico (p. 122).

17

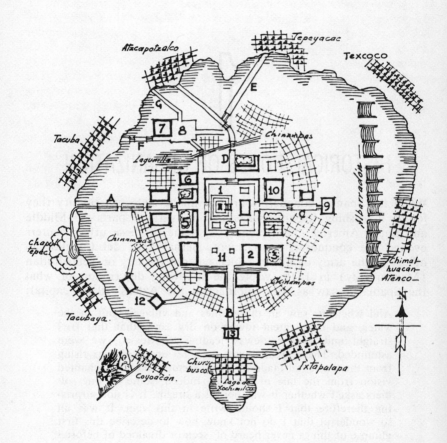

MEXICO CITY IN THE SIXTEENTH CENTURY
Map attributed to Hernan Cortes.

cities in Mexico antedated Tenochtitlán by almost fifteén hundred years.[2] Nor did they know that far to the south, in the central highlands of Peru, even greater urban centers awaited discovery among the Incas.

The *Valle de Mexico* (Valley of Mexico), site of modern Mexico City, has known urban civilization since the first millennium A.D. Lying twenty-five miles northeast of the ancient Aztec capital are the ruins of Teotihuacán, which was the earliest great urban center in Middle America. While Middle American civilization as such did not begin at Teotihuacán, civilized *urban* life of extraordinary proportions certainly flourished there at a very early date. The ruins of great temples, spacious palaces, ample plazas, and extensive residential areas testify to the enormity and complexity of this ancient metropolis.[3]

Religion seems to have permeated the Teotihuacán way of life. Up until the time of the city's fall to the Toltecs, the religious influence of the city extended throughout Middle America. With the founding of the Aztec capital of Tenochtitlán in 1312, the stage was set for a further development in the urban life of the Valley of Mexico, with the political and commercial aspects of the city rising to new prominence.[4]

For the Spaniards, the development of urban centers was an integral part of colonization. Although the initial impact of their arrival often entailed the destruction of existing cities, the conquerors generally did their best to maintain and develop the towns which had already been established by the native people.[5]

> The urban colonization of western South America was part of the largest town building movement in history. Systematic exploration, colonization, and urbanization began with the arrival of Francisco Pizarro's expedition on the northern coast of Peru in 1532. The following half-century was the formative period of the urban ecology of the region as well

---

2. *International Encyclopedia of the Social Sciences,* 1968, s.v. "Early Civilizations of the New World," by René Millon.
3. Ibid., pp. 207-13. Millon points out that "civilization" and "cities" are distinct ideas and should not be confused. "Civilization" refers to qualities pervading a whole society, whether urbanized or not; whereas a preindustrial "city" is a settled community with a concentrated and relatively permanent population.
4. Ibid. For the date of the founding of Tenochtitlán, see Carlos A. Loprete and Dorothy McMahon, *Iberoamérica: Síntesis de su Civilización* (New York: Charles Scribner's Sons, 1965), p. 293.
5. Carlos M. Sabanes, "Urbanization in Latin America," *International Review of Missions* 55 (July 1966): 307-8.

as of the Viceroyalty. By 1582 a pattern of cities and hinterlands, an almost complete framework of human habitation, covered the arable and otherwise useful areas of Peru, Ecuador, and Bolivia, with parts of Chile, Argentina and Colombia—what was then the urbanized region of the Viceroyalty of Peru.[6]

The history of Spanish colonization does much to explain the present urban situation in Latin America. The location of the great urban centers and the distribution of population throughout the hemisphere would be impossible to explain, in fact, without reference to the colonial history of the continent. By 1580, sixteen of the twenty largest cities of modern Latin America had been founded, all of them in accordance with plans and legislation laid down by the Spanish crown.[7]

The motives which the Spaniards had in mind when they established cities shed light on both the locations and the subsequent history of these urban centers. Colonial cities did not spring up spontaneously. Official authorization was necessary for the establishment of a city, and the principal reasons for such authorization were: (1) military occupation, which usually meant that the city waned when its military significance disappeared; (2) development of agriculture in a chosen area; (3) political administration, which was a key factor in the development of the major metropolises of the continent; (4) exploitation of mineral resources, which accounted for mushroom growth when new veins were discovered and rapid decline when the mines were exhausted; and (5) port cities on the coasts, linking the New World to Spain and Portugal, and inland centers through which goods and personnel moved from the hinterland to the coast. The teaching of Roman Catholicism has also been cited as a motive for the Spaniards' enthusiasm for the founding of cities because cities brought large masses together. In some cases, authorization for a new city was simply

---

6. Ralph A. Gakenheimer, "The Peruvian City of the Sixteenth Century," in *The Urban Explosion in Latin America: A Continent in Process of Modernization,* ed. Glenn H. Beyer (Ithaca, N.Y.: Cornell University Press, 1967), pp. 33-34. (This volume hereafter cited as *The Urban Explosion in Latin America.*)
7. Beyer comments that "details of the city planning of Philip II could be read with profit by some of today's city planners: orientation of streets in relation to the sun, width of streets, orientation of location to take account of prevailing winds, sizes of the squares, selection of places for public buildings—everything from a technical viewpoint was fairly completely covered" (*The Urban Explosion in Latin America,* p. 58).

a political favor or a way to deal with the problem of poor immigrants from Europe.[8]

The coming of independence in the early part of the nineteenth century brought relatively few social or economic changes to the internal structure of Latin America, and the overall urban pattern remained static throughout the hemisphere. Cities such as Lima, Mexico City, Bahia, Havana, Rio de Janeiro, Buenos Aires, Caracas, Santiago, and Bogotá stood out as centers of commercial, political, military, and cultural importance; but the rest of the hemisphere had to await the arrival of railroads and highways for corresponding growth and development. The nineteenth century was a period of quiet transition as far as Latin American cities were concerned. The social, industrial, and economic forces which were to make Latin America the most rapidly urbanizing major area of the world had to await the coming of the twentieth century.[9]

---

8. Gakenheimer, "The Peruvian City of the Sixteenth Century," pp. 36-43. Concerning the establishment of cities as centers of religious instruction, he cites Pizarro: "Since there is a good disposition of land and Indians in the region, a city ought to be founded for the service of God and His Majesty for teaching of the Catholic Faith. . . ."

9. Beyer. *The Urban Explosion in Latin America,* pp. 60-62.

2

CHARACTERISTICS OF MODERN URBANIZATION

The subject of modern urbanization is limitless, and it is not the purpose of this study to attempt to say the last word about it. An understanding of certain characteristics of urbanization is important, however; and the six factors which will now be discussed shed light on the subject.

Population Growth

Urbanization and population growth are closely related phenomena. Prior to the twentieth century the growth of Latin American populations was slow. In 1850 the total number of inhabitants in all of Latin America was only thirty-three million.[1] Economic development was slight, and so was the increase in population. Until the early decades of the twentieth century, one uniform pattern prevailed throughout Latin America; namely, that of one-crop agricultural economies, exporting their particular specialty to industrialized nations abroad. In this situation, the growth of towns and cities was minimal, and the only urban growth which did occur was due mainly to immigration from Europe.[2]

In 1900, the total population of Latin America stood at sixty-three million.[3] The economies of the various countries were largely

---

1. Sabanes, "Urbanization in Latin America," p. 308.
2. W. Stanley Rycroft and Myrtle M. Clemmer, *A Study of Urbanization in Latin America,* rev. ed. (New York: Commission on Ecumenical Mission and Relations, The United Presbyterian Church in the U.S.A., 1963), p. 37.
3. Sabanes, "Urbanization in Latin America," p. 308.

stagnant and the urban picture showed no marked alteration. Radical changes soon began to take place, however, as population figures began to soar.

Striking as the overall population growth has been in Latin America, the really phenomenal increase has been in the cities. Urban population growth has been characteristic of the twentieth century in all parts of the world, but in Latin America the picture is nothing less than startling:

> The growth rate of the total population in Latin America during the decade 1950-1960, estimated at an average of

FIGURE 1
PERCENTAGE OF POPULATION LIVING IN CITIES

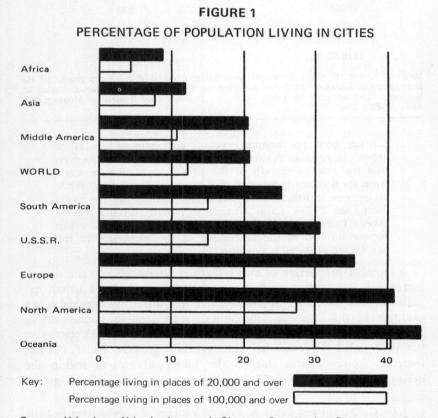

Key: Percentage living in places of 20,000 and over
        Percentage living in places of 100,000 and over

Source: *Urbanism, Urbanization, and Change: Comparative Perspectives,* Paul Meadows and Ephraim H. Mizruchi (Reading, Mass.: Addison-Wesley Publishing Co., 1969), p. 40.

TABLE 1

GROWTH IN LATIN AMERICAN POPULATION

1925	99million
1950	163 "
1955	175 "
1961	206 "
1965	226 "
1970	267 "
(1975)	291 "

Sources: United Nations—Economic and Social Council, *Preliminary Study of the Demographic Situation in Latin America,* p. 5; *1971 World Almanac;* Carlos M. Sabanes, "Urbanization in Latin America," *International Review of Missions,* LV (July, 1966), 308.

2.7 per cent per annum, exceeds the estimated rates of growth in all other regions of the world. It appears, however, that the rate of growth of the urban population in Latin America was nearly twice that of the total population. While an increase in urbanization was general throughout the world during the 1950's, Latin America surpassed all other regions except Oceania, both in the rate of growth of its urban population and in the magnitude of the increment to the percentage of urban population.[4]

A sizeable proportion of city growth is attributable to the overall increase in population, and it is a mistake to think of urban expansion only in terms of rural-urban migration. Venezuela is an example of this. Caracas, its capital, grew from a population of 359,000 in 1941 to 1,507,000 in 1963; and other Venezuelan towns equaled or exceeded this rate of growth. Most of this increase, however, was due to the biological growth within the urban centers themselves. If the general population had not grown

4. John D. Durand and Cezar A. Pelaez, "Patterns of Urbanization in Latin America," in *The City in Newly Developing Countries: Readings on Urbanism and Urbanization,* ed. Gerald Breese, Modernization of Traditional Societies Series (Englewood Cliffs, N.J.: Prentice-Hall, 1969), p. 184. (This volume hereafter cited as *The City in Newly Developing Countries.*)

at all, and internal migration had been the only factor in the growth of the cities, the increase would have been reduced by 57 percent and the slum conditions which have made Caracas and other cities so notorious would not have become so severe.[5]

Despite its rapid growth in population, Latin America cannot be considered an overpopulated area. The problem is that population, like wealth, is *unevenly* distributed, with heavy concentrations in particular areas, especially along the seacoasts and in capital cities, while vast areas in the interior remain virtually empty. The phenomenal growth in urban populations since the end of World War II is not due to a general overcrowdedness as far as land is concerned, but rather to a combination of factors, the first of which is the sheer rate of biological increase throughout the continent.

Slow Economic Development

The economic squeeze, as far as the cities are concerned, appears at the point where economic development does not keep pace with population growth and urbanization. This is the crucial difference between what is happening around the globe today and the urbanization which Western, industrialized countries experienced in the nineteenth and early twentieth centuries. City growth in the Third World is disproportionate to economic development and industrialization, and this makes it virtually impossible to draw parallels between what is happening today and what occurred in Europe and America in the past.

> It is in this respect that the non-industrial nations, which still make up the great majority of nations, are far from repeating past history. In the 19th and early 20th centuries the growth of cities arose from and contributed to economic advancement. Cities took surplus manpower from the countryside and put it to work producing goods and services that in turn helped to modernize agriculture. But today in underdeveloped countries, as in present-day advanced nations, city growth has become increasingly unhinged from economic development. . . .[6]

The poverty, the slum housing, the beggars on the street are all evidence of the simple fact that urbanization in Latin America is far out of proportion to the rate of industrialization and economic growth. There are various reasons for the slow growth of industry.

5. Kingsley Davis, "The Urbanization of the Human Population," in Breese, *The City in Newly Developing Countries,* p. 18.
6. Ibid., p. 19.

Among them are the lack of capital, the low educational level of large segments of the working force, and the general lack of skilled laborers. Especially do new migrants from rural areas find their agricultural skills unmarketable in the urban setting. As a consequence they must satisfy themselves with types of employment which are the most menial and lowest paid.

Complete unemployment, as it is found frequently in the United States, is not a characteristic feature of urban life in Latin America. No matter how little a man earns, he generally keeps himself busy doing something. With all members of the family working, a subsistence level is somehow maintained and life goes on. While "unemployment" figures, therefore, are comparatively low in Latin American cities, much of the so-called employment is of a very marginal nature as far as the economic picture is concerned; and it provides a minimum amount of income for the people involved. The fact, however, that relatively few people are entirely without employment makes it considerably more difficult to interpret available data on the degree of industrialization and the laboring force employed in it.[7]

Urban Agglomerations

The expression "urban agglomeration" is used to describe a city proper plus its suburbs, and it is a useful term with which to describe Latin America's great urban centers. Without some understanding of what urban sprawl is like, it is almost impossible to comprehend what has taken place in the last few decades. As fast as populations have shifted from hinterland to city, urban boundaries in many cases have become obsolete. They serve more to confuse than to facilitate an adequate comprehension of the city and its population. City limits have been overrun and the real urban population in virtually all the large centers extends into areas which officially are "rural," or are incorporated under other names.[8]

An example of this taken from South America is Buenos Aires,

---

7. Rycroft and Clemmer, *A Study of Urbanization in Latin America,* pp. 48-49. As an illustration of the low rate of "unemployment" in Latin American cities, the 1970 census reveals only 2.41 percent of the Mexico City population as unemployed. Nevertheless, 65 percent of the working population earns $100 or less per month. Estados Unidos Mexicanos, Secretaría de Industria y Comercio. Direccion General de Estadística. IX Censo General de Población. 1970 (Con Datos Sabre le Vivienda.) January 28, 1970. *Resumen de las Principales Características Por Entidad Federativa.* México, D.F.: Office of the Secretary of Industry and Commerce, 1970, pp. 115, 117. (Hereafter cited as *Census, 1970.*)
8. Rycroft and Clemmer, *A Study of Urbanization in Latin America,* p. 39.

TABLE 2

INDEXES OF URBANIZATION AND INDUSTRIALIZATION FOR SELECTED COUNTRIES IN LATIN AMERICA

Country	Census Year	Indexes of Urbanization[a]	Indexes of Industrialization[b]
ARGENTINA	1947	48.3	26.9
CHILE	1952	42.8	24.2
VENEZUELA	1950	31.0	15.6
COLOMBIA	1951	22.3	14.6
BRAZIL	1950	20.2	12.6
BOLIVIA	1950	19.7	15.4
ECUADOR	1950	17.8	17.8
PARAGUAY	1950	15.2	15.5
PERU	1940	13.9	13.2

Source: W. Stanley Rycroft and Myrtle M. Clemmer, *A Study of Urbanization in Latin America,* for the Commission on Ecumenical Mission and Relations, The United Presbyterian Church in the U.S.A. (rev. ed.; New York: 1963), p. 79, citing official census data.

[a]Percentage of total population in places of 20,000 or more inhabitants.

[b]Percentage of economically active men engaged in industry, construction, gas, and electricity.

where approximately 37 percent of the metropolitan population lives beyond the city limits.[9] The fact that this is typical of Latin American cities and is seldom taken into consideration when urban growth is discussed limits the value of most population tables. The trends and movements are plainly visible, but in most cases the precise nature of the urban situation in each area requires further analysis and description. In general, the actual size of the

9. Ibid.

TABLE 3

MEASURES OF DEGREE OF URBANIZATION AND URBAN CONCENTRATION IN LATIN AMERICA AT EACH CENSUS SINCE 1919

Country	Census Year	Percent of Total Population in Localities of Specified Number of Inhabitants			Percent of Urban Population in Localities of Specified Number of Inhabitants	
		20,000 or More	100,000 or More	Largest City	100,000 or More	Largest City
MIDDLE AMERICA						
Costa Rica	1927	19.3	—	19.3	—	100.0
	1950	22.3	22.3	22.3	100.0	100.0
	1963	24.0	24.0	24.0	100.0	100.0
Cuba	1919	24.3	14.7	14.7	60.4	60.4
	1931	27.6	18.5	16.0	67.0	57.8
	1943	30.7	19.9	17.4	64.9	56.8
	1953	35.5	22.9	18.3	64.7	51.4
Dominican Republic	1920	3.5	—	3.5	—	100.0
	1935	7.1	—	4.8	—	67.6
	1950	11.1	8.5	8.5	76.5	76.5
	1960	18.7	12.2	12.2	65.1	65.1
El Salvador	1930	9.0	—	6.2	—	69.0
	1950	12.9	8.7	8.7	67.5	67.5
	1961	17.7	10.2	10.2	57.6	57.6
Guatemala	1950	11.2	10.2	10.2	91.0	91.0
Haiti	1950	5.1	4.3	4.3	84.8	84.8
Honduras	1940	6.1	—	4.2	—	69.1
	1950	6.9	—	5.3	—	76.6
	1961	11.6	7.1	7.1	61.5	61.5

| Country | Census Year | Percent of Total Population in Localities of Specified Number of Inhabitants | | | Percent of Urban Population in Localities of Specified Number of Inhabitants | |
		20,000 or More	100,000 or More	Largest City	100,000 or More	Largest City
Jamaica	1921	10.3	—	10.3	—	100.0
	1943	16.3	16.3	16.3	100.0	100.0
	1960	24.8	23.4	23.4	94.0	94.0
Mexico	1940	18.1	10.2	7.4	56.4	40.8
	1950	24.1	15.1	8.7	62.8	36.0
	1960	29.6	18.6	8.1	62.9	27.4
Nicaragua	1950	15.2	10.3	10.3	67.7	67.7
	1963	23.0	15.3	15.3	66.3	66.3
Panama	1930	22.9	—	16.7	—	72.9
	1940	26.6	19.4	19.4	72.9	72.9
	1950	26.8	20.4	20.4	75.9	75.9
	1960	33.1	25.4	25.4	76.7	76.7
Puerto Rico	1920	9.2	—	5.9	—	64.7
	1930	14.1	8.3	8.3	58.7	58.7
	1940	18.8	10.1	10.1	53.8	53.8
	1950	27.0	16.1	16.1	59.7	59.7
	1960	28.0	23.3	18.4	83.1	65.6
SOUTH AMERICA						
Argentina	1947	48.3	36.8	29.7	76.2	61.5
	1960	57.5	45.5	33.8	79.2	58.8
Bolivia	1950	19.6	10.6	10.6	54.1	54.1
Brazil	1920	11.3	8.7	3.8	77.0	33.3
	1940	15.3	10.7	3.7	69.8	24.0
	1950	20.2	13.2	4.4	65.5	21.9
	1960	28.1	18.8	4.5	66.8	16.2

TABLE 3, continued

Country	Census Year	Percent of Total Population in Localities of Specified Number of Inhabitants		Largest City	Percent of Urban Population in Localities of Specified Number of Inhabitants	
		20,000 or More	100,000 or More		100,000 or More	Largest City
Chile	1920	28.0	18.4	13.6	66.2	48.6
	1930	32.5	20.7	16.2	63.9	50.0
	1940	36.4	23.1	18.9	63.5	52.0
	1952	42.8	28.5	22.7	66.5	53.2
	1960	54.7	33.3	25.9	60.8	47.3
Colombia	1938	12.9	7.1	3.7	55.4	29.1
	1951	22.2	14.7	5.5	66.2	24.9
Ecuador	1950	17.8	14.6	8.1	82.3	45.4
	1962	26.9	18.9	11.2	70.2	41.4
Paraguay	1950	16.5	16.5	16.5	100.0	100.0
	1962	—	16.8	16.8	—	—
Peru	1940	14.2	8.4	8.4	59.1	59.1
	1961	28.9	18.4	14.5	63.9	50.2
Uruguay	1963	—	—	45.9	—	—
Venezuela	1936	16.2	10.3	7.0	63.3	43.1
	1941	18.1	11.8	8.6	65.1	47.7
	1950	31.9	20.3	13.5	63.6	42.4
	1961	47.2	29.9	17.7	63.5	37.6

Ellipsis dots indicate that data are not available.

Dash indicates a magnitude of 0.

Source: Gerald Breese, ed., *The City in Newly Developing Countries: Readings on Urbanism and Urbanization* (Englewood Cliffs, N.J.: Prentice-Hall, 1969), pp. 170-71.

large agglomerations is underestimated in the published reports.[10]

Throughout most of Latin America, a pattern often referred to as "high primacy" can be found. By this is meant that in many Latin American countries there is a major concentration of population in one large city, which in most cases is also the capital. These principal cities expand far out of proportion to the second- and third-ranking cities. In sixteen Latin American countries, in fact, the population of the largest city is almost four times larger than that of the second largest city.[11] The Mexican capital is an illustration of the high primacy pattern of Latin American city growth. Eight million people out of a total population of forty-eight million live in metropolitan Mexico City; whereas the second ranking city, Guadalajara, passed one million only in the last decade; and the third city, Monterrey, has not yet reached one million.[12] The most extreme example of primary concentration is Montevideo in Uruguay, where nearly half the population of the country lives in the capital city.[13]

The Process of "Push" and "Pull"

In order to understand the causes of Latin American urbanization, factors involving both "push" and "pull" are commonly enumerated.[14]

> Among the advantages of the city (the "pull" factors) are: opportunities for economic and social achievement and mobility, the possibility of educational advantages, at least for one's children, better facilities for health care, and, in general, the hope for a better way of life. The disadvantages of rural life (the "push" factors) are the lack of opportunities for achievement, education, and health welfare, and the in-

---

10. Ibid., p. 40.
11. Ibid., p. 42.
12. *Census, 1970,* passim.
13. Luman H. Long, ed., *The World Almanac, 1971 Edition* (New York: Newspaper Enterprise Association, 1971), pp. 572, 582. (Hereafter cited as *World Almanac, 1971.*)
14. Numerous writers refer to "push" and "pull" in order to describe the causes of urbanization. Cf. Rycroft and Clemmer, *A Study of Urbanization in Latin America,* p. 44; Beyer, *The Urban Explosion in Latin America,* p. 97. The "pull" factors of the city are fairly well agreed on, but with respect to the rural areas, the forces of expulsion vary greatly from one country to another and from one time and local area to another. In Mexico, for example, the government is doing a great deal to alleviate the conditions which thrust people out of rural areas; and the "semi-feudal conditions" described by Sabanes do not exist in all Latin American countries in the same way. Sabanes, "Urbanization in Latin America," p. 310.

tensification of poor living conditions as a result of increasing mechanization of farms, soil exhaustion, and lack of incentives for farming, such as, among other things, credit facilities and good transportation.[15]

Probably no one can explain all the causes behind the present large-scale movement toward the cities. Educational opportunities for one's children and the hope of economic improvement undoubtedly are the two leading motives. In the Colonia Arenal, east of the Mexico City airport, four men were building a new shack. One day I engaged them in conversation and casually asked the question: "Why did you come to the city?" The spokesman for the group turned in the direction of the modern two-story school building the government had constructed in the center of the vast shantytown. "There is the answer," he replied; and without another word he returned to nailing the tarpaper walls.[16]

Urbanization has a strong, deleterious effect on the village and on rural life; for it means that the more ambitious and aggressive elements in the rural population are leaving for the city. By that same token, the rural communities are left with less capacity for reform and improvement. As the more dynamic members of the rural population go to the cities, losses in terms of human resources actually occur in both areas, though the area affected most acutely is the rural.

Those segments of the rural population which are most dissatisfied with the old ways and most open to new ideas get out and migrate to the cities. Those that stay behind resign themselves to a more or less static way of life, with few changes or improvements. A Mexico City newspaper recently commented on the contrast in mental attitudes between people who migrate and those who stay in the village:

> Mexico's rural poor are happy poor. At least they aren't unhappy. Those that don't like the misery of village life get out. They migrate to the cities in hope of something better.

15. Beyer, *The Urban Explosion in Latin America,* p. 97.
16. Personal interview with four shack builders, May 1970, Mexico City. William L. Wonderly has observed that while on the one hand differences in educational level between parents and children are clear indications of upward social mobility, for which many come to the city, these differences also are a potential source of tension within the family, as rural-oriented, uneducated parents see the gap between themselves and their urban-oriented, school-educated children grow wider. "Urbanization: The Challenge of Latin America in Transition," *Practical Anthropology* 7 (September-October 1960): 206.

Those who stay are content to keep things the way they are. Changing their way of thinking is the greatest challenge facing Mexico today.

A better way of life for the campesino has been a major goal of the Mexican Revolution. And inability to provide it has been the greatest failure. Once again pledges are heard that the rural standard of living shall be improved. And well it may be. But accomplishing this feat means saintly endurance in face of crushing frustrations.

Already, much saintly endurance has been chalked up. Young medical students have taken their knowledge into the bush and run into walls of suspicion—as well as hate from local herbologists. Public laundries stand empty as local women continue to wash in nearby streams. Schools go without scholars when harvest time arrives.

Efforts to provide drinking water, sewage systems and paved streets meet little but opposition. Gradually, young men and women fired by missionary spirit become cynics. Idealists eventually stoop to graft and play along with the system, convinced that no one really cares.

Yet the fight goes on. Mexico has awakened to the fact that it cannot develop if half its population wallows in misery. Even if there are many content to do no more than wallow. . . . What must be realized now is that money and technology are of secondary importance in raising rural living standards. The prime task is reaching the rural mind and convincing it of the need to demand a better life.[17]

Besides the losses caused by urbanization in the rural areas, losses occur in the city, too, as "this potentially usable talent is wasted in economically unrewarding jobs and struggling with the problems of slum life."[18] Great human potential, therefore, is being lost to both areas in the present situation. This undoubtedly does much to explain the widening inequalities between the urban and the rural, between the rich and the poor within geographic regions, and the general inability of potentially capable people to rise above the poverty level.[19]

---

17. Jim Budd, "Mexican Scene: Changing Tactics," *The News* (Mexico City), 22 December 1969, p. 3.

18. Beyer, *The Urban Explosion in Latin America,* p. 98.

19. Sixty-seven percent of Latin Americans live in the five largest countries (Brazil, Colombia, Mexico, Peru, and Venezuela), which are experiencing high rates of population increase along with rapid urbanization and considerable economic growth. Nevertheless, the inequalities between internal regions, urban and rural zones, and economic sectors of the population continue to widen despite the changes that are being made. United Nations, Economic and

Even as the benefits of modern life are introduced to the village community, they tend to stimulate ("push") the more aggressive elements toward the city rather than delay their departure. United Nations studies indicate that though the weak rural school—which is barely able to produce literate pupils—provides little stimulus for rural youth to migrate, the role of the small town school—where a somewhat better education is available—does much to persuade local youth to seek urban life and its benefits.[20] In other words, the taste of modern life is sweet; and when once the ambitious villager has savored it, he wants more. And "more" means migrating to the city.

Multitudinous Problems

The Latin American writer Alberto Lleras recently described what he called the "Monster of Urbanization" by comparing modern metropolises to the Biblical cities of Sodom and Gomorrah. Citing the nineteenth chapter of Genesis, where Abraham goes up to the place where he had met God and looks toward the two cities, and sees that "the smoke of the land went up as the smoke of a furnace,"[21] Lleras says:

> Contemporary man does not have to go up much farther than Abraham. He needs only to make an inspection by helicopter or plane over the immense megalopolises of our day, as full of sin as the two Biblical cities and likewise at the point of destroying themselves. "Like the smoke of a furnace," something mephitic, dirty, blackish, it extends below and through the clouds, at times with the suspicious color of a ripe orange. This atmosphere above the cities is like an overturned cup which preserves the material destined to poison the present generation, guilty as it essentially is, of the worst sin, though still without religious classification: the sin of [urban] agglomeration.[22]

In graphic, if not to say poetic, fashion, Lleras describes the problem-filled life of the city: the millions of motor vehicles, with their choking exhaust fumes, constant breakdowns, and temper-raising traffic jams; the slum housing; the high suicide rates; the blunders of government planners; and the problems raised by industry. *"La cuidad no trabaja"* (the city does not work), he

Social Council, *Population Trends and Policy Alternatives in Latin America,* E/CN.12/874, 8 February 1971, p. 19.
20. Ibid., p. 29.
21. All Scripture quotations are from the American Standard Edition of 1901.
22. "El monstruo de la Urbanizacion," *Vision,* 11 April 1969, p. 19. Translation mine.

says. It fails to provide what it promises; and no one any longer believes that these giant blots of iron, cement, and oil can give new life to men or be regenerated themselves.

> We Latin Americans say that this is the failure of the industrial empire, and the fault is not ours. Nevertheless, our case is even worse. Immigration from the countryside, the primitive rural regions of semicivilized people, continues to grow. The shanties increase and hold the old city in siege. Lacking sufficient electrical light, communications, transportation, and even cemeteries, hospitals, and police, the cities keep expanding every night like a cancer. What was once a source of their greatness now has become the chief factor in their misery: population. *Here the insecurity is worse than the villages left behind.*[23]

In Brazil the slums are called *favelas;* in Argentina, *bandas de miseria;* in Peru, *barriadas;* in Colombia, *tugurios.* But, by whatever name they go, the characteristics are the same. They are the rudest kind of slums, clustering like dirty beehives around the edges of Latin American cities.[24] The rate at which these "mushroom colonies" are growing may differ from country to country, but the overall picture is uniform. "For all of Latin America a growth rate of the urban marginal population from 1965 to 1975 of 2.9 per cent per year has been predicted."[25] In most instances, the largest share of this population increase will live in the urban slums, where, in the words of Lleras, life is "crude, cruel, insensible, and vicious."[26]

> In the new suburbs the basic social welfare services are completely lacking, and transport often comes to a complete stand-still. The problem manifests itself particularly harshly in the shantytowns which surround all the large towns of Latin America. These shantytowns are inhabited mainly by families who have emigrated from the poorer areas in the interior. They are an acute symptom of complex socio-economic problems to which no solution has yet been found.[27]

It may be asserted that these shantytown poor have always been poor, so their condition now is no worse than before. But there is one great difference. As the widely read Mexican magazine *Siempre* pointed out recently, these millions of urban poor now

23. Ibid. Translation and emphasis mine.
24. Beyer, *The Urban Explosion in Latin America,* p. 101.
25. Ibid.
26. Lleras, "El Monstruo de la Urbanizacion," p. 19.
27. Sabanes, "Urbanization in Latin America," p. 312.

live within sight of the rich.[28] They see the homes, the cars, the elaborate parties which the rich put on, the extravagant purchases they make, and the expensive vacations they enjoy. And they return to their slum hovels with the unmistakable feeling that somehow they have been cheated and the poverty to which they have been accustomed for so long is insufferable.

On a visit to Latin America in 1960, Ambassador Adlai Stevenson and Senator William Benton were shocked by the slums they saw, and they called them the "blight of the Latin American cities."[29] The two Americans visited slums in Lima, Bogotá, Rio de Janeiro, Santiago, and Caracas. The slums in Lima made the strongest impression on them (perhaps because they went there directly after eating lunch at the Club Nacional, one of the most luxurious men's clubs in the world). Benton wrote:

> Within a five-minute drive of this citadel of Lima's wealth we reached the most execrable slums I have seen in this hemisphere, vast stretches of one-room brick and mud huts in which people live in utter squalor, without plumbing and surrounded by filth and pigs—and empty beer bottles.[30]

Not all the slums in Latin America are equally debased, though the overall characteristics are universal.[31] Some squatter settlements in Mexico City, for example, have shown remarkable improvement within a matter of a few years.[32] Much depends on the location of the slum itself—whether it lies within a municipal area whose administration can be petitioned for assistance, or whether it lies in an area which has no local government structure.[33] Many slum dwellers are able to improve their housing and install modern services. In some Latin American cities, slum dwellers have shown tremendous initiative in developing their communities

28. *Siempre,* 9 June 1971, p. 33.
29. Rycroft and Clemmer, *A Study of Urbanization in Latin America,* p. 47, citing W. Benton, *The Voice of Latin America,* p. 18.
30. Ibid.
31. Bill Read and Chuck Bennett, "Urban Explosions: The Challenge of Latin America," *World Vision Magazine,* June 1969, p. 9.
32. After being away from Mexico City from the summer of 1970 to the spring of 1971, I was happily amazed at the signs of improvements in such *colonias* as San Isidro Fabela and Adolfo López Mateos.
33. For example, in Mexico City, the lower standards of living are noticeable immediately when one passes over the drainage ditch which divides the Federal District from the State of Mexico to the east of the airport. The conditions in *colonias* such as Las Palmas, State of Mexico, are substantially lower than in corresponding *colonias* on the other side of the administrative boundary.

through digging wells and building community centers, schools, and roads.[34]

Urban Anguish

More painful than the physical side of human suffering in the city are the mental anguish, the emotional insecurity, and isolation of the individuals involved. Many migrants to the city never really succeed in a personal integration. They live in the city physically, but not emotionally. They are part of the urban world, yet they establish few personal interrelationships. They view the city with a mixture of detachment, suspicion, and fear, even of antagonism and hatred; and this prevents them from ever entering into the life of the city with any degree of satisfaction.[35]

New urbanites, by and large, retain a rural outlook. The break with their former environment has involved geographical relocation; cultural, social, and sometimes language changes; and whole new family relationships between those who migrate and those who stay behind. But along with the breaks there is also continuity with the past, and in some cases an only thinly veiled rejection of what is new as it is symbolized by the city. The new immigrant retains his personal identification with the rural setting and continues to view the urban world from the outside, keeping it cautiously at arm's length. The potential that this condition has for inner suffering, longing for identification, and loneliness which in some cases leads to utter despair is immeasurable. Where but in the city are suicides so numerous?[36]

Tragically, the elaborate long-range strategies of industry and government do little to improve the condition of the individual as he relates to the city, Galo Plaza, former president of Ecuador, and secretary-general of the Organization of American States, expressed his hope for Latin America in the 1970s as follows:

> One of the highest priorities in the Latin American development strategy of the '70s will be the creation of new jobs in the cities. . . . Without this it will be impossible to achieve

---

34. Rycroft and Clemmer, *A Study of Urbanization in Latin America,* p. 47. Lima, Peru, is cited as an example of neighborhood associations formed for the purpose of community development. Obtaining ownership rights to the land always has first priority in such efforts, and after that come physical improvements and public services.

35. Peter L. Van Katwyk, "The Sense of Displacement," *Calvinist Contact,* 19 February 1970, p. 3.

36. For a penetrating analysis of the problems confronting the urban migrant, see Gino Germani, "The City as an Integrating Mechanism," in *The Urban Explosion in Latin America,* pp. 175-89.

economic growth rates for adequate living standards, reasonably full employment, and industrialization.

Continued heavy migration to the cities in Latin America will aggravate deficiencies in housing, sanitation, communications, and transportation, and call for heavy investments in these areas.[37]

Plaza is undoubtedly correct when he insists that Latin America needs greater industrialization. And everyone shares his dream of eventual full and rewarding employment for all urbanites. But the fulfillment of this goal will be a long and slow process. In the meantime, where does it leave the slum-dweller and his family? Life at the level of the individual and the family needs to be upgraded, and given hope, right now; and strategies must be devised which will affect this present generation as well as the next.

Glenn H. Beyer, in *The Urban Explosion in Latin America,* discusses the problems which the average rural-urban immigrant confronts as he tries to relate to the city and make urban life more liveable. The city possesses many different agencies and associations which might possibly be of help, but the new urbanite lacks knowledge of these associations and he would hesitate to approach them even if he knew of their existence. Limited as to information, and unaccustomed to the way city life operates, the immigrant-poor tend to withdraw from the mainstream of urban life. They eke out whatever they can and bear what they must, with few emotional or material supports.

The city as such is too large to help individual families effectively. If they are to be helped, Beyer suggests, it must be through local associations:

> One way is to help them organize by themselves: slum dwellers' organizations, meeting centers; or other agencies formed for community development.... Sometimes schools should be important vehicles; sometimes churches, especially neighborhood churches. Experience with Puerto Rican groups in New York City has shown that small units, such as neighborhood churches, can be effective in integrating people into city life and preventing anomie.[38]

Here is a specific suggestion which deserves attention. The immediate problems faced by thousands of urban families in Latin America require grassroots solutions on the level of the local

---

37. Galo Plaza, "Next Decade Better for Latin America," an article prepared for United Press International, *The News* (Mexico City), 17 January 1969, p. 8.
38. Beyer, *The Urban Explosion in Latin America,* p. 206.

neighborhood. Here the church can supply what is needed, both socially and psychologically, and above all, spiritually. It is something which neither governments, nor industry, nor the Organization of American States can do effectively, but which the church is specifically designed to do. Through the proliferation of countless cell units of fellowship, worship, and service, Christianity has the opportunity of providing the bedrock for an urban civilization in which the quality of life is raised to a new and higher level. Without this, it is doubtful that urban civilization can even endure.[39]

---

39. Lewis Mumford suggests that without the religious dimension, the forces which have dogged the city throughout history will finally overcome it, and urban life will become impossible (*The City in History,* pp. 575-76).

3

SIGNIFICANCE OF URBANIZATION
FOR MISSIONS

In the 9 June 1971 issue of *Siempre,* one of the most popular socialist-oriented magazines published in Mexico City, an editorial cartoon accurately expressed how the impoverished masses feel toward the sociological and anthropological studies being conducted among them.

The setting of the cartoon is a slum-dweller's shack. Five people are depicted. On the far left is a naked, undernourished child looking up in curiosity at the pith helmeted anthropologist who is studying him through a magnifying glass. In the center, a dull looking secretary wearing slacks and high heels sits with a tape recorder on her lap and earphones clapped over her ears. Mechanically, and without any sign of emotion, she records what comes in through the microphone held in the hand of a fat, bald-headed researcher seated on a wooden box next to the bed of a dying man. The man on the bed obviously is the victim of starvation. His face, unlike the faces of the three researchers which show no emotion whatsoever, is full of pain and despair. The climax comes in the question being asked by the overfed social scientist holding the microphone near the dying man's mouth:— ¿Y qué sentir usted cuando estar muriendo de hambre?[1] (And how does it feel to be dying of hunger?)

The urban masses in Latin America are weary of being made

---

1. *Siempre* (Mexico City), 9 June 1971, p. 57.

the objects of study, research, and investigations. They want less of the academic and more of the type of action which will change their desperate situation. Sociological studies and demographical reports about the city are necessary, but they accomplish nothing of any human consequence unless their findings are translated into action which improves the quality of life in the city.

TABLE 4
URBAN-RURAL DISTRIBUTION OF THE MEXICAN POPULATION 1900–1970

Urban area = localities with 10,000 or more inhabitants

Year	In Thousands		Percentages	
	Urban	Rural	Urban	Rural
1900	1,657	11,950	12.2	87.8
1910	2,034	13,126	13.4	86.6
1920	2,239	12,096	16.2	83.8
1930	3,272	13,281	19.8	80.2
1940	4,298	15,356	21.9	78.1
1950	7,542	18,338	28.9	71.1
1960	13,081	21,842	37.5	62.5
1970	21,888	26,429	45.3	54.7

Source: *50 Anos de Revolucion Mexicana en Cifras,* Nacional Financiera, S.A., Mexico, D.F., 1963, p. 22.

The same must be said of missionary studies. The city needs to be studied and understood in the most comprehensive way possible. The problems involved in periods of rapid urbanization require careful analysis. But having examined the urban scene in its broad dimensions, the question arises: What bearing does all this have on the spread of the gospel and the growth of Christ's church? Urban anthropology, unapplied, does the missionary cause little good. The question of the hour for Christian missions is not how fast are Latin American cities growing, but rather, how the teeming urban masses can be brought the Good News about Jesus Christ and living churches planted among them. Data concerning population growth, infant mortality, and slum conditions help to clarify some of the issues involved in urban missions, but the real need is for someone to show how the gospel can be applied to urban needs, how the church can grow in the urban environment, and then to lead forth in doing it.[2]

In any study such as this, it is important to recognize that not everything which is suggested can be applied universally. Generalizations must be made, but they always have their exceptions. Moreover, the problem is compounded when generalizations are applied to an area as wide as the twenty-two countries of Latin America. Urbanization has its unique characteristics in each country, depending on the historical, social, and cultural conditions of the land. Consequently, the relevance of urbanization to Christian missions will vary from place to place; and this should be borne in mind by the missionary in the field and the administrator at home. The gospel is the same, and the overall pattern of cultural change and its effects are the same, but no two countries or cities are exactly alike. Consequently, the secret of missionary success lies in applying the solutions of Christianity to the precise needs of each given community.

The solutions that Christians bring in the name of Christ must be as theologically valid as they are sociologically relevant. Therefore it is important that the missionary strategist stay close to the Bible while he theorizes about the meaning of urbanization for Christian missions. He must be aware constantly of the danger of allowing his approach to be other than Biblical. For if he fails in this, he forfeits his only source of authority as a missionary and he becomes guilty of religious imperialism—of taking advantage of lonely, bewildered, and unhappy people—and of manipulating people for his own purposes. If he loses the Biblical message, the missionary has nothing true or lasting to offer urban people, and his invitation to become Christians means nothing. As Calvin Guy has pointed out:

> We need to make effective use of the sociological factors that encourage response, but these must not be substituted for that demanding message from God which makes the response valid. For example, an invitation can be extended in such a fashion that a person reared in a culture which takes great care never to offend may answer yes out of courtesy. The offer of benefits to those who respond may lead to the patron-peon relationship so cherished in feudal societies. In other instances men may accept the invitation to profess faith in Christ, not because they love Christ but because they hate

---

2. Donald A. McGavran, personal letter, 28 April 1971.

something else. The first evangelical preaching in Rome after Victor Emmanuel II came to the Italian throne found spectacular response. But the church organized on this anti-clerical reaction had to be reorganized within four years. All this is to say that the message should offer what God offers, and make the demands He makes: repentance, confession, and total allegiance.[3]

The opportunities for church growth which urbanization presents are great and numerous, and Latin America offers fertile soil for evangelical expansion in this period. But great care must be taken that it is the gospel that is offered to the teeming urban masses, and not a mere human substitute.

It is possible that the missionary who lives and works in the city may be quite unaware of the social forces which operate in the urban environment. Much time, money, and energy are wasted when this occurs. Social forces should be understood and used for the spread of the gospel, and for that purpose the following five factors relating to the city are singled out for attention. The fifth factor, dealing with rural-urban "bridges," will be treated in a separate chapter, due to its importance and length. All of these factors are of significance for missions because each of them calls for, or sheds light on, the answer of the Christian gospel as it applies to the urban masses in Latin America. Each of these factors deserves continued study and research on the part of those concerned with missions in this hemisphere.

Frustration and the Search for Fulfillment

The frustration which the new urbanite encounters is summed up in the following statement by the United Nations Department of Economics and Social Affairs (UNESCO):

> Mere physical separation from kinsfolk and community of origin can deprive the individual of social identifications, and of material and moral support when these are most needed. "Anomie," the feeling of being lost and rootless, family disintegration, lack of supervision of children, the formation of delinquent gangs of youths, and collapse of personal morals sometimes results—though by no means always. . . . It is demonstrably false from evidence available today that a modern industrial society cannot have strong and stable family and community bonds, once the new society is es-

---

3. R. Calvin Guy, "Directed Conservation," in *Church Growth and Christian Mission,* ed. Donald A. McGavran (New York: Harper & Row, Publishers, 1965), p. 203.

tablished. But in the process of transition, of breakdown of old social forms and creation of new ones, there is a particularly dangerous stage when attitudes and behavior may be without anchors, controlled more by passing winds of demagogy, faddism, or mob spirit than by established values of home and community.[4]

As the UNESCO report indicates, anomie threatens most during the initial years in the city when the cultural patterns of the individual and his family are in rapid transition, old social forms are breaking down, and new ones are being created. During this traumatic period, people are in search of new forms of security and identification. They need to attach themselves to a community which can help them through the difficulties they are experiencing. The apartments and neighborhoods in which they live may teem with people, but still loneliness is everywhere. In the apartments where only an inch of plaster separates neighbors, and in the shantytowns where rusty tin sidings serve the same purpose, a man may have less intimate contact with his neighbor than did his father in the village with people living a mile away. In the city a man may fight with the people next door, but he does not know them. The city, especially for those who have newly arrived, is a lonely and frustrating place.

Evangelical Christianity stands in a unique position to satisfy the needs of urban migrants for identity, community, and moral undergirding. The present rapid growth of Pentecostal churches in such countries as Brazil, Chile, and Mexico justifies the assertion that the evangelical faith can meet many of the needs of large numbers of urban people.[5] William R. Read asserts:

> The Pentecostals have stepped into this vacuum. They have helped restore stability to family life. Membership in a Pentecostal church fulfills the need to belong to a vital social unit, a need often felt by people in rapid social change.[6]

An illustration of this fact is found in the Interdenominational (Pentecostal) Church in the Colonia Portales in Mexico City. This church is located in one of the most densely populated colonias of the city, an area which has been the recipient of waves of rural-

---

4. Cited in Emilio Willems, *Followers of the New Faith: Culture Change and the rise of Protestantism in Brazil and Chile* (Nashville: Vanderbilt University Press, 1967), pp. 124-25. (Hereafter cited as *Followers of the New Faith.*)
5. Willems, *Followers of the New Faith,* p. 122.
6. *New Patterns of Church Growth in Brazil,* Church Growth Series (Grand Rapids: Eerdmans Publishing Co., 1956), p. 212.

urban immigrants for a number of years. The seating capacity of
the auditorium is around three thousand, depending on the extent
to which the people are crowded in. The four pastors and twenty
elders all serve on a voluntary basis; no one receives any salary.
A building drive is presently underway for the purpose of enlarging
the auditorium.

Two-hour prayer services are held every morning during the
week at the Portales church. The meetings are conducted on a
rotation basis by one of the six deaconesses at an hour when
women especially can come for prayer and personal counseling.[7]

At a recent prayer meeting which I attended, seventeen persons
knelt at the rail of that church for special prayer. Represented in
these seventeen people was the whole gamut of urban society
with its needs. Two teen-age girls just in from the village were
without money and could not find the relatives with whom they
were to live. The deaconesses and others prayed for them sympa-
thetically and offered their advice. A mother of five children poured
out her tale of woe, including a drinking, abusive husband, a sickly
child, and insufficient income to feed and clothe the family. Prayers
and tears flowed together for her. A well-dressed, middle-aged
man was jolted visibly as the deaconess interpreted what his problem was before he himself expressed it. Family strife was tearing
his home apart. He was Presbyterian in background but came
regularly to the Pentecostal church for the mid-morning prayer
meeting. In the corner, with his face buried in the steps leading
to the platform was a young man in his early twenties. He said
nothing, but only wept. The white dust on his shoes and trousers
indicated that he was probably employed as a bricklayer's assistant
somewhere in the city. Whatever his problems were, he kept them
between himself and God, and the deaconess who prayed with him
did no probing.

On down the line the problems gushed out and the prayers
were offered. After a closing song and encouraging word from
Scripture, those who wished could leave and others could stay for
personal counseling. Everyone was reminded of the evening service
where one of the church's numerous choir groups would present
special music and a pastor would preach.

7. Ángel Arce, deaconess of the Portales church. Personal interview held at
the close of the daily prayer meeting in the Interdenominational Church,
Colonia Portales, Mexico City, 8 June 1971. The information concerning the
Portales church contained in these paragraphs stems from this interview, attendance at the prayer meeting on 8 June 1971, and from personal observation
of this church's program over the past eight years.

Prayer is the Portales church's principal response to the plight of the urban poor. Any man with a burden is welcome to speak out and present his need before the Lord and the church. The ministry does not end there, however; the Portales church has outdistanced most old-line denominations by operating a kind of credit union to help its members in times of financial crises. Moreover, the four pastors and their assistants serve unofficially as employment agents. In all, the Portales church is a true "Haven for the Masses,"[8] a place where God's concern for human needs, both spiritual and material, is reflected.

Places such as Portales, where a church's program is drawing thousands to it, teach valuable lessons to all who are concerned about the church's task in the city. Given Biblical insights into the nature of Chritsianity—fellowship, mutual concern, and care for the needy—no one should be surprised that human needs are being satisfied.

It is at this point that the understanding of a humble Christian who knows and trusts the Bible may exceed that of a trained sociologist who lacks spiritual discernment. Secular sociology can analyze the human dilemma and can describe with a degree of accuracy what is required to fulfill men's aspirations. But it may be the Christian believer who with neither embarrassment nor surprise supplies the answer.

This answer comes from the very nature of the gospel itself and the redemption which it proclaims. It says in plain language that urban man needs to repent of his sins and be reconciled to God through Jesus Christ. Divine revelation sheds vertical light on all the multiplied horizontal problems of urban society. The Bible speaks to man at the level of his need—and at more levels than any religious system not founded on it. No other system is able to match the solution it offers to man, for God deals with man in a way that is uniquely distinct from man's religious systems.

Wherever this is happening, regardless of the denomination, Christians should be listening, watching, and learning; for there the Spirit of God is at work.

Freedom to Choose One's Own Religion

Evangelical Christianity can offer little hope to urban people if these people are not free to investigate and accept it. But here,

---

8. Allusion is made here to the recent study by Christian Lalive D'Epinay, *Haven of the Masses: A Study of the Pentecostal Movement in Chile,* trans. Marjorie Sandle (London: Lutterworth Press, 1969). (Hereafter cited as *Haven of the Masses.*)

too, the phenomenon of modern urbanization provides a unique situation in Latin America.

In the past, village people were not free in most cases to inquire into or practice evangelical Christianity. Wherever the Roman Catholic Church was strong, evangelical Christianity had little chance of gaining a foothold.[9] Non-Roman Catholic Christians found it virtually impossible to obtain facilities for their worship services. When buildings were obtained, they were soon lost when the news got around that *protestantes* were holding meetings. Roman Catholic processions were held in protest against evangelicals, Bibles were burned, sympathizers were intimidated, and converts were persecuted. Pressures of every kind—social, economic, and religious— were brought to bear in order to restrict the individual's freedom in the choice of religion.

But what happens when such individuals arrive in the city? The old pressures are relieved and the individual—often for the first time in his life—is free to make a religious decision of his own. "The anonymity of the individual," says Willems, "makes it easier to adhere to a value system of his own choosing and to spend his free time in close association with those who share it."[10] The entire climate of the city is one of change, new discoveries, and individual freedom. In contrast to the village environment, where change was frequently resisted, the city is the very citadel of change.

> However, changes in an individual's life are usually accomplished more rapidly than in an entire group, especially if the individual is in a new cultural environment or in a group which is in process of rapid change. Accordingly, evangelistic work is more likely to be successful in a new town, or even in a new suburb of an old town, than in an old town; for in such new situations traditional socio-religious ties are not so strong. Often a person in such circumstances is not suspicious of intruders, but rather is looking for new friends.[11]

9. Donald A. McGavran, John Huegel, and Jack Taylor, *Church Growth in Mexico* (Grand Rapids: Eerdmans Publishing Co., 1963), p. 37. This is also the conclusion of Julian C. Bridges, "A Study of the Number, Distribution, and Growth of the Protestant Population in Mexico" (unpublished M.A. thesis, University of Florida, 1969), pp. 100-101.

10. Willems, *Followers of the New Faith*, pp. 167-68.

11. Eugene A. Nida, "Dynamics of Church Growth," *Church Growth and Christian Mission*, ed. Donald A. McGavran (New York: Harper & Row, Publishers, 1965), p. 173.

Many of the changes which take place affecting the lives of new immigrants to the city may be quite unrelated to religion. They may be changes involving employment, housing, and social relations in general. But they all have bearing on the individual's capacity to listen to and accept new religious ideas and values as well, for "culture change then acquires a snowball momentum."[12] The net result is a fresh attitude on the part of a growing number of persons in which they are prepared to receive new teaching about life and about God, which is an important precondition for their conversion to the evangelical faith.

Applied to a country like Mexico, what does this mean for Christian missions? It means that where social change is taking place the most rapidly, in new towns, border areas, frontiers, and in areas of rapid urbanization, men are likely to be the most free to listen to the Christian evangelist and respond to the gospel in a way which their former environment did not allow. For missionary planners, this should be an important consideration in the selection of areas to evangelize.

Consider, for example, Table 5, which shows the rate of growth of some of Mexico's principal cities. Other things being equal, the missionary planner can expect that where the growth of population exceeds 50 percent per decade, an environment exists where people will be relatively free to listen to the gospel and become members of evangelical churches. Some of the older urban centers may not be keeping up with the newer areas, and the very latest population figures should always be consulted before the location of a new missionary enterprise is decided on.

The last four cities in table 6 show growth ranging from 100 to 300 percent in the last decade. Each would require separate study before more precise predictions could be made, but in general it can be surmised that areas such as these offer tremendous opportunities to reach men with the Good News of Jesus Christ and to persuade them to become His disciples. Urbanization on this scale frees men from the tremendous social pressures which had prevented them from reading the Bible, attending evangelical services, or committing themselves personally to the gospel.

The Disadvantages Confronting Roman Catholicism in Urban Areas

For those who are accustomed to Catholicism's relative strength in North American cities, it comes as a surprise to learn that the Catholic church faces serious disadvantages in Latin American

---

12. Ibid.

TABLE 5

URBAN GROWTH IN MEXICO 1960-1970

City	Population 1960	Population 1970	Percentage of Growth
Guadalajara	740,344	1,196,218	61.56
Monterrey	601,085	830,366	38.14
Puebla	332,821	521,885	56.81
Merida	190,642	253,856	33.16
Torreon	203,153	257,045	26.53
San Luis Potosi	193,670	274,320	41.64
Leon	260,633	453,976	74.18
Ciudad Juarez	276,995	436,054	57.42
Veracruz	153,705	242,351	57.67
Mexicali	281,333	390,411	38.77
Chihuahua	186,089	363,850	95.52
Aguascalientes	154,211	222,105	44.03
Tampico	124,894	196,147	57.05
Morelia	153,481	209,507	36.50
Saltillo	127,772	191,879	50.76
Hermosillo	118,051	206,663	75.06
Neuvo Laredo	96,043	150,922	57.14
Matamoros	46,631	44,103	-5.42
Culiacan	208,982	358,812	71.70
Toluca	156,033	220,195	41.12
Mazatlan	112,619	171,835	52.58
Reynosa	134,869	143,514	6.41
Uruapan	61,221	104,475	70.65
Cuernavaca	85,620	159,909	86.76
Guadalupe (N. Leon)	38,233	153,454	301.32
San Nicolas de la Zarza (N. Leon)	41,243	111,502	170.35
Tijuana	165,690	335,125	102.26
Coatzacoalcos	54,425	108,818	99.94

Source: Estados Unidos Mexicanos, Secretaria de Industria y Comercio, Dirección General de Estadística. *IX Censo General de Población, 1970.* 28 de Enero 1970. Datos Preliminares Sujetos a Rectificación. México, D.F., May 1970.

cities. Due mainly to immigration patterns following the Civil War, Roman Catholicism dominates the urban scene in most of the United States outside the South. This is clearly reflected in the mass media, where events affecting the Church of Rome uniformly receive major coverage in city newspapers.[13] Protestantism, historically, has been associated with rural America, and Catholicism with the cities, with the result that the "country parson" and the "urban priest" have become virtual stereotypes in American movies and novels.

In Latin America, something of the opposite situation is beginning to develop in this era of rapid urbanization. Rural conditions since Colonial times generally favored the dominance of Roman Catholicism; and wherever Catholicism was strong, Protestantism was vigorously resisted and generally made little headway. A homogeneous rural culture did not permit any such divergences in religious adherence.

But today, as masses of people are on the move, Roman Catholicism faces two sets of problems in the cities. First, there is the attitude of the masses which demands greater freedom, more democratic government, a larger measure of equality in the distribution of wealth, and education for themselves and for their children. Catholicism, along with other institutions which traditionally have restricted freedom and retarded progress, is viewed with hostility; whereas evangelicalism, which by its nature calls for freedom, finds a new degree of openness toward its teaching in the urban setting. Catholicism is by nature anti-democratic. It teaches the absolute authority of the church and the passive obedience of the people. The individual is deprived of responsibility, except for the passivity required to submit to those above him. He need not even read or write: obedience, not knowledge, is what is required of him.[14]

To the extent in which this attitude is maintained, Catholicism is in for serious trouble in the cities of Latin America, where individuality, freedom of decision, and the importance of education are highly prized. Between the two systems, the Catholic and the evangelical, the latter stands closer to the modern scale of values held by urban people. Not only do large areas of religious

---

13. Martin E. Marty, *The New Shape of American Religion* (New York: Harper & Brothers, Publishers, 1958), p. 74.
14. For a discussion of Catholicism's inherent hostility toward the freedom which urbanites prize so highly, see Willems, *Followers of the New Faith,* p. 236. Willems cites A. R. Crabtree, *Historia dos Baptistas do Brasil* (Rio de Janeiro: Casa Publicadora Batista, 1927), 1:127.

doctrine separate the two systems, they represent sharply opposing attitudes toward life as well. The gospel of the evangelicals includes the principles of democracy, the freedom and responsibility of the individual, and the equality of rights. Catholicism, by nature, is opposed to these things. The church possesses absolute authority and the people must submit. The system as a whole is medieval. It represents the very things to which modern man is opposed.

The growth of democracy and freedom in Latin America depends to a large extent on the spread of evangelical values. Just as personal responsibility before God implies the right of the individual to read and study what God's Word teaches, individual responsibility in society and the maintenance of a democratic society as a whole require literacy, education, and the freedom of inquiry. Democracy and evangelical values go together and they depend for their development on freedom and education, both of which face deeply ingrained opposition in a Catholic environment.[15]

In an atmosphere such as that of the city, where skepticism, perplexity, and deep longing for change exist, the alternatives open to the individual are wide, ranging from strict conformity to past tradition to radical forms of rebellion and religious defiance.[16] It is too early to predict with absolute certainty what increased urbanization will bring; but if the example of Brazil and Chile are indicative of what may happen on a broader scale, the urban masses in Latin America may decide that a radical break with the authoritarian control of the clergy and the Catholic church is the only way to express their desire for greater freedom in the area of religion.[17]

The second problem facing the Roman Catholic church in the city has to do with the nature of the Folk Catholicism which rural-urban migrants bring with them.[18] Folk Catholicism does not belong in the modern city. It is predominantly a *rural* religion, adapted to the needs and problems of an agricultural people. The saints who are worshiped are *local* helpers, closely identified with some village church or shrine.

---

15. Ibid.
16. Ibid., pp. 258-59.
17. It is highly important that evangelical churches avoid forming false authoritarian structures of their own, for ultimately these structures will stifle evangelical growth just as they are now driving people away from the Roman Catholic church.
18. For more detailed treatments of Folk Catholicism, that peculiar blending of precolonial, pagan religion with elements of Roman Catholicism so typical of Latin America, see Eugene Nida, "Christo-Paganism," *Practical*

> Folk Catholicism is associated with crops and animals, with droughts and floods, and with the evil spirits and demons of the jungle and the country crossroads. Life in an industrial city poses different problems believed to require a different approach to the supernatural. Basically unaltered are only the problems which accompany the life cycle of the individual, namely birth, marriage, sickness, and death; and even these seem to gain a somewhat different significance in an urban setting.[19]

New urbanites cling to many of their former religious practices long after moving to the city, but distance and time gradually diminish their effect, and a spiritual vacuum results. Willems observed that in the changing society of Brazil and Chile, Folk Catholicism no longer served the functions which it formerly did in the rural environment; and gradually it lost its hold on the people.[20] The same is true everywhere, for the man in the city cannot resort any longer to the Catholic pantheon back in the village where he formerly worshiped, and he must find alternative solutions to his problems in the city. He may continue to travel to the village on special occasions, and in times of crisis he may still pray to the village saints, but estrangement increases and the rural orientation of his religious life gradually disappears. Bombarded by a host of new pressures in the city, he must turn in a new direction to satisfy his religious needs, and in that situation evangelical Christianity has a unique opportunity to impress him.

The Needs of the Family

The trauma of urbanization has various effects on the family. Generalizations are dangerous,[21] especially when large geographical areas and more than one country are involved, but the analysis given by UNESCO as to the effects of urbanization on family life in Buenos Aires appears accurate for the hemisphere as a whole:

> It is . . . a rather complicated matter to determine the "impact" of the city on groups of persons whose cultural pat-

---

Anthropology 8 (January-February 1961): 1-14; and William L. Wonderly, "Pagan and Christian Concepts in a Mexican Indian Culture," *Practical Anthropology* 5 (September-December 1958): 197-202; "The Indigenous Background of Religion in Latin America," *Practical Anthropology* 14 (November-December 1967): 241-48.
19. Willems, *Followers of the New Faith,* p. 132.
20. Ibid.
21. For a case study which concludes that for many people the urbanization process does not work serious havoc on the family, see Oscar Lewis, "Urbanization Without Breakdown: A Case Study," in *Contemporary Cultures and*

FIGURE 2

DYNAMICS OF RURAL-URBAN TRANSITION
THE REACTION OF NEW URBANTIES TO URBANIZATION

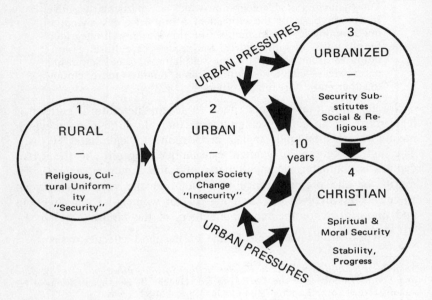

KEY:

1. RURAL—the original situation where traditional concepts predominate:

   homogeneous culture; Folk Catholicism; face-to-face human relations; agriculture

2. URBAN— the new environment where traditions are shaken loose by new pressures:

   heterogeneous culture; religious pluralformity; political unrest; industrialization; education

3. URBANIZED—the way of life common to the city:

   adjustment to urban culture, social and religious; some rural patterns erected against external pressures; defense barriers erected against external pressures and associations

4. CHRISTIAN—the Christian way of life based on spiritual and moral security:

   identity, personal dignity, fellowship found in the church; family stability; upward socio-economic mobility

terns would, if judged by urban standards, be regarded as symptoms of "disorganization." The observations made of the groups covered by the study lead to the conclusion that the city produces two opposite effects: on the one hand, the majority of families acquire urban ways of living, including those relating to the family; on the other hand, the well-known factors of disintegration which are particularly active in certain parts of the city affect a minority, destroying or undermining a certain number of previously well-integrated family units. In other words, the process of cultural assimilation to urban society has the simultaneous—and somewhat paradoxical—effect of knitting some families more closely together and disorganizing others.[22]

Studies show that urbanites tend to accept the cultural pattern of legal marriage to a far greater degree than do rural people, which means a correspondingly higher proportion of "legitimate" births.[23] The high percentage of women, especially young girls, in the urban centers is characteristic of all parts of Latin America, caused primarily by the preponderance of women in the rural-urban work force.[24] This involves the changing role of women—a new freedom and importance for the female members of the family.[25]

Work outside the home is one of the most effective ways

Societies of Latin America: A Reader in the Social Anthropology of Middle and South America and the Caribbean, ed. Dwight B. Heath and Richard N. Adams (New York: Random House, 1965), pp. 424-37.
22. Gino Germani, "Inquiry into the Social Effects of Urbanization in a Working-Class Sector of Greater Buenos Aires," in Urbanization in Latin America, Seminar on Urbanization Problems in Latin America, Santiago, Chile, 6-18 July 1959, ed. Philip M. Hauser (New York: International Documents Service, Columbia University Press, for the United Nations Educational, Scientific and Cultural Organization, 1961), p. 215.
23. Ibid.
24. Ibid., p. 100. Also Thales de Azevedo, "Family, Marriage, and Divorce in Brazil," in Contemporary Cultures and Societies of Latin America: A Reader in the Social Anthropology of Middle and South America and the Caribbean, ed. Dwight B. Heath and Richard N. Adams (New York: Random House, 1965), pp. 304-5.
Azevedo illustrates the higher percentage of women in the urban centers with data drawn from six geographical districts of Brazil, all of which follow the same pattern. The higher mortality rate among men and the preponderance of females in the urban migration cause proportionately fewer women in the rural areas and more in the urban centers.
25. The woman's role in Latin American households is oftentimes highly ambiguous. On the one hand, as the mother, she enjoys affection and a position of great influence in the family. But as the wife, she suffers from low status and a position of subservience to her husband, who, frequently, moves from one extramarital affair to another and shows a negligible amount of

of breaking down the so-called 'cloister" pattern of upbringing; even though a girl may work for only a few years before her marriage, they can have an effect on her throughout her lifetime.[26]

The new freedom and dignity which women enjoy is of significance also in the area of religion, where they are expected to assert a more active role than traditional patterns have allowed.[27]

The UNESCO studies reveal four classes of people that are found in higher percentages in the cities than in the rural areas: (1) unmarried young people, due to the fact that young people make up a high proportion of the rural-urban migration and urban inhabitants tend to marry at older ages; (2) married people, due mainly to the fact that legal marriage is more commonly accepted in the cities; (3) widows, probably because of higher job opportunities in the city, with the reverse with respect to widowers; (4) divorced and separated people.[28]

In the structuring of their missionary outreach in the city, Christian churches and missions need to bear in mind the needs and characteristics of particular groups within the urban society. The needs of the working girls, for example, are of special significance. Beyer speaks of the "stream of female migrants, especially working girls, from rural areas into the cities."[29] The estrangement which these girls must feel when confronted by the middle-class oriented youth programs of most urban churches ought to be considered. Prostitution among girls as young as nine or ten years years old sometimes is the result of poverty and the need to make a living.[30] But more often it is the result of the natural hunger for companionship and affection, conditions

responsibility for the family's welfare. Cf. William L. Wonderly, "Urbanizaiton: The Challenge of Latin America in Transition," *Practical Anthropology* 7 (September-October 1960): 206.

26. Beyer, *The Urban Explosion in Latin America*, p. 84.

27. In the Pentecostal churches which were studied in Mexico City, I observed a uniform pattern of more active participation on the part of women than is customarily found in the historic denominations.

28. Hauser, *Urbanization in Latin America*, p. 105.

29. Beyer, *The Urban Explosion in Latin America*, p. 84.

30. In "We Can Bring Christ's Love to These Neglected Children," *Latin American Evangelist*, March-April 1970, p. 9, Lois Thiessen tells of a documented study conducted among five thousand slum dwellers in San José, Costa Rica. Next to malnutrition there is the problem of loneliness. Mothers must often abandon their children during the day, locking them up in their one-room shacks, for the mother's employment is the family's only source of income. But equally hard is the feeling that no one cares, of never having

which make village girls in the city easy prey for unscrupulous men.[31]

In the Church Growth Seminar held at Winona Lake, Indiana, in 1967, the impact of urbanization on the family was discussed. The problems of loose marriage standards, illegitimacy, lack of family cohesiveness, alcoholism affecting the economic and emotional stability of the home, and the double social and moral standards for the man were discussed in relation to the city.[32] These problems, typical of Latin American society for generations, are accentuated by the urban environment.

It is important to observe that evangelical Christianity, with the emphasis on the Biblical concept of the home, fidelity in marriage, parental responsibility, and the moral conduct of men as well as women, fits the need of urban migrants in a very significant way. By incorporating both the male and female members of the family into the religious life of the church, which in itself is a major accomplishment in a society which traditionally leaves the practice of religion to the women, evangelical Christianity builds family unity on a religious and moral foundation, which is society's greatest need. Willems tells of what his research revealed in Brazil:

> In a number of cases we witnessed the unusual phenomenon of family gatherings during which passages from the Bible were read, prayers recited and hymns sung in unison. Particularly in rural communities, such gatherings are preceded by the evening meal which congregates all family members around a large table. Needless to say, all meals begin and end with a common prayer. Such commensural behavior stands in the sharpest possible contrast to the eating habits of the lower class of rural Brazil, where the family members, especially the men, seek to isolate themselves and swallow their food without uttering a word.
>
> Where schools are unavailable or distant, fathers are sometimes seen teaching their own children the rudiments of reading and writing, a rare sight indeed in a society that knows only the choice between government-provided schools and illiteracy. The father-teacher apparently assumes a responsibility above and beyond what non-Protestant fathers would be willing to recognize as their personal responsibility. It

---

anything to look forward to or be excited over. Early prostitution, she concludes, results from the natural hunger for both food and love.
31. Willems remarks that fornication on the part of men is commonly accepted, and the working girls in the city, especially those that work in factories, are considered easily accessible. *Followers of the New Faith,* p. 51.
32. "Problems Related to Church Growth and Possible Solutions in the Hispanic World," Church Growth Seminar, Winona Lake, Ind.; Findings of the Area Discussion Groups. Winona Lake, Ind., 1967 (mimeographed).

may be considered a sample of what our numerous inform-
ants had in mind when they referred to the "greater sense
of responsibility" inherent in the role of the Protestant
parent.[33]

No one can argue, in the light of these observations, that the
growth of evangelicalism in Latin American cities is irrelevant.
Evangelical convictions change lives, as every missionary knows.
Secular sociologists may express amazement that such changes
take place, and without religious insight they remain largely in-
explicable. But to the evangelical the reasons are clear enough,
for they stem from the transforming power of divine grace which
makes new creatures out of old (II Cor. 9:18).

Two writers who have done much to make the world aware
of the plight of urban working-class families in Latin America are
the American anthropologist Oscar Lewis, who deals principally
with Mexico, and the impoverished yet poetic resident of a Sao
Paulo *favela,* Carolina María de Jesús.[34] Both of these writers
have recorded in autobiographical fashion the struggles, hopes,
and frustrations of the urban poor. Since an accurate comprehension of the home and its functions is of utmost importance to
Christian missionaries, the works of these two authors should be
studied closely. One thing they show the missionary is that the
home in Latin America, especially among the lower classes, operates differently than most Anglo-Saxons have assumed. The
missionary who hopes to communicate the gospel relevantly to
the urban masses should begin by acquainting himself thoroughly
with the writings of these two people.

33. Willems, *Followers of the New Faith,* p. 172.
34. Oscar Lewis's principal works on Mexico City are *Five Families: Mexican
Case Studies in the Culture of Poverty* (New York: Basic Books, 1959) (hereafter cited as *Five Families*), and *Children of Sánchez: Autobiography of a
Mexican Family* (New York: Random House, 1961). A similar study by
Lewis, this time of a Puerto Rican slum family that moves between San Juan
and New York, is *La Vida* (London: Panther Books, 1968). As powerful
as any of Lewis's books is *Child of the Dark: The Diary of Carolina María
de Jesús,* trans. David St. Clair (New York: E. P. Dutton & Co., 1962).

4
URBAN-RURAL BRIDGES: BONUS GIFT TO MISSIONS

In the present period of rapid urbanization, the kinship relations between urban and rural people may prove to be one of the most decisive factors in winning large numbers of both groups to the Christian faith. These natural "bridges" must be recognized, and their potential developed and utilized, if a unique opportunity for the spread of the gospel is not to be missed.[1] They are the city's "bonus gift" to missions.

Before examining the way in which the progress of the gospel in the city may become a vital factor in its spread in rural areas, two ways in which rapid urbanization *weakens* the existing Christian community need to be examined. First, migration to the city often works chaos in rural churches as the more intelligent, aggressive young people and families leave for the city. There are villages today in Mexico where house after house stands empty due to the mass exodus of villagers to the city. This drains off the strength of the villages as a whole, and of the churches which are established there. In the Mexican town of Mier y Noriega, in the state of San Luis Potosí, the attractive building of the Independent Presbyterian Church stands nearly empty each Sunday

---

1. The use of the term "bridges" recalls Donald A. McGavran's *Bridges of God: A Study in the Strategy of Missions* (New York: World Dominion Press, 1955), from which the basic idea is borrowed.

because the majority of the members have moved to Monterrey.[2] No matter how many converts are made in the village, if the rural-urban migration continues at its present pace the development of strong village churches will be extremely difficult in the future.

The second way in which the strength of the Christian community is affected by rural-urban migration has to do with the migrants themselves and what becomes of them in the city as far as the Christian faith is concerned. Fife and Glasser have pointed out that in the process of urbanization the church loses members. In one report cited, a society in India claimed that it lost over 10,000 rural Christians as they moved into the city of Calcutta.[3] In the Mexico City program of the Christian Reformed Mission, approximately one-third of those gathered in the new house-churches were persons of rural background who had been evangelicals before coming to the city; but they had drifted along without any fixed church relationship after arriving in the urban center.[4] In many cases, the failure of existing urban churches and foreign missionary agencies to reach the city in the areas where the majority of the new migrants are located represents the largest and most tragic "leakage" of the Christian community in the Third World.

There is no valid excuse, in my opinion, for the continuation of this membership leakage, at least to the degree in which it is currently taking place. Rural pastors should help their members who plan to move to the city by supplying them with names and addresses of city pastors and churches. Any pastor who is concerned that his people do not become spiritually lost in the city should be willing to draw upon his contacts, write a letter or two for each family that is migrating, and see the matter through to conclusion, if necessary, when he himself visits the city. Missionary agencies involved in both rural and urban work could do the same. In a matter such as this denominational jealousy certainly ought to be overcome. Referrals should be made to other evangelical denominations in those areas of the city where one's own denomination does not have a church.[5] The cause of Christ is too great,

2. The plight of the Independent Presbyterian Church in Mier y Noriega is known to me from personal observation between 1962 and 1969, and from conversations with missionaries as recently as June 1971.
3. Eric S. Fife and Arthur F. Glasser, *Missions in Crisis: Rethinking Missionary Strategy* (Chicago: Inter-Varsity Press, 1961), p. 182.
4. See chap. 15.
5. This is one of the suggestions proposed by the Church Growth Seminar, Winona Lake, Ind. "Problems Related to Church Growth and Possible Solu-

and the migrant's need too urgent, for the maintenance of denominational exclusiveness in such a situation. A coordinated program between rural and urban churches, both within each denomination and across denominational lines, would work for the strengthening of each group and would save thousands of rural Christians from being lost in the maze of the city.[6]

Along this same line, A. R. Tippett calls attention to the spiritual vulnerability of rural church members who migrate to the city:

> Christians who become isolated in the world when they migrate away from their home group are spiritually vulnerable in many ways. Sometimes, without witness and involvement they rationalize a theory of "Christian presence." Sometimes they surrender their distinctiveness to the world in conformity. In either case they are lost in the records, to the fellowship, and to the abundance of spiritual resources that come from participation in the life of the body of Christ.[7]

Tippett goes on to call for letters or certificates of membership to be given to those members of rural churches who plan to migrate to the city so that they can establish themselves in a Christian fellowship in their new place of residence. Christian leaders ought to be big enough, says Tippett, to tell them that if their own denomination is not operating in their particular area they should then join the evangelical church that is nearest them. "For what he needs is not a denomination but a *Church*—and the Church in that locality needs him."[8]

Crossing Old Bridges to the Countryside

In their discussion of the challenge of the city, Fife and Glasser score the church for having failed in three areas:

> First, she has failed to keep those members who have migrated from the country to the city. Secondly, she has failed

tions in the Hispanic World," in "Findings of the Area Discussion Groups" (Winona Lake, Ind.: 1968), p. 2 (mimeographed).
6. I am aware of the problems involved. Lost addresses, the rural pastor's resentment toward the city and its churches, and the urban churches' reluctance to search out migrant people are complicating factors known only too well to the leader that has tried to put some rural-urban plan into effect. One method which I have used is to collect addresses in the village from the parents and relatives of young people that have gone to the city. Any rural pastor could do the same and could forward the addresses to his denominational headquarters in the city or to some pastor with a heart for the migrants.
7. A. R. Tippett, "Membership Shrinkage," *Church Growth Bulletin,* March 1968, p. 286.
8. Ibid.

to make an impression on the city masses with the gospel. Thirdly, she has failed to produce the kind of city church with a missionary heart that reaches out to evangelize the surrounding rural areas.[9]

It is to this third "failure" that attention should now be directed, for there is strong evidence to suggest that the present urbanization process provides the Christian church with one of its most unique opportunities in history to evangelize rural areas.

The maintenance of close ties with relatives in the village is an observable fact among many, if not the majority, of urban migrants.[10] Relatives from the country visit their city "cousins," often sponging off them for weeks at a time, frequently driving their hosts into debt before leaving. And similarly, city people make periodic visits back to the village and live off their rural relatives during the time they are there. This continuity of relationships explains to a large extent the relative stability of many migrant families during the period of their adjustment in the city. With improved means of travel and communication, the movement back and forth between rural and city homes can be maintained at a high level, even when adjustment to city life has become relatively complete. Oscar Lewis, in his study of the village of Tepoztlán, found that the close ties between the Tepoztecans living in Mexico City and those still in the village was an enduring factor in the lives of these people:

> In considering stability or change in the way of life of Tepoztecans in Mexico City it is important to realize that the ties between the city families and their relatives in the village remain strong and enduring for almost all the city families studied. They visit the village at least once a year on the occasion of the Carnival. Many go much more often, to celebrate their own Saint's Day, to attend their barrio fiesta, a funeral, or the inauguration of a new bridge or school, to act as godparent for some child, or to celebrate a wedding anniversary, or the Day of the Dead. The ties with the village do not seem to weaken with increase in years away from it. On the contrary, some of the most ardent and nostalgic villagers are those who have been away from it the longest. Many old people expressed a desire to return to the village to die. Some men, who have been living in the city for thirty years, still think of themselves as Te-

---

9. Fife and Glasser, *Missions in Crisis,* p. 183.
10. See Lewis, *Five Families,* p. 26; *Tepoztlán: Village in Mexico,* Case Studies in Cultural Anthropology, ed. George Spindler and Louise Spindler (New York: Holt, Rinehart, and Winston, 1960), pp. 50-65.

poztecans first and Mexicans second. Fifty-six per cent of
the families studied owned a house in the village, and 30
per cent owned their private *milpas*.

The proximity to Tepoztlán, and the bus line which now
runs to the village, facilitate visiting. The young people enjoy
spending a weekend or a Sunday in their village. There is
also some visiting from Tepoztlán to friends and relatives
in the city.

In the past few years Tepoztecans in the city have organized a soccer team and play against the village team. The
organization of a team in the city means that Tepoztecans
from distant *colonias* must get together; however, the cohesiveness of Tepoztecans with their village is much greater
than among themselves in the city.[11]

The same high degree of interaction enjoyed by the Tepoztecans
cannot be experienced by migrants and their relatives when the
distance between them is much greater. Tepoztlán, after all, lies
only a short distance outside of Mexico City, so that the migrant
families from the village are in a position to maintain closer contact with the village than the average migrant can. But as every
resident of the city knows full well, the exodus of urbanites from
the city to the country during holiday time is so extensive that
if one plans to travel, he had better get his train or bus tickets
well in advance. For whenever he can, the man in the city goes
back to his rural home. And he takes with him, besides his city
clothes, the new ideas he has discovered, including ideas about
religion.

Of the 350 villages in the central part of Mexico in which the
Mazahua dialect is spoken, 41 villages have received the gospel.
According to Donald Stewart, leading member of the team of
Wycliffe Bible translators who translated the New Testament
in the Mazahua dialect in 1970, most if not all of these 41 villages heard the gospel through contacts made in Mexico City.[12]
Located from fifty to ninety miles north and west of Mexico City,
some of the villages which now have churches founded through
the Mexico City converts appear in the following table:

These fifteen churches came into being in various ways, but
the movement of men from the village to the city and back was
the principal factor in all of them. In the case of the village of
Santa María Citendeje, a migrant to Mexico City was converted

---

11. Lewis, "Urbanization Without Breakdown: A Case Study," p. 434.
12. Donald Stewart, personal interview held in Fort Worth, Tex., 24 May
1971.

there, and on his next visit to his relatives in the village left three Bibles with them. The change which the evangelical faith had made in his life led them to read the Bible seriously, and out of it four churches were eventually formed.[13] In the case of San

TABLE 6

EVANGELICAL CHURCHES IN MAZAHUA VILLAGES

Villages	Number of Churches	Denomination
CONCEPCIÓN DE LOS BAÑOS	1	Pentecostal
	2	Baptist
	2	Assembly of God
SAN PABLO	1	Baptist
	1	Seventh Day Adventist
SANTA MARIA CITENDEJE	1	Baptist
	2	Interdenominational (Portales)
	1	Assembly of God
SAN PEDRO ROSAL	1	Baptist
SAN JUAN DE LAS MANZANAS	1	Assembly of God
	1	Pentecostal
	1	Nazarene

Juan de las Manzanas, a contact in Mexico City brought a group of evangelists to the village. The first believer was a man named Joel Quintana, and eventually three churches were established.

13. From observation and interviews conducted in these villages in 1968, I learned that the proliferation of churches in such areas is often due to internal disagreements which develop between families, causing division and the establishment of new churches. From the doorway of one church in which I had preached, I could see two other churches not far away. The division of local churches along family lines is a difficult problem in rural villages. Commented Donald Stewart: "They can grow only to about twenty men and then they split." (Personal interview, 24 May 1871, Fort Worth, Tex.)

Emilio González was the founder of the first evangelical church in San Pedro Rosal. His brother was working in Mexico City and was drinking heavily. In desperation he went to an evangelical church near the place where he worked, and there he was converted. He went home and told Emilio, and a chain reaction was begun which led to the founding of a Baptist church.

The same basic pattern of events brought about the establishment of the first evangelical church in Concepción de los Baños. The first believer was José Ermita de la Luz, whose uncle brought him a Bible from Mexico City. José himself then went to the city and joined a Baptist church. Returning to the village, he called together his friends and relatives and began a Bible class, out of which a Baptist church was eventually established.

- The same kind of urban-to-rural movement of the gospel which so thoroughly typifies the Mazahua tribe is true also among the Zapoteco Indians in the state of Oaxaca, in southern Mexico.[14] Read, Monterroso, and Johnson mention that they found it happening also in South America, with urban churches benefiting from the influx of village believers, and in turn, helping to plant the gospel in rural areas:

> The rural background of the urban Church provides a ready-made mission field. The urban Churches are being fed by the rural Churches, and at the same time are carrying the gospel back to rural areas. We found many congregations in the interior of Brazil which had no official connection with any denomination but had been started by someone who had become an Evangelical in Sao Paulo or Rio de Janeiro and had gone back as a spontaneous church-planter.[15]

With this kind of movement taking place, it becomes obvious that the best thing that can happen for rural evangelism is the rapid growth of evangelicalism in the cities. Rural and urban mission work share each other's fortunes. It is not a matter of either-or; they need each other.

---

14. Roger Mohrlang, Wycliffe Bible translator, Northern Nigeria, on returning from a study period in Mitla, Oaxaca, personal interview held in Fort Worth, Tex., 24 May 1971. Mohrlang commented that in Northern Nigeria animism is breaking down in the villages, and people who never intend to leave the village are forsaking animism in large numbers. In Mexico, the great impact of cultural change does not come until one has left the village and moved to the city. In Nigeria, said Mohrlang, "if they move to the city it is almost 100 percent certain that they will convert to either Islam or to Christianity."

15. *Latin American Church Growth,* p. 242.

In fact, in some instances the only way to penetrate an Indian community effectively is through the kind of personal contact that has been opening Mazahua villages to the gospel. John T. Dale, director of the Mexican Indian Mission in the state of San Luis Potosí, describes how his home- and family-centered approach in Aztec Indian villages depends on a personal contact with someone from inside the community:

> In the areas where we have work, we can regard the population as rural and deeply related to the land and its cultivation. The people hold the land in communal fashion, in *ejidos,* and also in the form of private property. There are various types of villages and small ranches in our area of work. We can say that where the normal indigenous standard is maintained, there the life is communal, and where the mestizo element dominates, there the way of life is individual.
>
> In our plan of operation we have considered the first steps to be of prime importance for they form the mold of all future work. In the villages where the mestizo element predominates we take into account the structure of the community, but we do not lose sight of the fact that it is principally of the individualistic type. Our plan of evangelism is house-to-house, and individual. In the indigenous communities, however, we do just the opposite, and here we want to explain our work more in detail, taking as the basis our work among the indigenous people which speak the Aztec language.
>
> It has appeared to us to be of fundamental importance to take into account the fact that the life of these communities is communal, with everything which this word implies. In order to penetrate this type of society, one must take the family as the base of evangelization, but at the same time in relation to the barrio. The idea of "barrio" antedates the Spanish conquest, when the Aztec villages were made up of *"calpuli."* Possibly in the beginning these barrios were made up of families related to one another by blood lines. At present, however, the barrios in the Aztec communities are not necessarily comprised of related families but of families that are linked to one another socially and economically. For example, the land in the barrio is considered the property of the community, and each family has the right to use the land that it needs in order to live.
>
> The spirit of solidarity is maintained in the barrio and it extends to the community at large through reciprocal obligations. When a man wants to erect a house, he brings together first the material and then he invites his neighbors for a day of "house-raising." He does not pay his neighbors

for the time which they spend helping him, but is obligated only to feed them abundantly. The communal idea means that he in turn is obligated to give his services in the same way to the other people of the barrio when they so desire.

We have found that in order to penetrate and establish work in a community in which the social force of the communal spirit dominates, it is necessary to take into account the barrio or the barrios. *The evangelistic contact has to be through a family of the barrio in order to affect the whole community.* Generally this contact with a family of a particular barrio is done through an Indian believer from another community who has relatives, a godfather, or a friend in that barrio. Members of the evangelism committee of his church can go with him or some fellow believer can accompany him, for the purpose of evangelizing the family with which he is familiar. This has been the most natural and effective way of evangelizing.[16]

Dale goes on to describe how, through periodic visits to the one family with whom the initial contact was made, suspicions are overcome and the entire Indian community is gradually penetrated. The gospel travels along family lines, through the normal channels of human relationships; and before long other barrios are contacted as well and a local people movement is underway. The same pattern is evident among the Aztecs that was found among the Mazahuas. Once the gospel has entered the Indian community, it can be expected to move from person to person until one or more churches are established.

Throngs of Indian people such as those with whom Dale works are today moving in and out of the great urban centers. One sees them in the streets and markets doing the most servile types of labor. One sees them also in evangelical churches. Of all those who suffer the tensions and anguish of cultural change, they are in the worst position. The evangelical community offers them what they desperately need; namely, peace with God, personal identity, moral and spiritual strength, and community. Thousands across the continent are finding these things in Jesus Christ during the time they spend in the city. As these Indian people return to their villages where the tight walls of community solidarity have for decades kept outsiders from entering with the gospel, they carry the evangelical faith into areas where it could not penetrate before. It is happening already, as the Mazahua villages illustrate. It is

16. "Evangelismo Práctico en el Campo Rural," *Promotor de Evangelización,* December 1965. Translation and emphasis mine.

further evidence that, in McGavran's words, "we stand in the sunrise of the missionary enterprise."[17]

Crisscrossing Bridges Within the City

Related to the communal relationships which Dale describes in the village community are the *paisano* relationships in the city. *Paisano* means, literally, a fellow countryman or compatriot; and the term is used among migrants in Mexico City with reference to persons who come from the same village or general area. *Paisanos* regard one another in terms of kinship relationships, even though they may not be blood relatives at all. Two Mayas, for example, meeting in Mexico City, feel immediately attached to each other, even though they may not have known one another back in Yucatan. This is true also among persons coming from the coastal areas around Acapulco. They address one another as *"paisano,"* they borrow from one another, often live in the same *vecindad,* and consult one another over their problems.[18]

Paisano ties move in two directions: within the city among rural immigrants from the same area, and between these immigrants' relatives and neighbors back home. *Paisanos* send messages back and forth via whoever may be making a trip home. Through the chain of *paisano* relationships they keep in close contact with one another in the city and with the home area; and as soon as anyone arrives after a visit to the village, *paisano* friends and neighbors begin dropping in to hear the news and collect whatever letters may have been sent them.

This *paisano* relationship harbors great possibilities for Christian missions. A converted *paisano* has an open door among immigrants from his home area. They will not treat him offensively or refuse to give him entrance into their home even when they do not approve of his religion, for to do so would arouse hostility on the part of other *paisanos* who are their mutual friends. In the cold, impersonal world of the city, *paisano* relationships are too precious to be put in jeopardy unnecessarily.

Paisano friendship and respect can open doors in both the city and the village. In the city, *vecindades* often are composed of sev-

17. Donald A. McGavran, "Bring in the Vacuum Cleaner: The Right Way to Say It," *Church Growth Bulletin,* May 1971, p. 148.
18. Discovery of the importance of the *paisano* relationship came to me during seven years of working with students from rural areas who were studying and working in Mexico City. *Paisano* ties constitute a whole network of relationships within the city, to which Oscar Lewis also refers in his study of the Tepoztecans living in the city. "Urbanization Without Breakdown: A Case Study," p. 434.

eral *paisano* families drawn together by mutual interest and concern; and when one of their number becomes an evangelical, house-churches can be planted among them with relative ease.[19] In the village, when converted *paisanos* act as couriers of the gospel, these same ties can open doors which otherwise would remain closed, as the spread of the gospel among the Mazahuas illustrates.

The problem is that missionaries and churches are often unaware of the opportunities which the *paisano* social stratum represents. So much of the activity which occupies the attention of urban churches is completely irrelevant to the needs of such people. Read, Monterroso, and Johnson have called attention to this situation in their study of church growth patterns in Latin American cities:

> For the first decade, or perhaps a little longer, the rural and therefore group orientation of new city dwellers provides, in itself, a bridge by which they may be reached with the gospel. As they endeavor to cope with their new environment they look for something which will provide continuity, which will answer the puzzling questions which city life poses, and which will give a new sense of community. This they can find in the Evangelical Church—*if the Evangelical Church speaks in terms relevant to their new situation.*[20]

In every evangelical church in the city there are visitors, inquirers, and members, whose recent village origins give them *paisano* relationships with scores of other people. These are natural bridges which pastors and missionaries ought to utilize. The social orientation of rural-urban migrants can serve either as a barrier or a bridge, depending on what the Christian evangelist does with it.[21]

---

19. This was borne out in the experience of the Mexican Christian Institute, to which reference will be made in chap. 14, where Bible school students eagerly visited their *paisano* acquaintances in the city with a view to converting them to the evangelical faith.

20. Read, Monterroso, and Johnson, *Latin American Church Growth,* p. 242.

21. No large-scale people movement has ever occurred among city dwellers, but who can say that it will never happen? People movements are the work of the Spirit and are not guaranteed by any human strategy. The potential of the cities today is very great. The likelihood of extensive Christian growth is there. Even the best situation, however, and the most thoroughly tested strategy mean nothing without the anointing of the Holy Spirit. For an incisive analysis of the people movement concept, see Stephen Neill, *The Unfinished Task* (London: Edinburgh House Press, 1957), pp. 122-25.

PART II
BIBLICAL MISSIOLOGY APPLIED TO LATIN AMERICAN CITIES

5

URBAN MISSIOLOGY: CONVERTS TO CHRIST

The task of the missiologist is not an easy one today. Conflicting opinions fly at him from every side, and the prevailing mood is one of uncertainty. For that reason, the need for a positive, Biblically defined approach to urban missions is all the more urgent. "In this period of confusion and transition in world mission," says Pierce Beaver, "the missiologist is called to be the pioneer and to blaze the trail. . . . The missionary will not escape from his uncertainty until the missiologist points the way, and the church will not move ahead in mission unless the missiologist sounds a prophetic call."[1]

By his research and writing the missiologist can make an invaluable contribution to the extension of the gospel, providing his theology is not only relevant but sound. For, as Calvin Guy has pointed out:

> Mission rises from theological foundations. It is a projection of basic theological beliefs. Its vigor and form reveal what it is based on. Men do not gather grapes from thorns or figs from thistles. Dynamic, growing churches do not spring up from enfeebled or distorted theological roots. If the vast missionary enterprise, proliferating into many cul-

---

1. "The Meaning and Place of Missiology Today in the American Scene," p. 10, as cited in Gerald H. Anderson, "Mission Research, Writing, and Publishing," in *The Future of the Christian World Mission* (Grand Rapids: Eerdmans Publishing Co., 1971), p. 140.

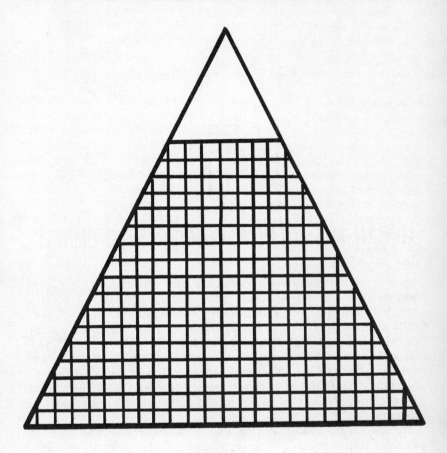

FIGURE 3

THE CHURCH IN SOCIETY — THE CREST OF THE ICEBERG

"The church, like the visible portion of the iceberg, has emerged out of society but remains in living relationship with it. Every Christian is still in the world out of which he has come. The bridges are still intact. Multiply these relationships by the number of Christians within the church and you get a network of high potential for an upward movement to Christ and the church. Every church member will have friends, relatives, and casual acquaintances who are still to be found in the submerged portion, the potential seeker layer. . . ." Takashi Yamada, *Studies in Extension Evangelism,* trans. P. W. Boschman, Church Growth Pamphlet Series No. 3 (Kobayashi City, Miyazaki, Japan: Jobayashi Kyodaisha, 1970), p. 17.

tural and economic activities, would safeguard its life, it must look closely to its theological foundations and make certain that they are found in the New Testament, commanded by Christ, and demonstrated in the growing Churches of nineteen hundred years of history.[2]

In many areas today, the advance of Christian missions is being hindered because of humanistic theology which produces a secular missionary policy on which neither sound churches nor solid social structures can be built. The two basic components of missionary theology and strategy are the theological and the anthropological.[3] The theological comes first because missions is concerned about God and His Word to and about mankind. God created man with an eternal soul, and since the Fall He has been speaking to man both of judgment and of grace. That message is the proclamation of Christian evangelism. But at the same time, missiology is concerned with anthropology, for mission work is directed toward human beings who live and move in an earthly environment marked by different languages, cultures, and races. To be concerned only with man's material and temporal needs is to neglect the spiritual and eternal; but to view mankind as simply so many souls to be saved and sent to heaven forgets that physical life, too, is God's creation, and is properly the concern of Christian missions.

In Latin America, urban missions of the secular-humanist variety find their chief representative and inspiration in the organization called *Iglesia y Sociedad en América Latina* (Church and Society in Latin America), with headquarters in Montevideo, Uruguay. Popularly known as ISAL, the movement is making a sizeable impact in many Latin American seminaries and among some church leaders. With funds available from the ecumenical movement for scholarships and trips abroad, many of the most talented young men from Latin American churches are being sent abroad to be trained for a secular-humanist ministry.

Peter Wagner, in his recent book *Teología Latinoamericana: ¿Izquierdista o Evangélica? (Latin American Theology: Leftist or Evangelical?),* has made a valiant attempt to arouse Latin American evangelicals to defend the Biblical Christianity which they have espoused against the encroachments of humanistic and secular theological movements of foreign origin that now are threatening to

---

2. "Theological Foundations," p. 56.
3. Alan R. Tippett, "The Components of Missionary Theory," *Church Growth Bulletin,* September 1969, p. 1.

capture the Hispanic world.[4] The long-cherished opinion that all is well theologically in Latin America needed to be exploded, and Wagner has done it. Heated as some of the reactions have been, Wagner will have accomplished his purpose if evangelical leaders now assume the responsibility of not only defending the faith but also articulating more effectively its meaning for modern Latin America. These are areas in which conservatives in Latin America have been ignobly silent.

In the pages that follow, an attempt is made to present a theological framework for urban missions in Latin America which is both sociologically relevant and theologically correct. It is based on the conviction that in spite of the changes that have occurred in the world, the basic issues which the church faces in missions today are the same as those which Paul confronted in the first century, and the theoretical principles on which he built his strategy are abiding.

Converts to Christ

The mission of the church in the city is first of all to present the gospel in such a way that people will be converted to Jesus Christ, believing in Him as their Savior and following Him as their Lord. Doing this they will be baptized and will seek membership in His visible body, the church.

This is basic New Testament missionary strategy. Any method, any approach, which does not seek to make converts has departed from New Testament principles. The kingdom of Jesus Christ can never be realized in this world without the conversion of sinners to faith in Christ. Conversion, the establishment of the church, and the broader manifestation of divine grace in all its implications are not distinct and separate purposes: they are all united in one single purpose, follow upon one another, and together spell out the task of Christian missions.[5]

It should not surprise anyone, however, that in this humanistic age, *conversion* as a goal of the Christian mission has become unpopular in some circles. Many today see the Christian ministry and missions, not in terms of calling men to personal faith and reconciliation with God, but rather in terms of man-centered programs of secular involvement.

That humanism has invaded the Church and plays a domi-

---

4. Pedro Wagner, *Teología Latinoamericana: ¿Izquierdista o Evangelica?* La Lucha por la Fe en una Iglesia Creciente (Miami: Editorial Vida, 1969), p. 24.
5. J. H. Bavinck, *An Introduction to the Science of Missions,* trans. David Hugh Freeman (Grand Rapids: Baker Book House, 1960), p. 155.

nant role in determining its mission can easily be seen. The recently elected moderator of the New York Presbytery of the United Presbyterian Church, the Reverend James D. Watson, was reported by the *New York Times* as saying that he calls himself "a Christian-humanist" with "more concern about man than about God." "I see the ministry in terms of social action," he said, "and not in terms of preaching or the rest of the nonsense we went through years ago."[6]

This same attitude has infiltrated a segment of the Roman Catholic church. The same editorial which carried the above account of an anticonversion spirit among certain Presbyterians told about a news release from the National Catholic News Service concerning the mission of the U.S. Catholic Relief Services in Cochin, India. Charges had been made that the relief extended to India's poor was nothing more than "bait" to dispose them toward conversion to Roman Catholicism. The priest in charge replied: "No. No. We have nothing to do with conversion. Our work is completely secular. There is nothing spiritual in it."[7]

Humanism takes the heart out of Christian missions. By concerning itself exclusively with the second table of the Law, and ignoring the first, humanism's direction is purely horizontal. It forgets that the fundamental issue is man's relation to God, against whom he has sinned and before whom he is responsible. Because it is entirely preoccupied with man and with men's relations to one another, the entire program of humanistic missions reflects a radically different orientation from that which is concerned fundamentally with God. J. H. Bavinck states it succinctly:

> The aim of missions is [to be] preoccupied with God, with his glory, with his kingdom. The man who is redeemed by Jesus Christ will finally see that peace is not to be found apart from God. Missionary activity is directed towards God's final purpose for the world, the eternal kingdom.[8]

The necessity of the conversion of non-Christians to faith in God as revealed in Christ follows naturally from a theocentric and Biblically defined approach to missions, but it is lost when man and his temporal welfare instead of God and His glory become the primary objects of concern. The Bible teaches plainly that the natural man needs conversion. Because of sin he is alienated from God and "cannot enter the kingdom of God" (John 3:3, 5).

---

6. Editorial, *Christianity Today,* 10 April 1970, p. 32.
7. Ibid.
8. Bavinck, *An Introduction to the Science of Missions,* p. 158.

Conversion is the universal need of all men—animists, Jews, Moslems, Buddhists, Hindus, Communists, as well as nominal Christians who simply inherited the trappings of Christianity without ever committing themselves heart and soul to Christ—and this determines the missionary's approach. In the following paragraphs Bishop Stephen Neill puts the matter plainly:

> It is constantly said that old ideas of mission must be completely replaced by those that are new and relevant. This is a statement that needs elucidation, and much useful discussion can arise out of it. But I wonder whether the heart has not gone out of the missionary enterprise in all the mainline Churches for another and deeper reason.
>
> If we put the plain question, "Do we want people to be converted?" from many of our contemporary ecumenical theologians the answer will be a resounding "No." If we are evangelicals, must not the answer be a resounding "Yes"?
>
> For years I have been looking for a word which will take the place of the now very unpopular word "conversion," and have not found it. I am well aware of all the possible objections to the word. But I have an uneasy feeling that those who hesitate to use the word are also rejecting the thing.
>
> Those of us who have come to Christ, even from a profoundly Christian background, have known what it means to be "without hope and without God in the world" (Eph. 2:12). Are we prepared to use Paul's language, however unpopular it may be? We desire all men to say Yes to Christ. But there are countless ways of saying Yes to Christ which fall short of the surrender that leads to salvation. Do we know what we are really talking about?
>
> It seems to me that the time has come when we ought to be done with circumlocutions and not be ashamed to say exactly what we mean.[9]

Bishop Neill puts his finger at the root of the problem. The reason conversion-aimed missionary strategy is so unpopular among many today is that they have rejected the conversion theology upon which such strategy rests. Universalism in one or another of its various forms has led them to believe that the follower of another religion does not need conversion, and therefore a missionary appeal for conversion is entirely out of place.

Fortunately, most Latin American evangelicals, as well as new Christians in other parts of the world, sense in their souls that

---

9. "Church of England Newspaper," 13 November 1970, cited in *Church Growth Bulletin*, May 1971, p. 145.

the universalists are wrong—that men do need conversion. Time and again one hears them testify to the difference Christ has made in their lives, and the reaction of a new convert to Christ is not to turn around and say to his unconverted friends: "Stay as you are; this is great for me but you don't need it." On the contrary, the burning desire of converts is that their friends and relatives come to know the gospel as they themselves have done, and many young Christians have risked their lives in order to win loved ones to Christ.[10]

Religion for multitudes in Latin America is an inherited thing. This is what distinguishes traditional Catholicism from the warm, personal faith of the majority of evangelicals. To attempt to rob evangelicals of this experience, through a reinterpretation of theology or a structuring of missions so as to exclude it comes close to being the ultimate disservice that one could render. Conversion —radical, personal, and based on conviction—is something which lies at the heart of Latin American evangelicalism, a fact which Roman Catholics increasingly recognize, and envy.

The Jesuit priest Ignacio Vergara, writing in the Jesuit edited magazine *Mensaje (Message),* has voiced his concern over the steady advance of the evangelical churches in Chile. While the nation's population increased one-sixth between 1940 and 1952, he points out that the number of evangelicals increased 100 percent, making a total of 700,000 in a population of 7 million. He attributes this growth to the evangelicals' "dynamic passion" as against the indifference of Roman Catholics, who "while claiming to be in the majority are religious only in name." Attempting further to explain what conversion to the evangelical faith means to Chileans, Vergara says:

> For Evangelicals, Christianity is above all total adherence to a living Person, whereas the only religion most Catholics know is a series of meaningless rites, wholly unconnected with daily living. The Evangelicals offer the people an ardent message which touches their needs. Many Catholics have become Protestants out of sincere conviction, out of genuine desire for God, of whom they probably never be-

---

10. It has been my experience that the most earnest witnesses to the importance of conversion are those who have very recently experienced its cleansing power and have come to know the richness of the life in Christ about which they knew nothing before. The conclusion cannot be avoided that those who question the necessity of conversion are either unconverted themselves or else have allowed their personal relationship to Christ to dwindle to the point where they can no longer distinguish between the life "in Christ" and that which is still outside of Him.

fore had an authentic experience. Furthermore, the Evangelical religion calls for a new way of life, a way to solve practically the problems of daily life. Catholic converts find that for Protestants Christianity is a way of living rather than a doctrine. People [who] have been victims of vice and turn Evangelical experience a radical change. The Evangelicals present to them a Christ who can change human beings.[11]

Quite obviously, conversion to the evangelical faith rates high with this Jesuit, both as to its influence in the life of the individual and its potential impact on society at large.

W. R. Estep, Jr., has said that "it is impossible to understand the deep-seated political and economic problems without an understanding of Roman Catholicism in Latin America."[12] Every culture is molded by its religion. Latin America demonstrates this very clearly. There can be no satisfactory solution to the social problems without a religious reformation. This means that if evangelicals lose their conversion approach to Latin American missions, their own future, as well as the continent's, is lost.

Paul's Attitude Toward Conversion

Turning to the New Testament, the first urban missionary strategist was the apostle Paul, and his attitude toward conversion is clear. Paul moved out into the highly urbanized Roman world of his day with a strategy that is plainly discernible in his actions. He fixed his eyes on the great concentrations of population, the nerve centers of world culture. The lines of his strategy ran from converts, to churches, to the whole Roman world with its culture, its institutions, and its religions. Paul knew what he was doing. Most, if not all, of the cities and towns in which he established churches were centers of Roman administration, of Greek culture, of Jewish influence, and of commercial and political importance.[13] His strategy called for the planting of churches in these centers of influence, and then, through the contagious witness of the converts, reaching the surrounding region.[14]

11. Cited in "News of the Christian World," *Christian Century,* 17 October 1956, p. 1205.
12. W. R. Estep, Jr., "Church and Culture in Latin America," *Southwestern Journal of Theology* 4 (April 1962), 27.
13. Roland Allen, *Missionary Methods: St. Paul's or Ours?,* 3d ed. (London: World Dominion Press, 1953), p. 19.
14. Michael Green, *Evangelism in the Early Church* (Grand Rapids: Eerdmans Publishing Co., 1970), pp. 260, 263. The author emphasizes the fact that Paul's strategy was provincial as well as urban, in the sense that Paul had entire provinces in view when he established urban churches. "He seems

Paul built his entire missionary strategy on the bedrock of repentance and conversion. The individual convert whose life had been changed by the divine disclosure of God's grace in Christ was the material with which he built churches and influenced the world. To Paul, the question of whether men *needed* to repent and be converted never existed. He himself was the prime example (I Tim. 1:16) of its necessity and importance. His earlier life had supplied him with religion, morality, zeal, and status (Phil. 3:4-6); but until he abandoned all these through radical conversion to Christ, at a definite time and place, he had nothing worth keeping (Phil. 3:7-9).

Religious conversion was not a popular notion in Paul's day any more than it is today. In his recent book *Evangelism in the Early Church,* Michael Green discusses at length the idea of conversion in Graeco-Roman society. He finds, contrary to certain modern writers that he mentions, that nothing in the other religions of that period resembled Christian conversion. The Christian faith which Paul preached demanded a complete break with all other religious commitments and a radical moral change in the lives of its adherents. All this was utterly contrary to the customary attitude of Hellenistic man, who did not regard belief as necessary for worship, nor ethics as part of religion, and could not understand why a person could not adopt a new faith while still adhering to some degree to his old ones.[15]

Regardless of its foreignness to the Graeco-Roman mind, Paul persisted in his conviction that repentance and conversion were absolutely necessary for entrance into the kingdom of God.[16] Any religious "kingdom of God" to which entrance can be gained, or its program realized in the world, without the demands of repentance and conversion being met, is not the kingdom about which Christ and the apostles preached. Conversion in the New Testament involves an exclusive change of faith, worship, and ethics. "All things are become new" (II Cor. 5:17).

Paul's theology made repentance and conversion as necessary for Jews as for Gentiles, for all were "under sin" (Rom. 3:9). "Dialogue" and "exchange" with followers of other religions were

to have made a point of setting up two or three centres of faith in a province and then passing on, and allowing the native enthusiasm and initiative of the converts to lead them to others whom they could win for Christ."
15. Ibid., pp. 144-46.
16. Gerhardus Vos, *The Kingdom and the Church* (Grand Rapids: Eerdmans Publishing Co., 1958), pp. 91 ff.

not characteristic of Paul.[17] Instead, Paul aimed at conversion. The conversion of his hearers to an exclusive and life-changing faith in Jesus Christ was the aim of Paul's preaching everywhere—among the Jews in the synagogue (Acts 9:20), along a river under an open sky (Acts 16:13), or in a Roman prison (Acts 16:29 ff.; 28:30-31; Philem. 10).

Paul was not blind to the evils of the Roman social order, but his building blocks were repentant and converted men. To them he gave his first attention. The all-of-life character of Christian conversion was the basic step in the transformation of society. There was nothing "other-worldly" about Paul's religion, if by that expression is meant a disregard for the here-and-now involvements of life. Pauline evangelism everywhere was a call to a radical change of life and an entire realignment of man's deepest allegiances under the sovereignty of God. All of a converted man's words, actions, and relationships now came under the direction of God's Word, and such a man could be expected to make a difference in society. Roman society needed changing, but Paul was not so foolish as to attempt it by using unchanged people in the process.

Paul's Means to Conversion

Paul wanted converts, but how did he get them? Luke seems particularly concerned to answer that question as he chronicles Paul's missionary journeys in Acts. Luke tells the *how* of apostolic convert making, and the two principal factors he brings out are not those for which sociologists or psychologists would look first. Luke emphasizes two distinctly *supernatural* factors: the Spirit and the Word.[18] The supreme agent of conversion in the New Testament is the Holy Spirit and the means is the Word. Without the Holy Spirit the whole missionary enterprise could not even begin (Luke 24:44 ff.) and without the Word there is no faith (Rom. 10:17). "Every initiative in evangelism recorded in Acts is the initiative of the Spirit of God";[19] and similarly, the salvation of men and women everywhere is taught to be utterly dependent on the missionary vocation, the sending, the going, the preaching, and the hearing of the Word of God, which make up missions (Rom. 10:13-15).

17. See Hans-Werner Gensichen, "Dialogue with Non-Christian Religions," in *The Future of the Christian World Mission,* ed. William J. Danker and Wi Jo Kang (Grand Rapids: Eerdmans Publishing Co., 1971), pp. 29-40.
18. Green, *Evangelism in the Early Church,* p. 148.
19. Ibid., p. 149.

If Paul is taken seriously the importance of personal conversion cannot be questioned. And taking conversion seriously, the *means* which bring it about become equally important. Paul never separated the Spirit and the Word. "The Word of God," says R. B. Kuiper, "is the one and only indispensable means by which the Holy Spirit works faith in the hearts of men."[20] Sociological and psychological factors may enter in, but they never serve as substitutes for the Word of the gospel. Historical conditions, in God's providence, may create openings for the gospel's reception; but the Word alone is the Spirit's indispensable instrument in conversion. Without a knowledge of the Word, conversion will not occur.

This being the case, it is not surprising to find Paul forever preaching. He proclaimed the Word everywhere in the great urban centers that he visited. Being "constrained by the word" (Acts 18:5), he stayed at Corinth; and being obedient to the heavenly vision, he remained there eighteen months "teaching the word of God among them" (Acts 18:11). It was "the word of God" which the Antiochans crowded to the synagogues to hear Paul preach (Acts 13:44), and through it there came for them and others the decisive moment of faith or rejection (Acts 13:46).

The message which Paul preached was essentially the same for men everywhere (I Cor. 15:1, 3-4), but he exercised remarkable flexibility in the way he applied it.[21] Everywhere it was the person and work of Christ, the gift of reconciliation, of adoption, of forgiveness, and of the Spirit. There is no evidence that he felt it necessary, or possible (Gal. 1:7-9), to change his basic message anywhere. The message of missions, for Paul, was a settled matter: "The word is nigh thee, in thy mouth, and in thy heart: that is, the word of faith, which we preach" (Rom. 10:8). And it was this message which made converts.

The Impact of Conversion on Individuals and Families

What happens when the Pauline emphasis on conversion is applied to persons, families, and society in the modern era? Does conversion in the Biblical sense have any relevance today in the cities, in the slums, and in modern industrialized society? Is it still

---

20. R. B. Kuiper, *God-Centered Evangelism: A Presentation of the Scriptural Theology of Evangelism* (Grand Rapids: Baker Book House, 1963), p. 123.
21. Green, *Evangelism in the Early Church,* pp. 150-51. Over against C. H. Dodd, who believed that the apostolic gospel was probably a very closely defined statement or formula, Green lays stress on the flexibility in approach and application which he sees evidenced among the early evangelists.

the approach which should be followed, or are the times too different?

Evidence seems to be pointing to one single, very significant answer: conversion to the evangelical faith is the most important single factor in the reorientation of individual and family lives and in their general upward mobility in the urban setting. Willems observes that in the lives of the evangelicals which he studied in Chile and Brazil, the former vices such as drunkenness, tavern brawls, wife beating, illegitimacy, neglect of children, untidy personal appearance, failure to improve poor housing conditions, and similar traits disappeared after conversion to the new faith. In their place appeared new attitudes and values that greatly changed the entire life style of the family. Describing the convert, Willems says:

> He refrains from alcohol, his attitudes toward his family change, instead of violence there is now patience and the "desire to forgive." If he lives in concubinage he seeks to legalize his union; he begins to enjoy home life and, thanks to his newly acquired money-saving virtues, he is soon able to ameliorate somewhat the shanty he may be living in. The place is kept cleaner and so are the children.[22]

Willems tends to ascribe these changes to the poor man's desire "to become respectable, that is, to adopt middle-class behavior."[23] But desire alone is not enough to explain what happens. The poor may have the *desire* for improvement, but desire by itself does not produce the change. The secret of Christian conversion lies in answering the question: What is the source of the convert's power to stop drinking, carousing, and fornicating and to begin living the kind of life that is a joy to himself and those around him?

That power, from the theological point of view, comes from the Holy Spirit who lives in the believer (Rom. 8:2-4, 9). That is what conversion is all about. The heart of man is changed—he thinks new thoughts, he wills new things, he loves what before he hated and hates what previously he enjoyed. Sociologists like Willems can describe what occurs when people are converted, but they fail to explain what makes it happen. Sociological studies are helpful but they supply only part of the answer. The spiritual dynamics of conversion can only be theologically explained.

Conversion is of special importance to the family. Increasingly today, the importance of the family is being recognized by students

---

22. *Followers of the New Faith,* pp. 130-31.
23. Ibid., pp. 131, 251.

of Latin American urban society.[24] A few years ago writers were saying that in the urban, industrialized environment primary groups (such as the family) were of less importance, and secondary groups (composed of one's fellow workers outside the home) were the most meaningful to the individual urbanite. This was one of the premises on which the industrial mission approach was built.[25] But today this is no longer being assumed. There is now an increasing body of research which suggests that this primary group, the family, is still very important in meeting the needs of urban people.[26] In the home circle certain needs are met—companionship, affection, basic security—which can be met nowhere else. Urban man's most basic identity still is connected with his home.

In one of the UNESCO studies emanating from Lima, Peru, it was found that in the urban area where there was much general tension, constant friction between neighbors, and a widespread feeling of failure and frustration, these factors were combined with a tendency to take refuge in family life and in the personal dependency which family membership involves.[27] The home, in other words, becomes even more meaningfully a man's castle when the storms outside the home are most severe.

As a consequence, it is logical to suppose that the key target area for the Christian missionary in the urban situation is the home and family. Not the man, the woman, or the children in

---

24. William H. Key, "Rural-Urban Social Participation," in *Urbanism in World Perspective: A Reader,* ed. Sylvia Fleis Fava (New York: Thomas Y. Crowell Co., 1968), p. 306.

25. One of the major premises on which the industrial mission approach is based is that in the urban setting the vocational, educational, recreational, and political relationships which the individual possesses take on larger significance than that of his primary group relationships, particularly those of the family. More time is spent with these secondary groups, and more satisfaction is derived from these contacts, than come from the home and the family. The places to reach such people, therefore, are the places where they work and spend their leisure time, and not primarily in the home with the family. See John S. Hazelton, "La Comunicacion del Evangelio en el Ambiente Urbano," *Promotor de Evangelizacion,* November 1868, p. 2, where the theoretical basis for industrial evangelism is explained. In the same issue the practical recommendations based on it are detailed in "Miembro de la Iglesia" and "Pastor de la Iglesia," p. 4. The entire focus is on encounter between Christian and non-Christian in the *places of employment,* without a word about the home. The new mission fields are the "factories, garages, offices, and all places of work." This, the articles conclude, constitutes the "new mission of the Church in contemporary society" (p. 4).

26. Key, "Rural-Urban Social Participation," pp. 306, 310-11.

27. H. Rotondo, "Psychological and Mental Health Problems of Urbanization Based on Case Studies in Peru," in *Urbanization in Latin America,* ed. P. M. Hauser, p. 257.

isolation from the other members of the family, but the family together, in the setting that means most amid the tensions of the city. The latest research, in fact, indicates that in many cases the family is more important in the urban area than in the rural. In the village, relatives and friends of long standing are all around —the whole village, in fact, provides the group support which the individual needs. But in the urban setting, surrounded by strangers, the primary group support of the family takes on an importance that it did not possess in the village. In the isolation of the city, kinship relationships become all the more meaningful.[28] It is in the home that urban people find their basic identification, and it is there that the most meaningful experience of life—religious conversion—should take place.

When thirty-six Presbyterian ministers in Brazil were asked to define the influence which, according to their own experience, conversion to the evangelical faith has on family life, they used such expressions as "more gentleness," "forgiveness," "better humor," "more understanding," "respect," "sincerity," "more attachment," "loyalty," and "affectivity" to define the changes that had affected the relationship among the members of the evangelical family.[29] Conversion has that kind of effect on individual and family life. Is there any doubt that conversion is relevant to the modern urban situation?

Paul's conversion approach to urban missions was *family centered*. The "households" mentioned in the New Testament (Acts 16:15; I Cor. 1:16; Gal. 6:10) were not unlike the extended families and kinship ties found in Latin America, and Paul used these households to establish the faith in each area he evangelized.

> While individual contacts and personal friendships marked the beginnings of a new church, it was through the Greek "household" that the new faith spread rapidly in St. Paul's world. The Greek *oikos* or *oikia* formed the basic social unity that was best fitted for the extension of the church. There is no exact equivalent in Greek for the English word "family." The *oikos* or household was a kind of extended family many

---

28. Key, "Rural-Urban Social Participation," p. 311.
29. Willems, *Followers of the New Faith,* p. 173. Willems attributes these changes to the social forces brought about by industrialization. It is inconceivable, however, to suppose that there is anything in the industrial revolution which can produce the things listed by these thirty-six pastors. On the contrary, in fact, respect, good humor, loyalty, and gentleness might be expected more often in the rural setting than in the industrial city with all its tensions. These qualities, moreover, are characteristic of converts to Biblical Christianity everywhere, whether in the village or in the city.

of whom lived together. It was composed not only of members of the family (in our sense) but also of employees, slaves, tenants, and other dependents.[30]

Thousands upon thousands of *vecindades* and extended family households all across Latin America represent the modern equivalent of the basic social unit Paul used as his base of operation. The Book of Acts and the Epistles often refer to the rulers of households. Through these men entire families were brought to conversion and baptism. Cornelius was "a devout man, and one that feared God with all his house" (Acts 10:2). When the Spirit fell on them, they were all baptized in the name of Jesus Christ (Acts 10:48). To the trembling jailor at Philippi, Paul said, "Believe on the Lord Jesus, and thou shalt be saved, thou and thy house" (Acts 16:31). The jailor then took Paul and Silas up into his house, the Word was preached to his entire household, and that very same night the jailor was baptized, "he and all his, immediately" (Acts 16:33). At Philippi, a woman named Lydia served as Paul's contact, and she and her entire household were baptized (Acts 16:15). Her house then became the center of the church at Philippi.[31] At Thessalonica, it was Jason and his house (Acts 17:5-9). At Corinth, Crispus, the president of the local synagogue, accepted the new teaching and was baptized along with his household (Acts 18:8). His home provided direct access to the Jews who were coming into the church. Paul, however, chose as his place of residence the house of Titus Justus, a Gentile and "one that worshipped God, whose house joined hard to the synagogue" (Acts 18:7). Being a Gentile, Titus could be the channel for other non-Jews to come to hear Paul preach. Scattered throughout the epistles are other references to the households where Paul stayed, preached, and established his first converts (I Cor. 1:15-16; Col. 4:15; Philem. 2).

Parents, children, servants, slaves, visitors, relatives, and friends all heard the gospel preached in the environment of the home, and there Paul generally made his first converts. They were baptized together and shared the Lord's Supper together. The first blow against pagan racial and social barriers was struck at the Communion table where master and slave, men and women, Jew

---

30. Joseph A. Grassi, *A World to Win: The Missionary Methods of Paul the Apostle* (Maryknoll, New York: Maryknoll Publications, 1965), p. 85.
31. I acknowledge my dependence on and appreciation for Maryknoll Father Joseph A. Grassi's emphasis on the family nature of Paul's missionary strategy (*A World to Win,* pp. 85-91). His approach is more Biblical and Reformed than that of many Protestant writers on the subject.

and Gentile sat together around the same table. The first and most basic lessons concerning the nature of the church as the "household of God" (Gal. 6:10; Eph. 2:19) were taught at the very beginning of the Pauline mission in each city as the faith was planted in the "extended family" of the Greek household. There, along the God appointed covenant lines, the gospel could travel its swiftest course until even distant relatives might be converted.

The Conversion of a Working Girl

Like thousands of other young girls, Lidia Falcon was sent to Mexico City at the age of fourteen to work as a domestic servant.[32] She drifted from one job to another, until, at the age of eighteen, she was employed as a seamstress in a clothing factory in one of the worst areas of the city. There she shared the low wages, the pressing temptations, and eventually the lonely, heartbreaking condition in which so many girls her age are found.

Opportunities for a better life came when Miss Falcon was offered a job with a missionary family that was moving to the city of Mérida. The way this family lived impressed her. In Mérida, she attended evangelical services at their church, and when evangelist Fernando Vangioni, of the Billy Graham Association, conducted a crusade in Mérida in September 1966, she attended the meetings. On the night of September 30, Lidia Falcon was converted under Vangioni's preaching and was baptized shortly afterward in the Independent Presbyterian Church of that city.

Miss Falcon became an aggressive evangelist almost from the night of her conversion. After about a year she enrolled in a Bible institute in Mexico City, and was so zealous in witnessing that she would go to the nearby market to distribute tracts and talk to people about Christ even during off-hours between classes.

One morning, I found Lidia talking to an older woman in the chapel. Just the two of them were there, and the older woman had a swollen, black eye. Smiling, Lidia introduced the woman to me as one who had just professed faith in Christ and wanted to be baptized. The two had met in the market where Lidia was distributing copies of the Scripture booklet *Dios Habla (God Speaks)*. "It's part of the Bible," Lidia was telling the people, when

---

32. Miss Lidia Falcón is a former student of mine. She also lived with my family for a year during the time when she worked in Mexico City, and later when she attended the Instituto Cristiano Mexicano. She is now married and has two children. Some of the information in this section was supplied by her answers to the questionnaire that appears in Appendix 1.

FIGURE 4

FACTORS LEADING TO CONVERSION

As given by fifty-eight converts
to evangelicalism between 1960
and 1970, interviewed in Mexico
City, 1968-70.

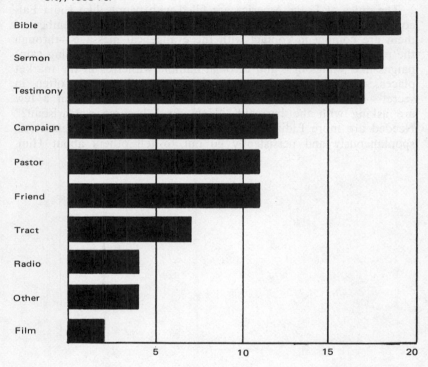

this woman slipped up to her and said: "I have a Bible and have been reading it. Can you tell me how to become a Christian?"

Telling people how to become Christians was Lidia's specialty; and she soon had the woman on her knees in the chapel, leading her through the basic steps of salvation. The woman related how she got the black .eye. She worked in a bar; and the day before, when she refused to give a man another drink after he had run out of money, he had beaten her severely. She hated her place of employment, but she had six fatherless children to support, and no other job was available.

The outcome of this was a short-term church-in-the-house; for this barwoman invited Lidia to come to her home every week to conduct a Sunday school, which later became a preaching center for a group of seminarians. A new housing project eventually abolished the squatter settlement where they lived, but for a time this woman's home was the center for evangelism among about twenty families, and many heard the gospel for the first time in her home.

The cities of Latin America are filled with people like Lidia Falcon and the barmaid with the black eye. A growing number of them are coming in contact with the evangelical message—through the personal influence of Christian families, through preaching campaigns like Vangioni's, and through humble witnesses in the market places. Bibles and Scripture portions are being read—often in secret—by thousands of men and women, and more than a few are asking with the barmaid, "How do I become a Christian?" Needed are more Lidias who, having found the Savior themselves, spontaneously and persistently go out to tell others about Him.

6

CHURCHES ESTABLISHED

Mission work, for many people, means a wide assortment of religious activities which, for the most part, do not produce or multiply churches. There are missionary training schools which teach about other religions, other cultures, how missionaries can stay healthy in hot climates, phonetics, languages, anthropology, sociology, and psychology; but they do not teach how people are converted and churches multiplied.[1] At best, such schools produce a type of missionary who serves well in keeping the machinery of missions running; but very little visible fruit in the form of converts and churches can be found even after years of missionary activity.

This is tragic. In a period of human history where large numbers of people in various parts of the world demonstrate a readiness to hear and believe the gospel, there is no excuse for mission work that does not result in men, women, and children being won to Christian discipleship. Fruitful, New Testament missions cannot be defined in any other terms than this. By New Testament standards, the authenticity of a missionary program that does not produce converts to Jesus Christ in a population that is demonstratively receptive, is highly suspect. By the same token, any strategy of missions that lays little stress on church planting, where circumstances permit such planting, is equally questionable. New

---

1. Donald A. McGavran, *How Churches Grow: The New Frontier of Mission* (London: World Dominion Press, 1959), p. 11.

Testament strategy demands both converts and churches, as Paul's approach to the cities of the first century illustrates so well.

Paul's Urban Church-Planting Strategy

Paul's church-planting mission work was placed in the Bible for a purpose. The Holy Spirit inspired Luke to record Paul's strategy because in it are found lessons from which the church in all periods can and should learn. The very weight of the narrative, highlighting Pauline missions, is evidence that this record has significance for the church universal and for mission work in all ages.

Within a period of ten years, by means of three missionary journeys, Paul founded churches in the four Roman provinces of Galatia, Macedonia, Achaia, and Asia. His sights were set on Spain, the farthest western frontier of the empire (Rom. 15:24, 28); and he may have gotten there. Everywhere Paul went he preached, gathered converts, and formed them into local, self-governing churches. The uniformity of his strategy is so outstanding that it can best be explained by examining the theological factors which lay behind it.

The first of these factors was Paul's insight into the meaning of history and God's purpose in the world. Paul's initial conscious awareness that God had intervened in the world to establish a new community of people which centered around Jesus Christ came at the time of his conversion near Damascus.[2] Paul, like any Jew well grounded in the Old Testament, knew full well that God had a goal in history—the formation of a people who would serve Him and carry out His purpose. Paul believed, too, that the Messiah would establish a community of men through whom God would, in the last days, act mightily and climactically in the affairs of men.

Therefore, when the glorified Lord said to Paul, "I am Jesus whom thou persecutest," Paul sensed at once what it was, and whom it was, to which Christ was referring. It was the church, the community of men and women whom Paul was persecuting, but who were so well known and so much loved by the risen Lord that He identified Himself with them.

That settled the issue for Paul. From that moment on he regarded the church as that unique community of believers in and through whom God was carrying forward His design and purpose in the world. The church is the long awaited messianic community

---

2. Grassi, *A World to Win*, pp. 21 ff.

and has worldwide dimension. It bears the Good News to all races and nations, and in this way fulfills God's plan in history.

It was this insight which turned Paul into an evangelist and a church planter. Seeing that God in Christ was now carrying on His unique, redemptive work in the world through the visible church, participation in this work and in the expansion of the church became the greatest joy and highest privilege a man could possess. Paul then gave himself to the task of church planting without reservation, in the deep conviction that the Christian communities he was establishing would be used by God to accomplish the divine purpose. The founding of a church, in Paul's view, was an act of incorporating men into a community of Christ, a fellowship where converts would grow into the kind of people God could use to fulfill His original purpose in creation and His ultimate design for mankind. As an establisher of churches, Paul was God's colaborer, building a community that would endure for eternity.[3]

With so strong a view of church-planting missions dominating his thinking, personal sacrifices in the line of duty meant very little to Paul. Though his missionary career was filled with suffering and difficulty (I Cor. 11:23-33), such difficulties were of small consequence when seen in the light of God's purpose and the privilege of participating in it. The multiplication and growth of churches was for Paul the most important activity that could occupy one's attention. It meant divine-human partnership, the kingdom of the Messiah manifested here and now, in which all the followers of Christ are called to labor (II Cor. 4:1).

Paul's church-planting missionary strategy developed out of his high view of the church and his strong sense of responsibility for the church's growth and expansion. In his own experience, conversion was followed immediately by baptism and incorporation into the fellowship of Christ's people (Acts 9:17, 18); and in the missionary career to which he was called Paul never separated soul winning from church planting. Paul never left converts isolated and alone, but drew believers together into living cells of fellowship, worship, witness, and service.

Moreover, Paul made the churches which he founded dependent, not on him or any other human resource, but on God the Holy Spirit.[4] Perhaps nothing is more relevant for urban missionary policy today than Paul's manner of teaching converts and their churches to lean on the gifts and guidance of the Holy Spirit

---

3. Ibid., p. 23.
4. Allen, *Missionary Methods: St. Paul's or Ours?*, p. 105.

(I Cor. 12—14). Luke's account of Paul's strategy tells of new believers being baptized and immediately *incorporated into* the visible assembly of believers, and being given both the privileges and the responsibilities of membership in the body of Christ. In sharp contrast to the policies found on many mission fields today, Paul trusted young Christians in the hands of the Spirit. After preaching in a certain place for a time, he dared move on, leaving behind him a church—not a "mission" or a "chapel," but a fully organized church—free from outside supervision or control and fully capable of growing and expanding by its own spiritual resources.[5]

> St. Paul's Churches were indigenous Churches in the proper sense of the word; and I believe that the secret of their foundation lay in his recognition of the Church as a local Church . . . and in his profound belief and trust in the Holy Spirit indwelling his converts and the Churches of which they were members, which enabled him to establish them at once with full authority.
>
> It is not easy for us to-day so to trust the Holy Ghost. We can more easily believe in His work in us and through us, than we can believe in His work in and through our converts: we cannot trust our converts to Him. But that is one of the most obvious lessons which the study of St. Paul's work teaches us.[6]

H. R. Boer points out that in the New Testament, the church, the Spirit, and missionary witness are inseparably related.[7] Whenever, due to ignorance, they have become separated either in theory or in practice, the missionary enterprise has suffered serious consequences. What God has joined together, men should not put asunder.

Still another vital factor in Paul's church-planting strategy was the kind of training he gave to his converts. Paul believed in the laity, the *laos* of God. What God had begun among them He would complete (Phil. 1:6), and through them He would carry out His purpose. The task of the apostles, of the prophets, of the pastors and teachers was to equip the laity—God's "holy ones"—for the work of the gospel ministry (Eph. 4:11-12).

To this end, Paul instituted the type of training program wherever

---

5. Harry R. Boer, *That My House May Be Filled* (Grand Rapids: Eerdmans Publishing Co., 1957), p. 73; Allen, *Missionary Methods: St. Paul's or Ours?*, p. 162.

6. Allen, *Missionary Methods: St. Paul's or Ours?*, p. ix.

7. Harry R. Boer, *Pentecost and Missions* (Grand Rapids: Eerdmans Publishing Co., 1961), p. 162.

he planted a church which, after a relatively short time, would allow him to leave the new believers in full charge of the local church's affairs. These included the continued preaching and teaching of the Word, mutual discipline, and the administration of the ordinances.[8] In an incredibly brief period, Paul and those who labored with him raised up local leadership in each place. Paul did not leave young churches with no one to preach, no one to teach, no one to baptize, and no one to administer the Lord's Supper. Nor did they have to wait weeks and months for a visiting apostle to appear before they could enjoy the full prerogatives of a church. Paul's converts learned to teach, preach, witness, and live as Christians, victoriously and fruitfully, beginning at the moment of their conversion experience. Because Paul trusted them, and the Spirit, and the Word, he dared to leave them, despite the perils which he knew existed (Acts 20:29-32).

The irrefutable evidence that Paul's strategy was correct is found in the fact that his converts became missionaries and the churches which he planted grew and multiplied. Witnessing was spontaneous. Paul did not have to harangue them on the subject of witnessing: they simply went out and did it, taking for granted the fact that they possessed both the obligation and the necessary spiritual equipment to transmit the faith to others.[9] How different from today.

> When we turn from the restless entreaties and exhortations which fill the pages of our modern missionary magazines to the pages of the New Testament, we are astonished at the change in the atmosphere. St. Paul does not repeatedly exhort his Churches to subscribe money for the propagation of the Faith, he is far more concerned to explain to them what the Faith is, and how they ought to practice it and to keep it. The same is true of St. Peter and St. John, and of

8. It is true, of course, that Paul made it a practice to delegate one or another of his coworkers to minister in certain areas until the churches were more firmly established. For examples of this, see Acts 17:14; I Cor. 16:12; Col. 1:7; and Titus 1:5. Once on their own, however, local leaders were fully in charge, administering baptism and the Lord's Supper as well as preaching the Word. The administration of the ordinances is generally the last thing modern missionaries entrust to new converts, yet Paul appears to have done so immediately. The words of I Cor. 1:14-17 seem to indicate that the majority of the converts at Corinth were baptized in his absence; and even when present, Paul did not usually do the baptizing himself. He baptized the first converts, and later ones were baptized by the local believers themselves. Cf. Allen, *Missionary Methods: St. Paul's or Ours?*, p. 126.
9. Boer, *Pentecost and Missions*, pp. 128 ff., following closely Allen, *Missionary Methods: St. Paul's or Ours?*, p. 121.

all the apostolic writers. They do not seem to feel any necessity to repeat the Great Commission, and to urge that it is the duty of their converts to make disciples of all the nations. What we read in the New Testament is no anxious appeal to Christians to spread the Gospel, but a note here and there which suggests how the Gospel was being spread abroad: "the Churches were established in the Faith, and increased in number daily," "in every place your faith to Godward is spread abroad so that we need not to speak anything"; or as a result of a persecution: "They that were scattered abroad went everywhere preaching the Word."[10]

Closely related to the spiritual independence of the young churches which Paul founded was their financial independence as well. Paul himself asked no financial assistance; he brought no financial help to those to whom he preached; and in no instance did he administer local church funds. The pattern of voluntary, unpaid leadership flowed from his own example. Each assembly of believers was financially independent from the start. "There is not a hint from beginning to end of the Acts and Epistles of any one Church depending upon another, with the single exception of the collection for the poor saints at Jerusalem."[11] In this way Paul avoided the multitudinous problems which later missionaries have found so burdensome. Nor did he or his coworkers ever have to limit church planting because the mission "budget" did not allow it.

Paul would not allow financial dependence on foreign sources to destroy the spontaneous freedom of the Spirit in his converts. Money always controls its recipients. Instead of controlling, and thereby restricting the young churches, Paul let them go. He gladly allowed their spontaneous enthusiasm and love for the Lord to be expressed in worship, service, and witnessing. There were risks involved, as he knew full well; and sometimes things got out of hand and disciplinary action was necessary. These occasional irregularities, however, were a small price to pay for growing churches and converts who in the freedom and joy of their salvation won their relatives and friends to the Lord.

As a result of Paul's consistent policy of dependence on local resources, spiritual and material, the churches he founded were by their very nature *structured for mission*. All that they needed for life, growth, and endless multiplication was available within the local group. No church was richer than another church: the Word and the Spirit, the transformed lives were held in common by all.

---

10. Allen, *Missionary Methods: St. Paul's or Ours?*, p. 8.
11. Ibid., p. 68.

Nothing that they did not need nor understand was imposed on them, nor was anything which they did need withheld. They could begin at once to move out in missionary outreach to their non-Christian neighbors. They could not leave evangelism to the "professional" missionary, for he (Paul) had already gone. There were no financial grants to their local church from foreign sources which might lead to suspicion as to why they had become Christians. All the sources of alienation which have worked such havoc in modern missions were carefully avoided in Paul's strategy. So mission structured was the Pauline church that it is impossible to distinguish between church and mission. Says Boer:

> One hardly knows where in Acts to look for a distinction between Church and missions. Restlessly the Spirit drives the Church to witness, and continually Churches rise out of the witness. The Church is missionary Church. She is not missionary Church in the sense that she is "very much interested" in missions, or that she "does a great deal" for missions. In Acts missions is not a hobby of an "evangelical section" of the Church. The Church as a whole is missionary in all her relationships.[12]

Paul would not even burden the church with buildings. "Use whatever is available" was his policy, and the majority of the churches which the New Testament refers to were house-churches. Paul promoting a "building fund" was unthinkable. As long as the "free course" of the gospel (II Thess. 3:1) was not hindered by lack of specially designed auditoriums, he dispensed with them. One cannot conceive of Paul tolerating the erection of pompous buildings and calling them "churches." Imagine what the writer of "Owe no man anything, save to love one another" (Rom. 13:8) would have said about enormous debts incurred by churches constructing splendid edifices in the same city where slum-dwellers go to bed hungry and children are without shoes.[13]

Paul taught the churches which he planted to *pray* for missions. This fact is often overlooked in the study of Paul's missionary strategy, but it had a strong bearing on the missionary zeal of the early Christians—a zeal that is so commonly lacking today.

---

12. *Pentecost and Missions*, pp. 161-62.
13. Examples of churches that are deeply in debt over their buildings and furnishings are too numerous to mention. History records some instances where churches owned slum tenement property and maintained their own lavish religious edifices from the rent obtained from slum housing. See Robert D. Cross, ed., *The Church and the City, 1865-1910* (Indianapolis: Bobbs-Merrill Co., 1967), pp. 78-81.

Where there is earnest prayer there will be corresponding endeavor. "Pray," wrote Paul to the Thessalonians, "that the word of the Lord may run and be glorified" (II Thess. 3:1). Paul's whole approach was bathed in prayer. Prayer is mentioned in the same breath as the other essential pieces of the "armor of God" (Eph. 6:14-18). Since the time when the upper room prayer meeting had been set aflame by the out-poured Holy Spirit on the day of Pentecost and the Word was preached resulting in three thousand conversions, prayer was an indispensable weapon for breaking down Satan's strongholds and the establishment of Christ's church. Was not Paul praying when Ananias found him and uttered those unforgettable words of incorporation into the fellowship of Christ's disciples—"Brother Saul" (Acts 9:17)?

As a result of all this, the churches which Paul planted in the urban centers of the Roman Empire were marked by prayer, freedom, spontaneous zeal, intimate fellowship, egalitarian spirit, and a burning desire to share the faith with others. In a cruel and hostile world, these cells of Christian love and communion fortified the believers to carry on their daily roles in the home, the market, the military, or public office, with a spirit and confidence that left its mark on all who knew them. Most of them were poor, unlearned people (I Cor. 1:26). But they had something which the world needed and did not have; and both in their living and in their dying the early Christians let the world know that Jesus Christ had come and had made all things new.

New Testament Church Planting in Twentieth-Century Cities

"There is the city," says Martin E. Marty, "and in the city there is the test."[14] Everything the church says, does, and tries to do is tested most severely in the city. And for Christian missions as well, the great cities are the supreme test. All missionary endeavor, in a greater or lesser degree, will henceforth be urban centered. There in the city the fiercest battles for men's souls even now are raging. The urban environment is the final arena for missions.

In applying Paul's church-planting missionary strategy to the rapidly growing cities of Latin America, four specific areas are found in which the New Testament approach seems particularly applicable to the modern situation.

---

14. *Second Chance for American Protestants* (New York: Harper & Row, Publishers, 1963), p. 164.

The Family Approach

Harry Boer has remarked that the great merit of McGavran in emphasizing the place of the *oikos* in missionary strategy can hardly be overestimated.[15] This is just as true in large areas of the city as in a rural environment. Urban populations are criss-crossed in every direction by natural human bridges over which the gospel can pass from person to person and from family to family. The lines of kinship, family, and "paisano" run from city to village and back again, and all across the city. The family is as strategic in today's cities as in the cities of the first century, and the Pauline pattern of church planting is repeatable still today.

Contact-people can be found in every corner of the cities if someone will go look for them. In the first century, Paul traveled from city to city following up his contacts with relatives and friends of Jewish Christians from Antioch.[16] Personal contacts were his bridges; and by means of these bridges Paul carried the gospel to the dispersed Jews, and beyond them to the Gentiles. This insight into *how* he was to carry out the commission God had given him was one of the secrets of Paul's successful church-planting ministry.

> Paul lived for one consuming purpose, that of knowing Jesus Christ and bringing others into the redeemed fellowship. His intellectual achievements and his mystical awareness of God were both tremendous. . . . Yet neither his dedication nor his communion with God in Christ was the sole secret of his amazing success. That lay in the combination of his deep understanding of, and fellowship with, the living Christ, with his intuitive and unherring [sic] co-operation with God in the extension of these vast stirrings of the people whom God purposed to disciple.[17]

There are "stirrings of the peoples" today, and scattered throughout the *colonias* and *barrios* of Latin American cities are people who are potential contacts of the highest importance. They are individuals and entire families who were evangelical Christians in the village before coming to the city, or they were converted soon after arrival in some other part of the city but since then have moved to their present location. They have joined no evangelical church. Some of them have been sympathizers for a long

---

15. *Pentecost and Missions*, p. 184.
16. This important thesis is developed by McGavran, *Bridges of God: A Study in the Strategy of Missions*, pp. 27-35.
17. Ibid., p. 26.

period of time but no one has ever approached them personally with the call to commitment.

A modern-day Paul, both in his perception of *how* the Christian faith can flow in the urban setting and his dedication to the actual task of church planting, is the Mexican pastor and medical doctor Moisés Lopez.[18] Dr. Lopez has done outstanding missionary work in and around Mexico City by following through on the contacts supplied him in his dual role as physician and Presbyterian minister. He has sought out and visited scores of members of downtown Presbyterian churches who have moved to the outlying districts. Likewise, he has gone to rural towns and villages where families were located whom he came to know in other ways.

As a result of his efforts, Dr. Lopez has established more than twenty churches in and near Mexico City. He follows two basic methods in locating the "bridges" he needs. First, when he preaches in older, established churches, he preaches on the theme of winning the city for Christ, and he gives an invitation containing three questions: (1) Who is willing to go out into the streets and evangelize? (2) Who is willing to become a teacher in one of the house-churches needing additional leaders? (3) If there are people in the audience that live where there is no gospel witness, are you willing to open your house for meetings?

"If you have the ark of the Lord in your house, His blessing will rest upon your household," Lopez promises; and he tells numerous stories about changes which have taken place in families that accepted his invitation.

His second method is to go personally and visit the families with whom he is acquainted, urging them to begin holding evangelical services in their homes. Dr. Lopez frankly tells them that due to his busy schedule, he cannot be expected to do much visiting after the initial group has been formed. The local people themselves, in New Testament fashion, are responsible for the leadership and the growth of the congregation. When there are special problems, they can call on him. But once started, they must expect to do the work of evangelization themselves.

In the house-churches which Lopez establishes, the head of the host family generally leads in the service, with a visiting preacher or teacher bringing the message if such a person is available. If

---

18. Information on the church-planting activities of Dr. López was drawn from two interviews in Mexico City, 7 February 1968 and 2 June 1971, and from my personal observation of two of his house-churches. Dr. López is referred to also in my article "Training Urban Church Planters in Latin America," *Church Growth Bulletin,* January 1970, p. 42.

there is none, then one from the group teaches the Bible lesson. Some services are held on Sunday, others during the week. Uncles, aunts, cousins, and friends from all parts of the city are informed of the services and come if they can. Neighbors are visited repeatedly, and long-time sympathizers with the gospel are found among them. There is fellowship, singing, praying for one another's problems and needs, and a twenty- to thirty-minute Bible lesson. Services continue in the home until larger accommodations are needed.

When asked what method of evangelism should be employed today, Lopez replied:

> Visitation in the new *colonias,* house-to-house, among unconverted people and whomever you find; but most important of all, the planting of centers for preaching in the homes of Christian families that are willing to open their homes for Bible study and services.[19]

Paul would like that.

The Proliferation of House-churches

The big consolidated downtown churches are not the answer. The need is for a proliferation of house-churches in all parts of the city. These evangelistic cell groups have a far greater potential for the spread of evangelical Christianity than anything else today. On this subject Paulus Scharpff asserts:

> "The one and only way to genuine fellowship is the creation of truly Christian cell-groups in the midst of the aridity of modern life; it is the indirect way to mutual reconstruction, to united witness, and outside service" (H. Kraemer).
>
> An evangelistic cell-group is a fellowship of pastoral care in which members first minister spiritually to one another before they unite in an outside witness. . . .
>
> Evangelistic cell-groups are a special means for cultivating the gifts of grace, for they are the best spiritual organisms available to the church of Jesus Christ. They are necessary so long as we are people of flesh and blood, and so long as the law of nature obtains that all organic life grows from small cells.[20]

Roman Catholic leaders in Latin America are coming to recognize the effectiveness of cell groups meeting in the home. As

---

19. Personal interview with Dr. Moisés López, 7 February 1968, Mexico City.
20. *History of Evangelism* (Grand Rapids: Eerdmans Publishing Co., 1964), pp. 339, 341.

part of the preparation for the celebration of the Thirty-ninth Eucharistic Congress, held in Bogotá, Colombia, from 18 to 25 August 1969, a program called *"Asambleas Familiares"* ("Family Assemblies") was carried out in all parts of Colombia.[21]

In every square block of all the important cities of Colombia, a house was chosen in which meetings were held for all the neighbors living in that block. Each neighborhood block, in other words, had its *"asamblea."* On the front of the designated houses a sign was hung which said: "Here a Family Assembly is held. Everyone is welcome." In some cities, such as Medellín, a flag was also hung out bearing the colors of the Catholic church and of the pope.

Each assembly had its *"animador,"* a person especially prepared to lead the Bible study and the discussion of the theme which followed. In Bogotá and other cities the assemblies met each Tuesday for the space of ten to twelve weeks. In some cities the meetings were held on consecutive nights until all the designated material had been covered. A special feature was the arrangement made in each city whereby at exactly 8:00 P.M. radio and television stations broadcast a message by a priest on the theme for the day. In each house where an assembly was conducted, people sat around their radios or television sets listening to the message. After it was finished they discussed what had been said, using the printed questions which had been circulated.

Two things should be noted about this Roman Catholic program in Colombia: first, that it bears striking resemblance to the home meetings by which evangelicalism is advancing in Latin America; and second, that the Bible was used by the Roman Catholics as their basic textbook. A copy of the Bible (Catholic version) was placed in each home where an assembly was scheduled to meet, and each day's discussion was centered around a theme taken from the Bible. The theme of the entire Family Assemblies program was "Where two or three are gathered together in my name, there am I in the midst of them" (Matt. 18:20).

Evangelicals were divided as to whether they should participate in these Catholic sponsored Family Assemblies. Some stayed away, but others joined in, and with favorable results in many cases. In the city of Medellín, some Presbyterians were asked to lead the Bible study; and after the Roman Catholic series of meetings was

---

21. The source of information concerning the *Asambleas Familiares* in Colombia is Rafael Baltodano, "Informe Especial Sobre Las Asambleas Familiares Católicas en Colombia," distributed by *En Marcha Internacional,* Apartado 1307, San José, Costa Rica.

ended many of the people who had attended began coming to the house-churches of the evangelicals. The overall impact made by the evangelicals who took an active part in the Catholic Family Assemblies was visible in a new openness to the gospel on the part of many Catholics, a general recognition that the evangelicals had something valuable to offer, and in some cases, numerical growth for evangelical churches.[22]

Neighborhood churches where whole families meet and worship fulfill both important religious and sociological needs. The dean of urban historians, Lewis Mumford, looking at the needs of city people from the viewpoint of a secular scientist, says:

> From the original urban integration of shrine, citadel, village, workshop, and market, all later forms of the city have, in some measure, taken their physical structure and their institutional patterns. Many parts of this fabric are still essential to effective human association, not least those that sprang originally from the shrine and the village. Without the active participation of the primary group, in family and neighborhood, it is doubtful if the elementary moral loyalties—respect for the neighbor and reverence for life—can be handed on, without savage lapses, from the old to the young.[23]

The very existence of a moral human society requires that family ties and neighborhood connections be maintained and have religious orientation. Christian missions does not take its starting point from this, nor does it map out its program on the basis of sociological observations. But it is significant that the testimony of secular scholars corroborates what Scripture teaches was Paul's strategy long ago when he directed his efforts in the cities to households, family groups, and through them to the community at large.

---

22. Baltodano tells of one instance, in the city of Cauca, where a twelve-year-old girl was refused entrance to the Family Assembly near her home by the nun in charge. The nun knew she was an evangelical, and therefore would not let her in. The girl, however, stayed by the window looking in. A while later a priest came by and asked her why she had not entered. She told him what had happened, to which he responded by taking her by the hand and bringing her into the Assembly. When the time came for questions, no one was able to answer. The girl, however, began by answering the first, then the second, then the third, until everyone in the meeting was wide-eyed with admiration. Finally the girl said: "I want to invite you all to my church where they can answer all the questions you may have." As a result of this, there is now a new and significant receptivity to the gospel in that neighborhood. Ibid., p. 2.
23. *The City in History,* p. 569.

It would be a modern missionary tragedy if the planting of local evangelistic cell groups was neglected in favor of large centralized churches. The power, the intimacy, the capacity for local leadership and aggressive evangelism would be largely lost. Missionaries have often tried to re-create the large metropolitan church known so well in Europe and the United States.[24] But the average church in the Third World is a small congregation numbering from forty to sixty in attendance.[25] The ineffectiveness in many ways of the large church, and the need for renewal via cell groups and house-churches is now recognized in the older Christian countries. What a pity it will be if their importance is overlooked in the Third World.[26]

The cities of Latin America need a multitude of neighborhood churches whose character and program are designed *specifically for their needs.* The gospel has so much to offer the urban masses of Latin America, but much of its influence will be lost if church planters simply transplant what they were accustomed to at home. Pompous buildings, for one thing, should be dispensed with, along with organs, padded pews, and stained-glass windows. Hand-made benches serve as well, and guitars please God as much. Where the fellowship is close and the Word is explained, cellular proliferation will occur; and the Good News will spread from neighborhood to neighborhood, from *barrio* to *barrio,* until the city is filled with gospel.

That is the goal: an evangelical church within walking distance of every person in the city. In a place where family cars are

---

24. Robert Calvin Guy, "Directed Conservation," in *Church Growth and Christian Mission,* ed. Donald A. McGavran (New York: Harper & Row, Publishers, 1965), p. 211.
25. Ibid. McGavran states that the average church in India numbers between twenty and thirty adult members. Church Growth Institute, Mexico City, June 1964.
26. Recent studies reveal that among American Protestant churches "congregations with the fewest members usually have the highest percentage of worshippers and workers." In Protestant denominations as a whole, "congregations with a membership of over 1,000 have only 20 to 40 per cent of the membership at worship services. In congregations of from 500 to 1,000 members the percentage fluctuates between 30 and 65 per cent. In congregations between 200 and 500 members the percentage rises to between 40 and 70 per cent. And, in congregations with 200 or fewer members the percentage climbs to between 65 and 100 per cent of the membership." Conclusion: "The smaller the congregation the greater the number of involved members." James Schut, "New Horizons for Smaller Congregations," *Church Herald,* 23 January 1970, p. 13. For the recognition of the importance of cell groups in the renewal of the churches, see Leighton Ford, "Evangelism in a Day of Revolution," *Christianity Today,* 24 October 1969, p. 11.

largely nonexistent and public transportation leaves much to be desired, only churches nearby can satisfy the need. These churches should not all be the same type, but rather they should fit the needs of the neighborhood and its people. Cultural, language, racial, and educational characteristics should all affect the ministry and structure of the church. Patterns of worship, witness, and service must be expressive of, and sensitive to, the particular subculture which each neighborhood represents. The gospel is universal, but in its presentation it must be communicated in the "dialect" of each group—not preached to "city dwellers in general" but to the people of each particular *barrio* and *colonia* as relevantly as is humanly possible.[27]

Periodic city-wide meetings serve a purpose: they create and maintain a sense of identity and oneness with the whole evangelical movement throughout the city. But the locus of weekly worship and fellowship must be the immediate neighborhood. Each tired worker returning from a long day in the factory, each mother who cannot leave her home except for brief periods during the day, and each boy and girl who should be enrolled in a Sunday school close enough that he can walk there without difficulty needs a place in his immediate neighborhood where the gospel is preached and God's people gather.[28]

The Witness of the Laity

When Paul approached a city, his first concern was to obtain active collaborators, not passive recipients.[29] It was with people like Aquila and Priscilla, to whom religion was not a mere appendage, that the gospel made its impact.[30]

The spread of the gospel in Paul's estimation was a joint effort

---

27. Donald A. McGavran, "Urban Church Planting and Evangelical Theology," *Church Growth Bulletin,* January 1970, p. 47.
28. Horst Symanowski, director of the Gossnerhaus Mission in Germany, describes "A Sunday in an Industrial Mission," in which religious services, including both the preaching of the Word and the celebration of the sacraments, are held in private homes in Germany, where the majority of industrial workers are almost completely estranged from the Church. The description which he gives, and the benefits of such house services which he enumerates, are directly parallel to those held among evangelicals in Latin American cities. ("El Domingo en una Misión Industrial," translated from the *Church Labor Letter,* Kyoto, Japan, by the Centro Urbano, Lanus, Buenos Aires, distributed by the Comite de Evangelismo Ocupacional, Monterrey, Mexico [Mimeographed].)
29. Grassi, *A World to Win,* p. 78.
30. A. T. Robertson, *Types of Preachers in the New Testament* (New York: George H. Doran Co., 1922), p. 69.

and a local responsibility. He never gave the impression that the evangelization of entire regions was his task alone. On the contrary, his converts were taught to tell others, win others, and continue what he had begun.

Carl G. Kromminga, in his thorough treatment of the subject of the communication of the gospel through personal witnessing to one's neighbors, sums up the New Testament evidence for the obligatory nature of lay witnessing:

> The obligation of all of these passages in the New Testament shows clearly that believers were actively engaged in the communication of the Gospel to others, to those with whom they came in contact in the conduct of daily affairs. The Lord and his apostles repeatedly taught that those who are citizens in the Kingdom of Heaven, those who share in the new life and the new order, are to love their neighbors without reservation. The Lord and his apostles also clearly taught that it is the obligation of those who share in redemption to confess openly the lordship of Jesus Christ and all that this implies. In obeying these commandments, believers follow in the footsteps of the Lord and his primary ambassadors. The manifestation of love for the neighbor and the open confession of Christ's name are acts of obedience to the requirements of citizenship in the Kingdom. . . . Concern for the salvation of others comes to expression in concern for the weak, the penitent, the fallen, the apostate, and those outside the Church.[31]

There is ample evidence throughout the New Testament that believers were active in propagating the faith. The new churches established by Paul and others and the members of older churches scattered abroad by persecution all brought the gospel *by both word and deed* to those around them.[32] The professionalism so characteristic of modern missions was not true of missions in the first century.

Modern missionaries might wish they knew more about *how* the apostles passed on their own zeal to others. At least part of the answer is found in Romans 16, where Paul's "fellow-workers in Christ Jesus" are listed. There is Phoebe, "a helper of many, and of mine own self" (v. 2), Prisca and Aquila are there, of whom Paul says, "for my life they laid down their own necks"

---

31. *The Communication of the Gospel Through Neighboring: A Study of the Basis and Practice of Lay Witnessing Through Neighborly Relationships* (Franeker, Netherlands: T. Wever, 1964), p. 66.
32. Ibid.

(v. 3). Mary, "who bestowed much labor on you," is greeted (v. 6). And so the list goes on: Andronicus and Junias, kinsmen of Paul and fellow prisoners, "who are of note among the apostles" (v. 7); Urbanus (v. 9); Tryphaena, Tryphosa, and Persis, all of them faithful coworkers of the apostle (v. 12). All of these people had been recipients of Paul's labors and were the beneficiaries of his sacrifices. But that is not why Paul remembers them, nor does it explain why their names are recorded. They are named because they labored—"fellow-workers" is their title—and here lies the secret of the gospel's early spread. Conversion was enlistment, and missions meant everybody.[33]

On this subject of lay witnessing, Latin American churches will learn little from the older churches of the West. European and North American Christianity has become so intellectualized and institutionalized that most of the fire has died out. It was not always that way: there was a time in the early days of the faith when Christianity was not a largely middle-class affair but rather had its greatest following among the working classes. The gospel, back then, was mainly spread by "lay" evangelists, by women as well as men, and even children played a role.[34] But by and large, that day has disappeared and professionalism now characterizes most missionary endeavor.

Revolt against professionalism is taking many different forms in the church. In Latin America, it appears especially in the Pentecostal churches; for they more than others make a radical break with the clerical monopoly of the Roman church. Witness any Pentecostal service: women take an active part; any person with a testimony, a petition, or a prophetic word may speak. The leaders are chosen on the basis of spiritual authority, not ecclesiastical privilege or educational superiority; and the pastors, like everyone else, must find remunerative employment to support themselves. The preference of the masses for these very egalitarian churches is to be explained, in part at least, by their more radical break with Roman Catholic professionalism.

As a result, Pentecostal churches, more than the historic de-

---

33. Ibid., pp. 66-67. In answer to the possible objection that this conclusion is too sweeping, Kromminga says on p. 67: "It is of interest to inquire as to the reason for the relative scarcity of direct injunctions in the New Testament —injunctions to honesty, love, sexual purity, etc. Here Van Swigchem offers a convincing explanation. He argues that the congregations were spontaneously carrying out their missionary obligation and needed no urging or correction in this matter. The situation was different with respect to the ethical conduct of the congregation."
34. Green, *Evangelism in the Early Church*, pp. 175-76.

nominations, have caught the New Testament meaning of an *evangelizing congregation.* The older churches have learned from long and bitter experience that organized evangelism is doomed to fruitlessness if it does not spring from an evangelizing church. Pentecostal churches, on the other hand, either consciously or unconsciously, have recaptured the spontaneous growth through lay witnessing which so characterized Christian missions in the first century. The gifts of the Spirit set down in I Corinthians 12—14 are viewed as all the equipment necessary for members and churches to witness and grow. No individual believer has all the gifts—one has the gift of prophecy, another the gift of healing, another of administration—but all members have what they need to serve fruitfully as living members of Christ's body.

J. H. Bavinck calls attention to the repeated references in the Book of Acts to the part played by unofficial lay preachers:

> After the persecution following the death of Stephen, refugees went through the land preaching the Gospel (Acts 8:4). Some were apparently driven to Phoenicia, Cyprus, and Antioch (Acts 11:19). Among them some began to preach the gospel to the Greeks (Acts 11:20). They thus broke down the separation and went unto the heathen. We find that Paul had a series of "fellow laborers.". . . We gain the impression that an intense role was played in the missionary activity of the early church by many men and women who held no other office than that of a believer. To the extent that these lay preachers were on their own, they were in danger of becoming involved in all sorts of confusion, and as a matter of fact this is just what happened. It is, however, the great strength of Paul that he did not suppress this spontaneous spreading of the gospel, but utilized and organized it instead.[35]

In line with this, it may be said that some of the gospel's most extensive forward movements across geographic and racial lines were accomplished by laymen. They left the confines of Jerusalem, preaching everywhere, while the apostles who had personally heard the Lord tell them to go "to all the world," stayed behind (Acts 8:1). Jewish Christian laymen first preached to the Samaritans, necessitating a delegation from Jerusalem to check into what was happening (Acts 8:14). Laymen, when unleashed, have shown from the beginning a capacity for evangelistic accomplishments which clergymen are hard pressed to match.

How ironic it is that, again today, God has hid great things

---

35. *An Introduction to the Science of Missions,* p. 40.

from the "wise and understanding" and has revealed them "unto babes" (Matt. 11:25). The so-called ignorant Pentecostals enjoy a measure of lay apostolate which the older denominations, with their traditions and accumulated wisdom, still are seeking. Nevertheless, they *are* seeking it, and that gives hope; for, as Hendrik Kraemer observes:

> Of all the voices that are raised around the laity, the call for the lay apostolate is the strongest. The Churches, rediscovering their missionary obligation and suddenly becoming aware of the hugeness of the task, turn to the laity with the argument that every Christian is *eo ipso* a witness and a missionary: to discover next that a laity which has been so long neglected and left ignorant is in its majority unable to respond to such a demand. But it is also true that in many parts of Europe new experiments of evangelization, which often show great originality, daring and inventiveness, are being tried.[36]

Evangelism-in-Depth, Campus Crusade, and other such organizations are teaching the churches something. Each of these movements approaches the task from a different angle, but together they represent something new and important. They are taking evangelism back to the laity, instructing ordinary church members in things which their churches failed to teach them about witnessing, sharing the gospel, and utilizing the Spirit's gifts. And in this confused, fragmented world, what else could be more important? As Suzanne de Dietrich writes:

> In many countries today the Christians are still—or are again—a tiny minority. We are in a situation more and more like that of the early church in the pagan world. . . . We must learn from it what it means to proclaim God's Word. The pagan world of the first century can scarcely have been more skeptical or more disillusioned than ours. . . . We must learn what it means to be "a witness" in whatever walk of life God has placed us.[37]

The Fellowship of the Holy Spirit

In the modern quest for less institutionalized structures, greater power, and authentic Christian unity, the Spirit's gift of *koinonia*

---

36. *A Theology of the Laity* (London: Lutterworth Press, 1958), p. 45.
37. *The Witnessing Community: The Biblical Record of God's Purpose* (Philadelphia: Westminster Press, 1958), p. 154, cited in Kromminga, *The Communication of the Gospel Through Neighboring*, p. 14.

should be the starting point.[38] A church which lacks the *koinonia* of the Spirit is institutionalized hypocrisy. Yet, it must be admitted sadly, that is the condition of many churches, both "older" and "younger," around the world.

Seated on the front veranda of my home in Colombo, Ceylon, I could observe at close hand the activities of the Fellowship Center, a Pentecostal church of the Bakht Singh movement from India. Entirely indigenous in leadership, structure, and support, the Fellowship Center was a splendid example of the *koinonia* of the Spirit and of witness.

Services were held almost every night of the week. They were long, and sometimes loud, and the overflow crowd often stood in the doorways and windows straining to hear what was being said inside. Prayer vigils often lasted all night, and by breakfast time a group was usually gathered for regular morning prayer meeting. People came and went at all hours of the day—women in their colorful *saris,* men in white suits or knotted *sarongs,* some, too, without shoes, and all carrying their Bibles. Converts from all three of the great non-Christian religions—Buddhism, Hinduism, and Islam—mingled together at the Fellowship Center.

The three pastors of the Center sometimes came to borrow Bible commentaries and ask questions. They were office workers in downtown Colombo and none of them had had formal theological training. They were honest, sincere men, who had both passion for the lost and compassion for the miserable (of whom Colombo had plenty). The Fellowship Center was always a beehive of Bible study. The members there did not believe in Bible institutes or seminaries, but taught that the church itself is the training school for all its members. Sometimes the lights would be on half the night as one group or another discussed a problem which they had encountered in their study.

But for all its good points, one thing was a bit irksome about the Fellowship Center. (It had nothing to do with the loud singing, long services, and continual traffic in and out.) The fact was that most of the foreign missionaries' converts ended up, not as members of the old-line denominations with which they worked, but of the Fellowship Center which had no missionaries. Somehow, the zeal and enthusiasm of new Christians would not allow them to settle down in the denominational churches. These churches had many things to offer, such as finer buildings, more clearly

---

38. Howard A. Snyder, "The Fellowship of the Holy Spirit," *Christianity Today,* 6 November 1970, p. 4.

defined doctrines, highly trained clergy, ritual, and prestige. But for some reason, new converts inevitably ended up at places like the Fellowship Center, with apologies (sometimes) to the missionaries who had led them to the Lord.[39]

Was there an explanation? Of course there was, and it lay in the nature of the two kinds of churches. The Fellowship Center was precisely what its name implied—a center of *koinonia,* where the freedom of the Spirit was recognized and His gifts were enjoyed, where things *happened* when men worshiped and the Word was not thwarted by archaic traditions.

So much of what passes as "fellowship" in the churches falls far, far short of the *koinonia* of the Spirit. At best, it is friendly fraternizing: appealing, but easily duplicated by clubs and associations outside the church. But the supernatural communion—and intercommunication of the Spirit with God's people, and between them as members of one family—is hard to find.

The early church experienced *koinonia,* not in large auditoriums amid lush furnishings and ritual, but in small groups, in private homes, and oftentimes with persecution. The churches in Latin America must find it, too, and strive not to lose what they already possess; for the *koinonia* of the Holy Spirit is the atmosphere of growth, witness, and service. If the patterns which missionaries have brought over do not serve, they should be dispensed with immediately. Some patterns, even highly revered ones, stifle the Spirit and destroy *koinonia.* It is better to look to New Testament patterns than to the traditions of the West, to growing, joyful, Spirit filled churches than to tradition-bound structures which have the smell of death about them. The communion of the Holy Spirit—that is the thing; that is the atmosphere in which churches grow and converts multiply.

---

39. There were exceptions, of course, but the pattern was too general to be ignored. I served as missionary-pastor of the Dutch Reformed Church in Ceylon, the oldest Protestant denomination on the island, which probably lost 90 percent of its converts to groups like the Fellowship Center.

7

BEYOND THE CHURCH: COMMUNITY

Arnold Toynbee, in his recent book on the history of cities, entitles one of the chapters "Capital Cities: Melting-Pots and Powder-Kegs." He may well have had Latin America in mind, for there it has been obviously true that "a melting-pot can easily turn into a powder-keg."[1]

The hope of most Latin Americans today—and this is particularly true in the cities—is strictly materialistic. They want a way out of feudalism and semicolonialism, and they see it in industrialization and cutting off economic dependence on the United States. The peasantry is restless, workers are suspicious, and students are turning more and more to "the barricades." Reports of urban guerrilla warfare are now becoming familiar from various parts of the continent.[2]

---

1. *Cities on the Move* (New York: Oxford University Press, 1970), p. 151. Toynbee attributes a large share of this powder-keglike nature of capital cities to the presence of "an urban proletariat in the sump beneath the capital's glittering upper-works."
2. For an analysis of labor's attitudes and hopes, see Henry D. Jones, "Christian Approaches to Labour in Latin America," *International Review of Missions* 40 (October 1951): 435-43. For a study of urban guerrilla warfare in Latin America, see Martin Oppenheimer, *The Urban Guerrilla* (Chicago: Quadrangle Books, 1969), especially chaps. 2 and 4. Oppenheimer concludes that there is little chance for the success of urban guerrilla tactics in accomplishing their goals. The picture of the United States as an oppressor is one not readily accepted by most Americans; but it is important that missionaries and American Christians in general realize that in the eyes of a growing

Revolutions have been a fact of life for a long time in Latin America.[3] Sometimes the upheavals are peaceful, but more often they are violent. There is such an air of inevitability about revolution in Latin America that it seems to be nothing more than a joke to many people, and the seriousness of what is happening right now is underestimated. Actually, however, the tide of revolution now sweeping across Latin America represents *the most important social and economic factor affecting the church and missions in that part of the world today.*

This revolutionary tide also carries with it the principal moral and religious countercontender for the minds and hearts of Latin Americans. In Africa it is Islam; in Asia the great historic religions as well as newer faiths are arising; but in Latin America, it is Marxism that pits its growing strength against Christianity.[4]

For everyone involved in Christian missions in Latin America, a prime requisite for effective action is knowledge of what is actually taking place. Many people do not want to know. Others have never had an opportunity to inform themselves as to the broad issues of social injustice and economic oppression as they exist in Latin America. The problems which urban squatters face, the failures of planned relocation settlements, and the factors which hinder upward mobility are generally given only passing attention, if any at all, by church administrators and missionaries. They know the slums are there, with their teeming poor, filth, and unsanitary conditions. But few they are who actually dig beneath the surface to find out what is taking place.

Three types of opinion can be identified with respect to the social and political issues facing Latin America; and evangelicals, inside and outside of Latin America, generally fall into one or another of these three categories:

1. The Establishment. Interested in development, this group insists that changes be made without disturbing existing structures. The continuation of traditional institutions is a precondition of development and improvement. The stability of the country, and of religion, must be assured.

---

number of Latin Americans, this country is cast in an imperialist-colonial role, from which Latin America must be liberated if ever it is to enjoy the benefits of modern society. See Gary MacEoin, "Neocolonialism in Latin America," *Christian Century,* 2 June 1971, pp. 685-97.
3. Horace L. Fenton, "Missions and Revolution," *ELO Bulletin,* Winter 1970, p. 3.
4. W. Richey Hogg, "The Oikoumene," in *The Future of the Christian World Mission* (Grand Rapids: Eerdmans Publishing Co., 1971), p. 22.

2. *The Gradualists.* More radical than the Establishment, and generally represented by social and religious liberals, this group looks for changes and development through a gradual whittling away at the sources of injustice and the growth of new institutions which will deal more adequately with the needs of the poor. Though they want change, they do not want violence.

3. *The Radicals.* Revolution is the keynote of this group. They regard the present system as beyond improvement or repair, fit only to be overthrown. Their strategies include violence whenever and wherever they consider it expedient. In Latin America, revolutionists invariably regard violence as necessary to accomplish their purposes.

Sitting in the lunch room of the largest university in Latin America,[5] I had occasion recently to reflect as to which of these three categories appeals most today to (1) the university students of Latin America, who will be the leaders of Ibero-America in just a few years, and (2) the Christians, broadly conceived, including both Catholics and evangelicals. The walls of the lunch room were literally plastered with two kinds of pictures—naked women and Communist heroes. The students' tastes seemed to run uniformly along these two lines; and since the posting of large pictures and announcements is permitted by university authorities, full vent was given to their feelings. The same could be said of the majority of the titles in the three bookstores on the campus. The impression was inescapable that if Communism fails to capture the allegiance of the student population, then its failure will be gigantic; for the amount of effort being put forth to promote Communism on the campus is nothing less than astonishing.

But what about the Christians—evangelicals and Catholics alike? Where do they fit into the three categories comprising the general attitudes toward change and revolution in Latin America? The majority belong to the first two groups, certainly, with a preponderance probably found in the Establishment. But not all of them are there; and among those who ask questions and dig for the facts, agitation is increasing for a more radical approach.

The following document was prepared by eighty Catholic priests in Chile. These eighty priests work among the urban masses. Their open letter, presented at a press conference in Santiago, Chile, is dated 16 April 1971. It represents one strong and clearly articu-

---

5. Universidad Nacional de México in Mexico City, which has approximately 100,000 students including those enrolled in campuses related to UNAM in various parts of the country. These observations were made in June 1971.

lated response to the urban social crisis from a Catholic Christian viewpoint.

As a group of 80 priests who live with the working classes we have come together to analyze the real situation in which Chile finds itself upon beginning to build socialism.

The working class still remains in a condition of exploitation which implies malnutrition, lack of housing, unemployment, and little opportunity to share in the fruits of culture. There is a clear and precise cause for this situation: the capitalistic system, product of a foreign imperialist domination and maintained by the dominant classes of the country.

This system, characterized by private ownership of the means of production and the increasing inequality in the distribution of income, converts the worker into a mere cog in the production system and fosters an irrational apportionment of economic resources and an unwarranted transference of surplus outside the country. This causes stagnation and prevents the country from rising out of underdevelopment (*subdesarrollo*).

Such a situation cannot be tolerated any longer. We affirm that the coming to power of the Popular Government and its decisive action in favor of the building of socialism represents the hope of the working masses. And this intuition of the people is not erroneous.

We do not deny the difficulties and mutual mistrust which have been caused in great measure by past historical circumstances which today have ceased to be a factor in Chile. There still remains a lot to be done, but the evolution that has taken place between Marxists and the Christians today permits common action in the historic project to which our country has committed itself.

This collaboration will be facilitated on the one hand to the extent that Marxism is presented more and more as an instrument of analysis and transformation of society and on the other hand to the extent that Christians continue to purify our faith of everything which impedes us from assuming real and effective involvement.

In effect socialism, characterized by the appropriation by society of the means of production, opens the way to a new economy which makes possible an autonomous and more rapid development, since it overcomes the division of society into antagonistic classes. However, socialism is not only a new economy. It ought also to generate new values which make possible the emergence of a society more united and fraternal in which the worker assumes the dignity to which he is entitled.

We feel committed to this process and we want to contribute to its success. The profound reason for our commitment is our faith in Jesus Christ who enfleshes himself in the circumstances of history. To be a Christian means to be united. To be united at this moment in Chile is to participate in the historical project which our people have laid out.

As Christians we do not see any incompatibility between Christianity and socialism. Quite the contrary, as the Cardinal of Santiago said last November: "There are more evangelical values in socialism than capitalism." In effect, socialism opens up a hope that man can be more complete and by the same token more evangelical. In a word, more in conformity to Jesus Christ who came to free men from all that enslaved them.

In this sense it is necessary to destroy the prejudice and mistrust which exists between Christians and Marxists.

To Marxists we say that authentic religion is not an opiate of the people. On the contrary, it is a liberating stimulus for the constant renovation of the world. For Christians we recall the fact that our God has involved himself in the history of men and that in these times to love our neighbor fundamentally means fighting that this world may resemble as much as possible the future world which we hope to see and which we have already begun to create.

By the same token we support measures which extend to the appropriation by society of the means of production, such as the nationalization of mineral resources, the socialization of banks and industrial monopolies, the acceleration and intensification of the agrarian reform, etc.

We believe that socialism is constructed through much sacrifice and implies a unified and constructive effort in order to overcome underdevelopment and create a new society. This undoubtedly will provoke strong resistance on the part of those who may lose their privileges. For this reason the mobilization of the people is absolutely necessary. We affirm a certain preoccupation that this has not yet been achieved to the hoped-for degree.

We believe it is also necessary to lay the foundation for the construction of a new culture which will not be reflective of capitalist interests but of the real values of the people. Only thus will the New Man be able to emerge, the creator of a truly united community (convivencia).

It is evident that there are significant groups of workers who, though being in favor of the changes and favorably disposed to them, still do not involve themselves actively in the current process of change. The unity of all the workers, whatever might be their party affiliations, is decisive in this unique opportunity which is being provided our country to replace the actual dependent capitalistic system and advance the cause of the working classes in all of Latin America.

The lack of class consciousness is fomented by the dominant groups principally through the media and political parties, instilling mistrust, fear, and finally resistance and passivity.

It is necessary to recognize that everything that happens is not necessarily positive and worthwhile. But at the same time we affirm that criticism should take place from within the revolutionary process and not from outside.

At this time, full of risk as well as hope, it behooves us priests as it does any Christian to modestly offer our support. For this reason we have wanted to reflect and prepare ourselves in these work-meetings concerning the "participation of the Christian in the building of socialism."[6]

The "profound reason for our commitment" to the Marxist strategy is "our faith in Jesus Christ," say the Chilean priests. Differing interpretations, both as to their motives and the solutions which they espouse, have come from both secular and religious sources;[7] but the most serious reaction of all comes from the indifferent. To shrug off this communique is the height of folly. Anyone who thinks that these eighty priests speak only for themselves or for a tiny, inconsequential minority of religiously committed people in Latin America is simply deceiving himself.

The name of Camilo Torres is magic to millions. Torres was the priest-guerrilla, ex-professor, and influential writer who was killed in a battle between Colombian government soldiers and guerrillas in 1966. Torres lost his professorship at the university when he began increasingly to challenge the status quo in politics and economics and sided with the revolutionists among the students. Torres became involved in various projects to assist the poor, organized peasant grievance meetings, and spoke and wrote in favor of radical social changes, even to the point of advocating violence. The Roman Catholic Church excommunicated him, and he left for the hills to join the guerrillas. Shortly afterward he was killed in battle against government troops.

Torres is now a symbol of Marxism and Catholic Christianity working together in harmony and "real brotherhood." His sayings are quoted everywhere:

6. Communique to the Press by priests taking part in a Work-Meeting concerning "Participation of Christians in the Building of Socialism," reported in *Frente Amplio, Unidad Popular,* published by CAGLA (Chicago Area Group on Latin America, 800 West Belden, Chicago, Ill. 60614), June 1971.
7. Ibid. Introduction, "Chilean Jesuits: Write On!"

> I took off my cassock to be more truly a priest.
> The duty of every Catholic is to be a revolutionary.
> The duty of every revolutionary is to make the revolution;
> The Catholic who is not a revolutionary is living in mortal
> sin.[8]

Thousands of Catholic clerics are asking uncomfortable questions all across Latin America.[9] Injustice, hunger, exploitation, racism, oppression, poverty, infant mortality, and military operations for no visible purpose than to make some men richer cannot remain unanswered and unabated forever. No one can escape the conclusion that most Latin American governments are operated for the benefit, not of the majority of the people, but for the privileged minority.[10] Said Father Emerson Negreiros to his poor, exploited parishioners of Santa Cruz, in northeastern Brazil:

> You should raise a goat to give milk to your children. If the landlord comes to kill your goat, he is threatening the lives of your children. Do not let him kill your goat: kill him first.[11]

What do evangelical leaders say about the needs of the community beyond the church? Most, it seems to me, have very little to say about it. C. René Padilla pricks the evangelical's conscience when he states:

> Is not more harm than good done to the cause of the gospel when we close our eyes to the problem that is posed by the customary divorce between evangelism and social responsibility, between the individual and society, between personal salvation and the creation of a new humanity in Christ? Is not the radical leftist theology itself, at least in part, a reaction against the deadly reduction of the Christian mission that has characterized Latin American Protestantism?[12]

The negligible impact of the evangelical church as a whole on

---

8. John Gerassi, *Revolutionary Priest: The Complete Writings and Messages of Camilo Torres* (New York: Random House, Vintage Books, 1971), pp. vii, xiii.
9. Ibid., p. xiii.
10. Vincet T. Mallon, a Roman Catholic, makes this observation in "Medellin Guidelines," *America*, 31 January 1970, p. 94.
11. Gerassi, *Revolutionary Priest: The Complete Writings and Messages of Camilo Torres*, p. 8. Cited also in John Gerassi, *The Great Fear in Latin America* (New York: Macmillan, 1965), p. 98.
12. "A Steep Climb Ahead for Theology in Latin America," *Evangelical Missions Quarterly* 7 (Winter 1971): 101.

the gradually emerging new society and the isolation of the churches
from the totality of human life are intimately connected with a
theological deficiency that has narrowed the concern of the church
to "saving souls," but fails to see the Christian's responsibility in
society.[13] Why have most thinking Latin Americans so far rejected evangelical Christianity as being irrelevant to their countries'
problems?[14] Is it not because evangelicals have failed to teach and
apply a New Testament social ethic, leaving no viable alternative
other than Marxist revolution?

A survey was made not long ago of the Protestant community
in Mexico City.[15] Scientifically conducted by trained personnel,
the purpose of the survey was to find out to what extent evangelicals differed from nonevangelicals with respect to basic moral
attitudes, both on a personal and social level.

The results of the study reveal that while, on the one hand,
the gospel's impact has improved to a marked degree the position
of the woman within the home, with a consequent lessening of
the *machismo* attitude of the man, and the overall condition of
home life has been affected, nevertheless, the basic moral and
social attitudes of evangelicals in Mexico City are not notably
different from those of many of their nonevangelical neighbors.
The study showed, moreover, that the "new life in Christ" is
commonly interpreted negatively—no smoking, no drinking, no
fornicating, no parties—and a sharp line of demarcation is drawn
between the "church" (which represents everything good) and
the "world" (everything bad).[16] So drastic is this cleavage that,

13. E. R. Wickham, *Church and People in an Industrial City* (London: Lutterworth Press, 1957), p. 14. Regarding the church's estrangement from the
working classes, see Horst Symanowski, "El Hombre Enajenado de la Iglesia
en el Mundo Industrial," *Promotor de Evangelización,* November 1968, pp. 1-2.
14. Says Charles F. Denton, "In general, thinking Latin Americans have rejected evangelical Christianity as being irrelevant to their countries' problems"
(*World Vision Magazine,* March 1970, p. 11).
15. The results of this survey were published in English under the title *Convictions of a Young Church: A Survey of Some Attitudes of Protestants in
Mexico,* and in Spanish, ¿*Los Evangélicos Somos Así?,* coauthored by William
L. Wonderly and Jorge Lara-Braud (Mexico, D.F.: Casa Unida de Publicaciones, S.A., 1964). The information used herein is drawn from the Spanish
edition.
16. Wonderly and Lara-Braud point out that included in the "world" is the
Roman Catholic church, with its members, and evangelicals make no distinction between orthodox Catholicism and Folk Catholicism with all its
syncretistic elements. Every Catholic, as far as the evangelicals are concerned,
is a polytheist and a "pagano," no matter how educated and cultured he may
be (p. 55).

as Peter Wagner has pointed out, the lines of communication between neighbors and even relatives are broken; and the natural bridges over which the gospel normally flows are consequently broken down.[17]

The Wonderly—Lara-Braud survey points up one major lesson which evangelicals must take to heart: evangelical churches and seminaries need to widen their perspective and begin teaching Christians what it means to live under the lordship of Jesus Christ in all areas of Latin American society. While not diminishing for a moment their emphasis on the primacy of conversion and the need to spread the gospel to sinners everywhere, they should also teach the full implications of the gospel for Christians where they live, work, and spend their time. Living the Christian life is more than not smoking, drinking, or carousing. It means, more importantly, a love and concern for men everywhere, in their misery and need, and an impulsating dissatisfaction with everything which keeps men enslaved. It means looking at life from a Biblical perspective and challenging all false kingdoms with the word of our sovereign Lord.

The trouble with so much of mainline Latin American evangelicalism is that it has become thoroughly middle-class, and the middle-class in Latin America is the staunch defender of the status quo.

> There was a time in Latin America when it was thought that the middle classes had a key role in the future. But in this sense the course of events has deceived us. On the one hand, the middle class is not a very large sector of the population: 13% in Bolivia, 15% in Brazil, 39.7% in Argentina, 31% in Uruguay. On the other hand, it has taken the path of mental and structural dependence upon the oligarchy to the point that one enthusiastic observer of another generation (1955) writes less than a decade later (1964) concerning the role of the middle class: "The middle class is less and less a factor of social change and is now becoming a part of the vast Latin American parasitology." *It will be other groups or social classes which will produce change. And they are precisely the ones who are not being reached by the Gospel. Why?*[18]

This middle-class contentment with itself, and the subsequent with-

---

17. Wagner, *Teología Latinoamericana,* pp. 68-69.
18. Samuel Escobar, "The Social Responsibility of the Church in Latin America," *Evangelical Missions Quarterly* 6 (Spring 1970): 137. Escobar cites Victor Alba, *Parásitos, Mitos y Sordomudos,* CEDS, Mexico, 1964. Emphasis mine.

drawal from the urban masses with all their problems, is the primary cause for the ineffectiveness of the Latin American middle-class denominations in both social renewal *and* evangelistic outreach. So concerned are the middle classes with their status that they have erected subtle but effective barriers around themselves and their churches to prevent being mistaken for anything but what they are—middle class, comfortable, and harmless.

This is brought to light in the Wonderly—Lara-Braud survey in Mexico City. The Pentecostals, drawn mainly from the lower classes, are more concerned with civic affairs than the members of the historic denominations, and they possess a sense of history, a feeling that they belong to something new and dynamic that is going to change things.

> One gets the impression that the Mexican Pentecostalists are more conscious of their place in the history and life of the nation than the members of the denominational churches. The denominations have *inherited* a history: see the emphasis upon the Protestant Reformation which gave them their origin, not really to them but at least to the churches which have sent them missionaries, and in this way they are able to enjoy an intellectual perspective that is clearer than that of the Pentecostalists. But the Pentecostalists are, for the most part, of more recent origin and have grown in a much more accelerated manner. Instead of having inherited a history, they set themselves to make history, and at the same time they are gripped by the conviction that they are fulfilling the destiny for which God has prepared them in times like these. Instead of looking back and resting on their traditions, they tend, on the one hand, to await more attentively the return of the Lord. And on the other hand, they labor with a greater sense of eschatological urgency in the present situation, and play the role to which they have been assigned. One of the results of this has been that they throw themselves into situations where they are more exposed to persecution (in many cases) than the denominational groups which tend to exercise more caution and expose themselves less to hostile treatment on the part of the majority group.[19]

Unless the mainline churches do an about-face soon, they are going to be left behind—numerically, evangelistically, and in respect to social evolution. Change is being produced, not by the middle classes, but by the masses of the lower class.[20] They are the ones

---

19. Wonderly and Lara-Braud, *¿Los Evangélicos Somos Así?*, pp. 47-48.
20. D'Epinay is critical of the Pentecostalists of South America for their

who must be reached, churches multiplied among them, and the full implications of the comprehensive Christian gospel explained to them. The historic denominations must awaken *now*. Whatever the reasons may be for their hesitancy with respect to the total implications of the gospel, there is no excuse for continued indifference.[21] They need to examine afresh both the Bible and their consciences, and both should prick them mercilessly.

Paul's Approach to the Community

Paul's strategy moved from converts to churches and on to the community beyond the church: the structure of society and its needs. The manner in which he approached society is important. After the initial work had been accomplished and a church had been organized, Paul's efforts were directed toward the "perfecting" of the converts, instructing them how they should live "Christianly" within society. The First Epistle to the Corinthians, for example, is devoted mainly to current problems confronting the Christian church in that city.[22] There is a breadth in Paul's perspective which can only be explained by the fact that Paul deeply understood the universality of Christ's kingly authority. Paul hardly could mention Jesus Christ without calling Him *Lord,* and he meant by this a here-and-now lordship which affects the Christian's approach to life and the world, as well as a future lordship at the end of the age. It seems to me that this is an underlying supposition in all of Paul's writings.

In this connection, it is important to observe that the epistles of Paul themselves are missionary literature and were part of his methodology. The epistles were written by a missionary to young converts and to churches only recently organized. They con-

---

alleged withdrawal from social responsibilities (*Haven of the Masses,* pp. 103 ff.). Recent events in Brazil and Chile, however, indicate a different situation. Pentecostalists are asserting their demands for social justice at the ballot box and are supporting political parties which have a platform geared to the masses' needs. See Glasser, "The Evangelicals: World Outreach," in *The Future of the Christian World Mission,* ed. W. J. Danker and Wi Jo Kang (Grand Rapids: Eerdmans Publishing Co., 1971), p. 112.

21. Samuel Escobar traces the history of Latin American evangelicalism's fear of anything which might be termed the "social gospel" back to the modernist-fundamentalist controversy in the United States during the period when most of the churches in Latin America were being established. "Our historical background explains our negligence," says Escobar, "and it also demands of us a re-examination of our conscience with its resultant corrective measures." "The Social Responsibility of the Church in Latin America," p. 131.

22. Grassi, *A World to Win,* p. 119. For a detailed study of I Corinthians considered in its missionary context, see William Baird, *The Corinthian Church —A Biblical Approach to Urban Culture* (New York: Abingdon Press, 1964).

tain the missionary message, the essentials of the gospel, *and* its application to the spiritual and social needs of the early believers. The letters deal with questions and problems which arise almost everywhere in the missionary situation.

The treatment of problems—religious, social, ethical, disciplinary, ecclesiastical, personal—characterizes Paul's writings. In every one of the epistles some problem is dealt with. It can be said that precisely because Pauline Christianity touched on the real problems which men faced, and treated them in such a way that the oppressed and downtrodden received hope and a new sense of freedom as God's children, Christianity caught the imagination of multitudes and spread like wildfire across the Roman world.

To a world of slaves, of underdogs, of masses held in physical and moral and spiritual bondage, Christianity proclaimed spiritual freedom, justice, and righteousness.[23] The key concepts of the gospel—freedom, forgiveness, sons of God, hope, peace, heavenly inheritance—rang across the sea of misery which was the Roman Empire, and the world listened. Jesus' cry was heard again: "Come unto me, all ye that labor and are heavy laden, and I will give you rest" (Matt. 11:28). The message got through, and multitudes followed Him. Each one came with his particular burden, finding in Christ the gospel rest which was promised. And that rest was not slumber, inactivity, but God-oriented action. Life now was new, and every facet of it was under the sovereignty of God.

For this reason, H. R. Boer says that "every missionary is a walking social revolution."[24] He has been commissioned to preach the most revolutionary message the world could hear. To attempt to make a revolutionary out of Paul, in the modern sense, is specious: he never attempted to overthrow the government, not even a totalitarian one. On the contrary, he taught the churches to obey and respect the "higher powers" (Rom. 13:1 ff.). Paul organized no frontal attack on the existing social order, corrupt though it was. Following closely the example of his Lord, he avoided questions of politics, economics, and social order. Robert E. Speer reflects on this:

> Jesus did not come as a social reformer. He refused to deal with political and politico-economic or social questions. The interpretation of His mission or of the development of early Christianity as the product of a class struggle has no basis in fact. On the other hand and in actual fact, however, a

---

23. Grassi, *A World to Win*, pp. 123-27.
24. Boer, *Pentecost and Missions*, p. 241.

new type of life, of a different and original quality, had come
into the world in Christ, which did exercise and will forever exercise a very profound transforming influence and will
venture on the most searching interference with the social
order. . . . It will succeed in destroying and breaking down
evil institutions and in inaugurating new ones. . . . Beyond
all national and other forms of unity, it will push forward
toward an ideal religious unity which will be spiritual, inward and living.[25]

The people of Christ became social revolutionaries in a totalitarian world.[26] But they did so, not by storing armaments in their
places of worship, nor by violence. They did it by changed lives,
which is the foundational change. Anyone can throw rocks. But
only the power of God can make a new man out of a lost sinner
and enable that man to live and work by the laws of God in
every relationship of life.

This comprehensive message which Paul preached was devastat-
ing to the pagan social structures of his day. The Christian message brings all human society under judgment and calls for its
complete renewal.

The gospel is good news for the *whole* of life. The Spirit
renews humanity and the natural world. He renews the life
that He gave at creation. The result of His work is a new
creation flowering in a new humanity, a new heaven, and
a new earth.[27]

This was Paul's understanding of the church's task, the proclamation of the life-embracing message of the whole Word, the "all
things whatsoever I commanded you" of Christ's commission (Matt.
28:20). Such proclamation releases a transforming energy into
society which ultimately exorcises the demons that control it. Invariably the gospel issues in revolution—religious, social, political,
and economic. To the impulsive and impatient, the Pauline approach seems slow. But without question it is thorough. The history of the first three centuries of the Christian era testifies to this.

William M. Ramsay calls the early Christians the "reforming
party" of the Roman Empire. The more astute emperors feared
Christians because they recognized that the Christian church would

---

25. *The Finality of Jesus Christ,* p. 225, cited in "The Revolutionary Masses
and Church Growth," *Church Growth Bulletin,* May 1971, p. 142.
26. Bengt Sundkler, *The World of Mission* (Grand Rapids: Eerdmans Publishing Co., 1965), p. 39.
27. Boer, *Pentecost and Missions,* p. 241.

be the ultimate foe of their autocracy.[28] Had Paul spent his time merely treating the symptoms of social injustice, he would have accomplished little of lasting significance. But Paul understood the basic issues at stake, the underlying evils in Roman society; and he threw his efforts into spelling out the gospel's message as their remedy.

A large part of the New Testament epistles is made up of practical teachings which are the basis for the Christian understanding of a just and righteous social order. In Paul's follow-up instruction by letters to the young churches we find the basis of distinctively Christian socio-economic and political perspectives which are diametrically opposed to all tyrannical systems, ancient and modern. Eventually, Rome sensed this; and the emperors themselves were required to respond to Christianity's challenge, either by persecution or capitulation. They did both. A converted empire was the Pauline goal, but a converted empire required the elimination of the god-emperor at Rome. One by one the smaller gods fell, until finally the emperor was next; and he himself could no longer resist. But the road to Rome was a long one, and preaching the gospel, making converts, and planting churches were Paul's basic approach to a society and an empire that needed changing.[29]

The Strategy Applied

The degree of the convert's transformation depends largely on the breadth of the gospel he hears. A narrow, truncated message produces the same kind of Christian. But when gospel proclamation is Biblically comprehensive, when Christ's promises and commands are taught in such a way that the new convert accepts his responsibility in all of life's multiple relationships, things begin to happen in society. Then the message of repentance takes on broader meaning. It includes sorrow for sin, both individual and corporate, and a radically new outlook on life as well. A new dimension is added to religion, a total dimension which brings hope for human society as a whole.[30]

---

28. William M. Ramsay, *The Cities of St. Paul: Their Influence on His Life and Thought* (Grand Rapids: Baker Book House, 1960; reprint of the 1907 edition by Hodder and Stoughton, London), pp. 73-75.

29. Ramsay, *The Cities of Paul,* p. 429. Ramsay examines closely Paul's provisional peace with the empire during the period when it afforded him a useful medium for missionary expansion. It did not imply any basic agreement with the religious, moral, and social system which the empire represented. Paul saw Rome's tyranny as an ultimate foe; but as long as there was peace, he would make use of it to spread the gospel (pp. 425-30).

30. Emilio Castro, "Evangelism in Latin America," *International Review of Missions* 53 (October 1964): 454.

William M. Pinson, Jr., points out that any practice or situation which adversely affects human life is a legitimate concern for Christians because it is a concern of God. Latin America is filled with such situations, as every urban slum testifies. The Christian is "under orders from his Heavenly Father to discover and to correct urban problems," says Pinson, and a kind of Christianity which concerns itself only with converting people but not about the society in which they live is "as ridiculous as for parents to be concerned only about getting a baby born and not about the food he eats, the clothes he wears, the house in which he lives, or the persons with whom he associates."[31]

The great failure of missionaries in China, say Fife and Glasser, is that they "trained men as they themselves had been trained, with limited Christian perspective on the local church's place in society." They illustrate this by relating that

> great tribal churches were led by men who were abysmally indifferent to the corruption around them—opium traffic, feudal slavery, rapacious landlords, social injustice—and this in areas where the Church represented a significant and sizeable segment in the total society. In the end, God judged His people and drove out the foreigners who had reproduced in the minds of their converts their own incomplete understanding of the Church and its message to society. Today Christians in China must perforce participate in the reconstruction of society.[32]

These mistakes must not be repeated in Latin America. Some of the social ills of China have their Latin counterparts, and so do the missionaries with their "incomplete understanding of the Church and its message to society." If the evangelical churches of Latin America will not reform themselves now, the history of China is bound to be repeated.

Fife and Glasser point to a key factor in carrying out the church's social responsibility—namely, the number of Christians in the population. The tragedy in China lay in the fact that "in areas where the Church represented a significant and sizeable segment in the total society," it failed to make a social impact.[33] The church must be established before it can minister; but where it is established, ministry must be performed. Guilt cannot be placed on small, often persecuted minorities, whose main concern is survival and growth.

---

31. "Issues and Priorities," in *Toward Creative Urban Strategy,* comp. George A. Torney (Waco, Tex.: Word Books, 1970), pp. 55, 51.
32. Fife and Glasser, *Missions in Crisis,* pp. 104-5.
33. Ibid.

However, it does rest wherever evangelicals are, in the words of Rubén Lores, "a respectable minority, and in numerous places . . . actually a practical majority as compared with Roman Catholics."[34]

This brings the discussion back to the matter of priorities and the particular problem which each situation presents. European and American missionary strategists make a grave mistake when they project their own situation on the Third World, applying everywhere what they conceive as the church's mission locally. The problem must be narrowed to the precise area under discussion, as McGavran does when he focuses on a factory community:

> What does mission mean in it? Before we can answer, we must know more about the factory community. Is it a hundred percent Hindu, Protestant or Roman Catholic? Are sixty percent of its people baptized, of whom a few are earnest Christians? Are the owners of the factory Christians or violently opposed to Christ? Is the problem renewal—getting the many existing Christians to carry their Christianity over from the worship service on Sunday to the shop meeting on Wednesday night? Or is it conversion—getting some of the Marxists or Hindus who make up the labour force to become baptized, practising disciples of the Lord Jesus? Or is it social action—getting the Christian majority to devise and institute Christian solutions to human problems?[35]

Before there can be Christian social action, there must be Christians. Before social, economic, and political institutions can be Christianized, there must be born-again believers in great number and churches proclaiming the Word of God by which men's lives are directed. It is all well and good to talk enthusiastically about Christian political action, labor organizations, confrontation, dialogue, and industrial renewal; but none of these things will ever be accomplished without first converting men to faith in Christ, baptizing them into membership in visible churches where the Word is preached, and instructing them in the full implications of the gospel.

To advocate a social and political strategy for world missions which intentionally or unintentionally bypasses the long hard road of conversion and church growth is foolish and un-Biblical. It is ridiculous to pretend that what Christians in London, Amsterdam, New York, and Toronto can do, and should do, is possible

34. "Why I Am Concerned for Social Needs," cited in Rycroft and Clemmer, *A Study of Urbanization in Latin America,* p. 138.
35. "Wrong Strategy: The Real Crisis in Missions," *International Review of Missions* 54 (October 1965): 456.

also in places like Mexico City where the evangelicals are less than 2.0 percent of the population. No amount of vague, sophisticated language can make it true. Nothing inhibits the reconciliation of men to God today more than to imagine that urban missions can be carried out without conscious planning for and striving toward the conversion of men to Christ and the growth of the church.[36] To minimize the importance of conversion, and to scorn the idea of church growth, is to cut the heart out of missions and make Christian social action impossible.

"The church," wrote J. H. Bavinck, "may not creep away into a separate nook of a city or into a special Christian village, but it must remain standing in the center of national life, no matter how dangerous this may be."[37] True that is; for despite the risks involved, that is the only possible way for the church to perform the task Christ has given it. But before that can be done, the church must be planted. That means men must be converted— which means preaching, knocking on doors, distributing literature, talking to the ones and twos in the street, in private homes, and in the factories. And that spells urban missions.

Evangelical Christianity, soundly Biblical and profoundly relevant, can provide the all-important bedrock for urban civilization in Latin America—an urban civilization in which justice and equity prevail because society at large is permeated with Christian truth. In order for this to occur, however, evangelicals must learn what the gospel means in its glorious comprehensiveness, as including all of life and all human institutions. And having learned this from the Word spoken in the churches, they must carry it outside the churches to a community beyond that sorely needs its influence.

---

36. Ibid., p. 459.
37. *An Introduction to the Science of Missions,* p. 166.

8

TOWARD COSMIC DIMENSIONS

"There is no way of getting so involved in our world," says Richard R. De Ridder, "as by mission."[1] And that world is far larger than Christians generally realize. Even human society is not the outer limit of Christian concern. As the scope of God's love is cosmic ("For God so loved the *cosmos...*," John 3:16), and as the whole creation shares both in man's bondage and, ultimately, in his liberation (Rom. 8:19-23), so the mission of God's people is cosmic in its dimensions.

Interpreting "mission" in the broadest sense, Eugene Rubingh says:

> Because Mission is God's work in this world through the sending of men for salvation, the scope of that salvation is determinative for the scope of Mission. As the salvation is cosmic, so the Christian Mission has a Kingdom mandate. Its work involves calling men from eternal death to eternal life, but also the attack on misery and chaos in the created order, now subjected to the incursions of the Satanic.[2]

Not for a moment does this minimize the importance of individual conversion and church planting. Yet the Biblical view of missions

---

1. *The Dispersion of the People of God* (Kampen, Netherlands: J. H. Kok, 1971), p. 220. "Mission" in the singular means the whole work of God in the world.
2. *Sons of Tiv: A Study of the Rise of the Church Among the Tiv of Central Nigeria* (Grand Rapids: Baker Book House, 1969), p. 24.

does not stop with that. The cosmos is the Lord's; He wills its salvation. Christian mission is that *Missio Dei* in the world.[3]

The new believer in Christ Jesus looks around him and says: "This is my Father's world! And that yellow, sometimes almost purple, putrid smog engulfing Mexico City, reaching almost to the tops of the mountains and turning the entire valley, once known for its clear, blue skies, into a coughing, choking incinerator disfigures my Father's handiwork! That is wrong, and it is my duty to do something about it."

The cosmos—which means the sum of all things God has made: the mountains and oceans, the planets, the stars, the whole of man's natural environment—is given him in trust. This is part of the message which the missionary proclaims. Satan's contaminating influence is visible in every place, but those "on the Lord's side" roll back Satan's forces from the land they have occupied so long. "Thy will be done, as in heaven, so on earth" (Matt. 6:10) means this, too.

The message of Christian missions calls the new believer in Christ beyond the Damascus Road experience to enter the ecological struggle as well. Urban ecology, the study of men in the urban community, needs the contributions of Christ motivated men and women who view the city from a Biblical standpoint and see human relations through God's eyes. The gigantic ecological problems festering through ravishing the soil, polluting the air, and turning clear streams into industrial sewers are all of great concern to men and women of God. For, despite the marks of sin it bears, they know that "the earth is the Lord's and the fullness thereof" (Ps. 24:1); and they cannot be indifferent to its devastation.

Young people will listen when the gospel is explained in its Biblical comprehensiveness, for many of them are searching for a unifying principle around which they can view the universe and their task in it. Addressing the twenty-ninth annual convention of the National Association of Evangelicals, meeting in Los Angeles, Billy Graham said that dedicated evangelicals should take advantage of the tides of sentiment that now are running strong in support of historic Biblical Christianity. Liberalism and organized ecumenism, he said, are losing ground while movements reflecting the teachings of historic Christianity are flourishing. This is particularly true among young people, who are looking to Biblical Christianity for meaning and orientation in their lives. "Whether

3. Ibid. See also Georg F. Vicedom, *The Mission of God: An Introduction to a Theology of Mission,* trans. Gilbert A. Thiele and Dennis Hilgendorf (St. Louis: Concordia Publishing House, 1965), p. 45.

we realize it or not," said Graham, "the ball is being passed to evangelicals. Will we throw it away, lose it, or let it go dead?" He continued:

> What would happen if all the evangelicals in America pool their resources and march on Washington and tell the nation that we believe in God, that Christ is our Saviour, that we believe in love of neighbor, that we are concerned about race, war and pollution—but that our greatest concern is for the spiritual welfare of America and of the world![4]

The delegates of the N.A.E. responded by pledging their "willingness to support all proven solutions (to the problems of wastage and spoilage of the environment) even at the cost of personal discomfort or inconvenience." They condemned those who advocate abortion "for reasons of personal convenience, social adjustment or economic advantage," and they condemned the practice of homosexuality while at the same time declaring their desire to extend "the healing ministry of our churches to this group in their desperate need of God's love."[5]

These are problems about which Christians throughout Latin America should be speaking on the authority of God's Word. Instead of so many sermons against smoking, evangelicals need to hear what the Bible says about abortion, bribery, dishonesty, and the proper use of nature's resources. These are the "weightier matters of the law" which are so commonly neglected.

It is the Biblically instructed evangelical who is in the best position to keep ecological concern in proper perspective. Real as the ecological Armageddon very soon may become, he knows that another Armageddon is approaching with even greater certainty. It is the spiritual Armageddon, where the pollution of souls will be examined. And it is this pollution crisis that is being ignored by many people today. Like Jonah on the hillside, they are distraught because a plant died but are callous to the death of cities full of people.[6]

The Biblically oriented missionary will not make the mistake of substituting ecological concern for evangelism. He knows that even if it was possible to clean up all the world's slums, rivers, lakes, and air, the oldest problem of all—man's personality—would

4. The report of Graham's N.A.E. address was published under "News of Religion: Graham Suggests Extraordinary Steps," *Presbyterian Journal*, 5 May 1971, pp. 4-5.
5. Ibid.
6. Portions of this section appeared in *Missionary Monthly*, January 1971, in my article entitled "Ecology and Missions," pp. 26-27.

still remain in its former condition. There is something more polluted than the slimiest stream, and it is the human heart (Jer. 17:9). Only God's grace can clean that. "Save our cities" is more than an ecological slogan on a postage stamp.[7] It requires that the cities' inhabitants be saved—not just from the slums but from sin, which is precisely what urban missions is all about.

In conclusion, what the cities of Latin America, and the entire world, need more than anything else is the Word of God in all its fullness, spoken and acted out. Only this can provide a viable alternative to the challenge of Marxism.

Pope Pius XI said to the bishops of France in December 1937: "You will convert those who are seduced by Communistic doctrines in proportion as you show them that faith in Christ and love of Christ inspire devotion and goodness, in proportion as you show them that nowhere else can there be found a like source of charity. Stress this point."[8] Christians of all denominations can ascribe to this. Words without actions will not suffice. Latin Americans have heard promises long enough. Today they say, *Show us!*

The Word of the gospel enjoins those who hear it to become its doers (James 1:22). "Word bears fruit in deed; deed lends authority and power to word; and word without deed, like faith without works, is dead!"[9] The crisis of the cities is a crisis of faith, yes—but faith as it is held, taught, and applied by people who live, act, hunger, and respond to human needs. It is not a disembodied faith: its supreme Object became flesh and blood, and dwelt among men (John 1:14). Christ and His Word demand a radical reorientation of perspectives: new eyes, new ears, and new value systems. If Marxism demands as much, should less be required of Christians? The words of DeKoster apply to the urban missionary challenge in Latin America:

> Until Christians take deeds as well as words into the marketplace, their denunciations of Marx will be futile, for his strength lies in the market-place. Until we see in each man a living spirit of "more value than many sparrows," we are not really anti-Marxist. Until we see slums in terms of persons, especially of children, and not as rents or investments, we are not really anti-Marxist. Until we see world

---

7. Ecology was the theme of a series of four postage stamps—"Save Our Air," "Save Our Water," "Save Our Soil," "Save Our Cities"—issued in the fall of 1970 by the United States Post Office Department.
8. Cited by Lester DeKoster, *Communism and Christian Faith* (Grand Rapids: Eerdmans Publishing Co., 1956), p. 114.
9. Ibid., p. 115.

hunger in terms of God's opportunity to our charity, and God's demand for an accounting of our stewardship, we are not really anti-Marxist. Until we see factories as associations of persons, not as statistics of production, we are not really anti-Marxist. In short, until we earnestly endeavor to bring every economic relation under the dominion of love, we are not effectively engaged in anti-Marxism.

Only then may we humbly bear to those who labor in the toils of the Marxist effort to save themselves the Master's compassionate and compelling

Come unto me, all ye that labor
And are heavy laden,
And I will give you rest.[10]

---

10. Ibid., p. 118.

PART III

CHRISTIAN ROLES AND RESPONSIBILITIES IN LATIN AMERICAN CITIES

9

LATIN AMERICAN CHURCHES

In his chapter entitled "The Unfinished Task in the Younger Churches," Stephen Neill challenges the churches of Africa, Asia, and Latin America with this thought:

> So far from the evangelization of the world having been nearly accomplished, it may rather be said that the pioneer stage has at length been passed through, and that this is the moment at which serious and constructive evangelization ought to begin.[1]

This pioneer stage, during which the initial church planting took place throughout the Third World in the modern era, has now about ended; and younger and older churches face a new day together for carrying out the great commission. What must be understood, however, is that most of the world's three billion people still need to be evangelized; and the new stage of missionary drama which now has been reached does not mitigate in the least the urgent need for aggressive evangelistic missions.

This needs to be taken very seriously by the leaders of younger churches. Leaders of younger churches are very influential administrators, and they face a great responsibility in this present period. Men "in the know" in missions are aware that in many areas established churches are experiencing only minor growth.[2]

---

1. *The Unfinished Task* (London: Lutterworth Press, 1957), p. 115.
2. Guy, "Directed Conservation," p. 201.

Many, in fact, are virtually stagnated. It cannot be too strongly emphasized, therefore, that the leadership of the churches in Latin America should take inventory of what is happening, think deeply about the causes of slow growth, and ask searchingly how their churches can be turned into healthy, growing centers of witness and service.

Where foreign missionaries are laboring alongside national workers, an atmosphere of free and honest exchange is important. National leaders in Asia have complained that the need for radical restructuring of the missionary system, because of its "unfortunate consequences," is not understood by the churches of the West.[3] Distrust and suspicion are found where confidence and open communication ought to exist.

> In defining goals for future work and conserving the results of past labors, the freest exchange of ideas between secretaries, nationals, and missionaries ought to be encouraged. Yet frequently there is not enough joint thinking. Despite efforts to share thought, a wide gap often develops between the mental processes of the men on the field and those of the board executive. This is even truer for nationals than for missionaries.[4]

This seldom admitted situation is one of the greatest weaknesses in world missions at the present time. National church leaders have the greatest stake of all in the matter of church growth and missions, yet missionary enterprises generally operate as though these leaders did not count. Some of the most creative ideas in evangelism today are coming from national church leaders. National leaders know the future depends on the expansion of the church in their areas. What God is doing through urbanization is to them of supreme importance. It is hoped that they will consider seriously the opportunities which urbanization offers, for it can mean the evangelical expansion about which their forefathers dreamed.

Evangelical leaders owe it to their countries to take urban church growth seriously. Cities represent a national problem everywhere today, and these problems basically are religious and moral. The sicknesses that infect the city are sicknesses of the soul. The families which fall apart because there is no spiritual center, where no one knows how fathers, mothers, and children should behave because no one has ever taught them; the young people without moral standards, purposes, or goals, ruining their bodies—

---

3. "Globe at a Glance," p. 20.
4. Guy, "Directed Conservation," p. 198.

and their minds as well—through drugs, sex, and alcohol; the masses living numbly, meaninglessly, in the drab conformity of an urban culture which deals with humanity as a bulk commodity and not as individuals; the racial conflicts; the political agitation; the growing conviction that happiness is to be found only in material possessions—all these illnesses are fundamentally spiritual problems, problems of values and priorities, of morals and goals, which can be diagnosed and cured only by Christian missions at work in the city.[5]

Behind every social problem in the city lies a religious factor for which only the message of the Bible offers a cure. When churches retreat from the city or ignore it in favor of quieter, less troublesome sectors of population, they leave the field where the battle rages most, and they forsake their calling and abandon their Lord. In order to avoid doing this, the problem areas for the church should be isolated and studied, and specific solutions applied to each one.

Three Major Problem Areas

It is possible to identify three major problem areas in regard to Latin American churches and the city. First, some national church leaders simply are *unaware* of what is going on as far as urbanization is concerned; second, others are *unwilling* to do what needs to be done to bring the receptive urban masses into the church; and third, other leaders, again, are *uninterested* in missionary outreach, being content with the management of churches already organized.

Many pastors of city churches—and this is even more true of village pastors—are largely unaware of the nature of urbanization and the opportunities which it poses for evangelization. This becomes evident in talking with these pastors. Some of them reveal utter amazement over facts about their own city's growth. Similarly, they have scant idea of urbanization's impact on the masses. They have seen the slums, mostly from a distance; but they know little or nothing about the actual conditions within the depressed areas of the city, nor of the conditions within industry where increasing numbers of men are employed. National church leaders should take pains to inform themselves and those under them of the extent of urbanization in Latin America and the opportunities

5. David W. Barry, "The Task of the Church in the Inner City," in *Cities and Churches: Readings on the Urban Church,* ed. Robert Lee (Philadelphia: Westminster Press, 1962), p. 140.

which it presents to evangelicals. A virgin mission field lies at their doors. There is need for heightened awareness.

Besides awareness, however, there remains the question of willingness. Evangelical churches in Latin America are generally linked with the middle class, and the problem of missions among the urban masses becomes one of motivation.[6] "For the middle class and recently arrived home owner to become really involved with the hungry poor is 'next to unthinkable.' "[7] This is a problem that goes beyond education: only grace can solve this one.

A wide cultural gap exists between city evangelicals and the new urbanites, and it is this gap which hinders the former from evangelizing the latter. There is little understanding or empathy between them. With some city evangelicals there is actually fear of identifying with the newcomers, as though such association might jeopardize one's status as a middle-class person.

In defense of Latin American evangelicals, it must be pointed out that this culture gap is found in North America as well; indeed, it is almost universal. The culture gap is a most common curse of churches which literally cannot win their neighbors. In America there are ardently missionary churches which send their sons and daughters abroad and raise ample support for missions, but which are utterly unable to draw people from the other side of the tracks (or even from their own neighborhoods) into their churches. In Liberia, the very fact that the Americo-Liberians, who number about 100,000, have been Christians and literate for generations has prevented the spread of Christianity to the 900,000 animists in the interior.[8] In Ceylon, the Dutch Reformed Church, the oldest Protestant denomination on the island, is almost exclusively burgher and middle class. It has been virtually impotent as far as evangelism is concerned. Why? Because of the cultural gap between peoples.

What will it take to solve this problem of the culture gap? One solution, which I tried in Colombo, Ceylon, is to fight it. I tried everything I could to turn a culturally exclusive congregation —as well as the entire church, through the denominational paper— into a heterogenous mixture in which people of every class, race, and culture would feel at home. And I failed. The Tamils still pre-

---

6. Read, Monterroso, and Johnson, *Latin American Church Growth,* pp. 229-30.
7. Roger D. Perkins, "Sufficient Attention to the Masses," *Church Growth Bulletin,* September 1967, p. 8. Perkins' observations are based on Brazil.
8. Donald A. McGavran, replying to A. C. Krass, "A Case Study in Effective Evangelism in West Africa," *Church Growth Bulletin,* September 1967, p. 5.

ferred their own services, the Sinhalese sang best by themselves, and the middle-class burghers continued their Western style services in the English language.

There is a better solution, and it is being applied in scores of Latin American middle-class churches where leaders are sensitive to both the problems and the challenges. It is simply to bypass the problem of the class-bound church and lead out with individuals who are free and have vision and passion for the lost. Urban strategists should not become preoccupied with the exclusivistic class-conscious local church. Certainly they ought to pray for it, preach for it, and provide for its needs; for that church, too, is the body of Christ. But they should not leave the city masses waiting until the established churches at last decide to give them attention.

It will take a visionary like Winston Gauder in Ceylon, who pleaded with his denomination until finally it allowed him to leave the dignified, middle-class church which he pastored to take up work in Makundura, where he could reach the Buddhist masses. It will take a Moises Lopez, who will add the care and concern of a dozen Mexico City house-churches to his already overloaded schedule because he cares for men's souls. Such men are there, though they may have to be searched out. Often they will be laymen with natural empathy for the masses. But whoever they are, they will respond to the call of God's Word to move out of their sheltered middle-class nests and go looking for the harvest fields which God's Spirit has prepared.[9]

Anne Parsons points out that an excessive amount of "privatization" can come over middle-class people and rob them of their sense of responsibility for the religious and social needs of others.[10]

---

9. It may be argued that almost all evangelical churches, no matter how many middle-class or upper-class members they may have, also contain members from the lower strata of society. This is true, but it does not disprove the assertion that urban evangelical churches in Latin America are predominantly middle class not only in membership but also in general orientation; that the lower classes do not take active roles in the program of the church, do not figure prominently in the youth organizations, and are generally treated in a rather accommodating manner. Willems, in *Followers of the New Faith,* points out that this distinguishes the historical churches from the Pentecostal denominations. The latter prove more attractive to the masses because their entire program is more in line with the lower-class way of life (p. 252).

10. "The Pentecostal Immigrants: A Study of an Ethnic Central City Church," *Practical Anthropology* 14 (November-December 1967): 250. The study is based in North America, but many of its observations are equally valid in Latin America.

The lower classes view religion and life as more of a unity, whereas middle-class people tend to view the world of business as one thing, religion as another, and social responsibility as something separated from both. This tendency is destructive of the truly Christian life in which the outward practice of religion (worship and activities centered around the organized church), social responsibility, and evangelistic witness are integrally related. Privatization may be one important factor in explaining middle-class indifference to the spiritual and social needs of the urban masses in Ibero-America as well as elsewhere.

The decade of the seventies, says Dennis Clark, will be the watershed in the history of missions.[11] Certainly it is a time of transition. Above all, it is vital that the churches of Latin America not be "copiers"; for to copy the mother churches of North America can be disastrous. Be innovators. Let the Spirit of God lead. The older churches have made too many mistakes to be copied except with extreme caution. Today, among the teeming masses pouring into the cities, there is fresh ground to begin a new program, implement new insights and new visions, without the burden of a tradition of mission work which has proved itself unfruitful but which refuses to be discarded. This is a day of unparalleled opportunity.

The third problem that vexes Latin American churches in regard to the city is one which, again, is universal, and has been called the "paradox of mission."[12] It is the tension which exists between concern for the established church and concern for missionary outreach, between separation from the world and going out into the world for the salvation of the lost. On the one hand, God's people are "an elect race, a royal priesthood, a holy nation" (I Peter 2:9); and on the other hand, they are like leaven hidden within the mass of mankind, indistinguishable to the physical eye, men among the many for the sake of the many, a redemptive but at the same time dispersed multitude.

This distinction finds concrete illustration in the tensions existing in many churches. One group in the church wants to reach out and bring in newcomers to the city and the neighborhood; whereas others want to keep the church just the way it is, without the new faces and their problems. I was told by a Mexico City pastor of an instance in which "old stock" members of his church let the

11. "A Virile Freedom in the Young Churches," World Vision Magazine, April 1970, p. 15.
12. Kromminga, The Communication of the Gospel Through Neighboring, p. 248.

air out of the tires of certain visitors to let them know they were not welcome to return. The older members were zealous for their church. They worked hard for its smooth operation, and they wanted it preserved just as it was. They resisted every effort by the pastor and other members to turn the church outward in mission to the city.

This attitude, of course, is based on a serious misunderstanding of the nature of the church. Somewhere in its history this group of believers was given the impression that the Christian community exists only for its members—for their self-preservation as Christians, and nothing more. The carrying out of the great commission, they came to believe, did not necessarily involve them. The "paradox" had disappeared. They solved the problem by absolving the church of missionary responsibility.

Preachers of the Word must never try to eliminate that paradox. The church must both be preserved and increased. In the answer to Question 123 of the Heidelberg Catechism, the petition "Thy kingdom come" in the Lord's Prayer is given this explanation:

> That is: so rule us by Thy Word and Spirit that we may subject ourselves more and more to Thee; preserve and increase Thy Church; destroy the works of the devil, every power that exalts itself against Thee, and all wicked counsels conceived against Thy holy Word, until the perfection of Thy kingdom arrive wherein Thou shalt be all in all.

Precisely right. The tension must not be erased, for both the *preserving* and *increasing* of the church are necessary. It is not an either-or proposition, but both-and. While the cords need to be "lengthened," the stakes, simultaneously, must be "strengthened" (Isa. 54:2).

What Some Churches Are Doing

Evangelism in the Latin American denominations which have their origin in the Protestant Reformation of the sixteenth century generally follows the traditional patterns of Western missions. Pentecostal evangelism, on the other hand, is generally something quite different. It grows out of the spontaneous enthusiasm of new converts who have experienced the gospel's power in their lives and cannot help but witness to others. They open their homes for neighborhood services without prompting from their leaders.[13] They

---

13. In three instances in Mexico City, I was invited to take over the supervision of house-churches already organized which had asked the large Portales church to take them under supervision. They had been turned down because Portales already had more house-churches than it could handle.

offer land for church buildings and freely give of their labor to erect the edifices.[14] Avoiding dependence on foreign assistance, either economic or by way of personnel, Pentecostals enlist their entire membership in evangelism. This is the secret of their success both as churches and as missionaries. No member is isolated or left inactive. Everyone has a place, a mission, a responsibility. This explains the capacity of the Pentecostal movement to grow in Latin America.

Between 1968 and 1970, I conducted twenty-five "depth" studies of evangelical city churches in Mexico. Most of them were in the capital. (See Appendix 2.) The purpose was to find out which churches were growing and which were not, and why the difference. One very obvious conclusion that came out of the study is that the churches whose leaders have a vision for growth and multiplication are having a great day, but the churches whose leaders are turned inward are stagnated.[15] Urban church growth is possible, far out of proportion to most expectations; but it takes men of vision and energy to seize the opportunity.

For example, in the Mexican border city Ciudad Juárez, missionary John Huegel wrote glowing reports in 1963 of the possibilities for evangelical missions in this area of rapid population growth and social change.[16] Because I was eager to find out how some of the churches in Huegel's report were progressing, I traveled to Ciudad Juárez in 1969 and interviewed some of the pastors. The First Baptist Church was outstanding.[17] It had planted eight

---

14. The ability of Pentecostal groups to secure property in the city is amazing. Nearly all of it is donated by some grateful convert. That is how the Portales church began, as well as most other Pentecostal city churches. The magnificent church belonging to the "Luz del Mundo" ("Light of the World") movement in Guadalajara cost one million pesos, seats 2,600 persons, and was erected almost entirely by the labor of the members themselves. Even women and children worked on the construction, which took two years to complete. Interviews: Angel Arce, Portales Interdenominational Church, Mexico City, 8 June 1971; eight members, Light of the World movement, Colonia Provincia, Guadalajara, 17 April 1970.
15. For the overall picture of church growth patterns in Mexico, see *Church Growth in Mexico,* by Donald A. McGavran, John Huegel, and Jack Taylor (Grand Rapids: Eerdmans Publishing Co., 1963).
16. "A Bridge into Mexico," an unpublished report of evangelical churches in Ciudad Juárez, prepared for Disciples of Christ, El Paso, Texas, 1963 (mimeographed).
17. Information contained in this paragraph stems from my interview with the Rev. M. M. Currola, pastor of the First Baptist Church, Ciudad Juárez, Chihuahua, Mexico, 3 June 1969. Despite his advanced age, Currola showed great zeal for further church planting. He said that a city-wide mass meeting held in the Plaza Toros, featuring the world yo-yo champion, had provided

daughter churches in the past three years. Four of these churches already had their own buildings and parsonages, and two had regular pastors. Of the remaining four, two expected to organize and call pastors within a year's time. The pastor of the mother church, M. M. Currola, spoke with great enthusiasm about these daughter churches. There is nothing to hinder Christians from the city of El Paso, on the United States side of the border, from coming over to help; and those who make themselves available are doing a remarkable service.[18] Prospective leaders are trained in the Baptist seminary in Torreon, and eventually all eight of the young churches will have full-time pastors.

In sharp contrast to Currola's enthusiasm and encouraging progress in church growth and outreach, the pastor of another denomination just a few blocks away gave a most discouraging report. "We have three missions," he said, "but they are not growing. The women do the evangelism in our church, and a few of the young people go with them. The men are not interested."[19] They had just bought a piece of land with money from the United States and hoped soon to erect a building for one of the missions. The overall picture, he reported, was not too encouraging, though complete freedom to evangelize was there.

So frustrated have some denominational churches become in recent years that they have virtually abandoned the urban masses to the Pentecostals. This is a sad mistake. The urban masses need not, and ought not, be left to the Pentecostals alone. Willems, in his study of the growth of evangelicalism in Brazil and Chile, points out that with the exception of the Baptists, the Pentecostal movement has dealt an almost paralyzing blow to the growth of the historical churches in some areas.[20] Preaching, praying, and singing in the streets and public parks are looked upon as being too "undignified" by straight-laced church people. They have grown too sophisticated, too class-conscious for such public demonstrations. But on the other hand, as Willems points out, where the historical churches have awakened and have refused to leave the urban

---

the Baptists with the opportunity to distribute hundreds of copies of Dios Llega al Hombre (Good News for Modern Man), and from this had come many converts and opportunities for additional house-churches.
18. An example of this is the service rendered by the Rev. José Rosales, Southern Baptist minister living in El Paso, Texas, who crossed the border almost every night to care for a new house-church in the town of Zaragoza. Interview with José Rosales, Ciudad Juárez, Chihuahua, Mexico, 3 June 1969.
19. Interview with Rev. Samuel Martínez, Methodist Church, El Centro, Ciudad Juárez, Chihuahua, Mexico, 3 June 1969.
20. *Followers of the New Faith,* p. 121.

masses to the Pentecostals, they have found that they can meet the competition and have shown substantial gains in converts and churches.[21]

Evangelismo-al-Fondo (Evangelism-in-Depth) is proving to be a great awakener of many denominational churches. To the many sleepy churches tucked snugly away in the middle-class corners of the great cities, involvement with Evangelism-in-Depth is precisely what they need. Writes the pastor of one of the largest Presbyterian churches in the metropolitan area of Mexico City:

> Despite our sins and limitations, God is blessing our church. Evangelism-in-Depth has put us on our feet. At the present time we are training a group of 70 persons who go out to evangelize in the streets and house-to-house. These people come back and tell the church of the beautiful experiences they have had, and the blessings they received, through evangelism. Besides, we have a group of 15 children who also go out to evangelize, and their testimony has been a great blessing to the church.[22]

This pastor goes on to say that not everyone is entirely happy with Evangelism-in-Depth, nor are they all cooperating. "But our vision is to motivate the whole church," he writes, "so that in the future they will all go to evangelize."[23] From my own observation, there can be no doubt that the 1971-72 Evangelism-in-Depth campaign in Mexico has already helped to revitalize the church.

Nationwide campaigns such as Evangelism-in-Depth are no cure-all for every tired, listless church that has lost its spiritual momentum. But, as Kenneth Strachan so rightly perceived, the strength and progress of a church is in direct proportion to its success in mobilizing its entire membership for the continuous propagation

---

21. Ibid.
22. Efren Haro Robles, personal letter to me, 17 May 1971.
23. Ibid. I find it difficult to understand how Emilio Castro can conscientiously say: "If all the members of the Church in Latin America were to devote themselves to a conscious programme for the spread of Christianity on the exhaustive lines of Evangelism in Depth, it would be a tragedy for the Gospel in Latin America; for we should then be taking our members away from their places of responsible witness in society." "Evangelism in Latin America," *International Review of Missions* 53 (October 1964): 455. In most countries, evangelicals are fewer than 2.0 percent of the population. In Mexico City, they number only 111,957, or 1.67 percent of the population (Census, 1970). In such a situation there is no greater need than massive outward movement for growth and multiplication.

of the Christian faith.[24] Thousands of churches across the continent, accustomed to letting the foreign missionaries do the evangelizing or hiring professional evangelists to do it, need to hear
that the great commission involves them.

> Evangelism in Depth has been hailed by some as a new
> strategy of evangelism. But in fact it involves nothing basically
> new. If there is anything different about it, it is perhaps
> the fact that it represents a formal effort to relate in a long-
> range programme the best elements of personal witness and
> mass evangelism, integrated in the continuous testimony of
> the local church and linked to the total witness of the
> entire Body of Christ. It also involves a challenge to all
> Christian bodies to plan and carry out their respective evan-
> gelistic programmes in a simultaneous, co-ordinated effort
> aimed at the ultimate goal that the Great Commission en-
> joins. To many individuals, moreover, it comes as a personal
> summons to take the Lord's command seriously and to ad-
> venture with other Christians in obedient involvement and
> witness in the world.[25]

"Evangelism-in-Depth," says Juan Isais, director of the movement in Mexico City, "was born out of our failures."[26] Because
it is essentially Biblical,[27] it has universal application; and "because it was born in Latin America it has certain external characteristics in its program and practice that are inherent to the culture
of the continent that saw its birth."[28]

Does this explain the missionary's difficulty in appreciating Evangelism-in-Depth? Among the fifty-two denominations in Mexico,

24. R. Kenneth Strachan, "Call to Witness," *International Review of Missions* 53 (April 1964): 200.
25. Ibid., p. 197.
26. Juan M. Isais, ed., *The Other Revolution: The Dramatic Story of
Another Revolution in the Dominican Republic* (Waco, Tex.: Word Books,
1970), p. 158.
27. Says Ruben Lores: "More than a methodological structure, more than a
missionary strategy, Evangelism-in-Depth is a practical expression of a theological reflection upon the inescapable consideration of the church's mission
in this world." "Algunas Reflexiones de Torno a los Fundamentos Teológicos
de Evangelismo a Fondo," p. 1 (mimeographed; translation mine). Lores's
contention is that Evangelism-in-Depth's major contribution lies in awakening the local church to its missionary responsibility and helping Christians
who have never witnessed for Christ before to get started. Lores does good
work in providing the Biblical and theological foundation for Evangelism-in-
Depth's program.
28. Isais, *The Other Revolution*, p. 158.

cooperation with the movement is spotty, to say the least.[29] The potential benefits, as Isais enumerates them, are fourfold: (1) greater confidence in witnessing; (2) training for witnessing; (3) increased aggressiveness through united effort; and (4) changed mentality.[30] This last one, *"cambio de mentalidad,"* is the most important. The attitude of defeat, which in many cases borders on a persecution complex, needs to be changed. A new day has dawned, and both the fears and the failures of the past must be discarded. Evangelism-in-Depth, as an organization, is of little importance. But as a concept, it is urgently needed. After the movement which bears its name has died out, the thing it stands for must live on in a hundred thousand churches throughout the continent. And most of those churches, at this time, still need that *cambio de mentalidad.*

Cell Groups and New Structures

In the atomized society of the city it is of utmost importance that the organization of the church help supply men with a sense of personal community. Historical evangelical churches can do this as well as the sectarian groups, *providing they are willing to structure themselves in a way which fits men's needs.* The inherited structures of North American, rural-based churches do not always meet the needs of Latin American cities, and even in the mother countries the inadequacies of these structures are slowly being realized. The formation of multitudinous new Christian organizations in the last few decades is largely due to the fact that the urban churches have not supplied men with the meaningful, person-to-person relationships they desire. Says Hugh A. Koops:

> It is unfortunate that the organized church has shown an institutional lag in its response to the heterogeneity of its urban population. Since the church has been reluctant to change the structures it has inherited from its rural origins, the membership of the church has formed many interest groups outside the organization. Such organizations as Campus Crusade, the Christian Businessmen's Clubs, the Christian Medical Society, the Inter-Varsity Christian Fellowship, the Southern Christian Leadership conference, etc., are illustrative of specific adaptations to diverse interests of dedicated Christians in education, profession, and social concern. These

---

29. In June 1971, the mission of the Christian Reformed Church was the only foreign missionary organization in Mexico which had officially decided to cooperate with Evangelism-in-Depth. Headquarters of the movement were located in the mission's downtown Mass Communications Center, and students of the mission's three schools were enlisted in the program.

30. Juan M. Isais, personal interview, Mexico City, 9 June 1971.

new structures, unlike the Men's Society, the Ladies' Aid, and the Young People's Society, are built upon the diversities of heterogeneity in urban interests rather than the natural diversities of age and sex.[31]

Who can deny that the majority of weekly program bulletins of Latin American denominational churches read exactly like their counterparts in North America? Structures imported from the rural America of the nineteenth century to the urbanized America of today, to the village churches on a hundred mission fields, and to the urban congregations of Mexico City, Rio de Janeiro, and Buenos Aires inhibit the life and growth of evangelicalism everywhere.

Moreover, rural church patterns cause tensions within individual congregations, where the members complain that the pastor is more distant and less personal in relation to his parishioners than the pastors they knew in the village. Of course he is. So is everyone else in the city, and the rural-urban roles which the pastor is trying to fulfill drive the poor man in every direction. Try to find a conscientious pastor of a large Latin American city church at home and at ease with his family sometime. If you find him at all, and engage him in conversation, he will be interrupted constantly by people at the door asking to see him. The rural patterns of close, personal, time-consuming relationships press down on the city pastor relentlessly. He must invite to his pulpit outside preachers far too often for his own or his people's good, for the simple reason that the rural pattern of demanding the pastor's personal attention to everything leaves him no time to study.

City life requires that the church revamp its strategy and its structures to meet the needs of urban people. New Testament *koinonia* in an urban environment can be realized effectively only when the church responds to the life patterns of its members and of those it is trying to reach in positive and relevant ways. Urbanization is the dominant sociological characteristic of the day. It affects every part of human culture, and the faster the church shifts gears to an urban style of work and witness the sooner the great harvest which God is preparing will be brought in.[32]

The nongrowing situation in which many churches find themselves is the concern of thoughtful leaders everywhere. Latin America has no monopoly on nongrowing churches; proportionately, there

31. "Toward the Holy City III," *The Reformed Journal,* December 1966, p. 16.
32. Ibid., p. 20.

are probably more of them in Europe and North America than anywhere else. Especially as countries become more industrialized, and hence more urbanized, increasing numbers of the working-class people feel that the church is far removed from their problems and really does not care about them. The large institution—whether Catholic or Protestant—is so cold, so impersonal. Unless the warm glow of the Holy Spirit is there it will turn more people away than it attracts.

In discussing this situation with a leading Pentecostal pastor in Mexico City, I was startled to hear him say:

> Your denominational churches are full in the morning and mostly empty at night. Do you know where your best members are? They aren't sitting home watching TV as you may think. They are attending Pentecostal services, where they hear the music and the preaching that they like! Our best crowds are at night, and one-third of the audience is made up of people from the old denominations. When are you going to wake up to what your people are looking for?[33]

That is a most enlightening observation and a very provocative question. When *are* the denominational churches going to wake up? And when will they dare to examine their programs, and those of the groups which are growing the fastest, and then ask themselves how and why the Lord is using some and not using others to win the urban masses to a living, vital faith in Jesus Christ? The *koinonia* which the denominations *talk about,* the humble Pentecostals are *achieving,* on the local level where it makes a difference in people's lives and promotes the growth of the gospel in numbers and influence.[34]

Bishop James Armstrong of the United Methodist Church returned recently from a trip to Brazil.[35] He went there for the spe-

---

33. Personal interview with Manuel J. Gaxiola, 20 November 1969, Mexico City. Gaxiola is the author of *La Serpiente y la Paloma* (South Pasadena: William Carey Library, 1970), and presently serves as president of the Iglesia Apostolica de la Fe en Cristo Jesus of Mexico.
34. In this connection it should be said that the Spanish edition of Christian Lalive D'Epinay, *Refugio de las Masas,* should be studied by every city pastor in Latin America. His conclusions are not those of an evangelical, but his analyses are most helpful.
35. Information concerning Armstrong's trip to Brazil and the data concerning the condition of Protestant and Pentecostal churches in that country are from "Pentecostals Make Marked Gains in Brazil," *Christian Century,* 6 January 1971, p. 7, and "Pentecostal Growth," International Roman Catholic Press Review, *Christian Heritage,* May 1971, p. 13. The full name of the church which de Mello leads is *Igreja Evangelica Pentecostal Brasil para Cristo.* Willems refers to it in *Followers of the New Faith,* p. 120.

cial purpose of observing the Pentecostal movement which is out-performing the traditional denominations. Called *"Brasil para Cristo"* ("Brazil for Christ"), the movement has a constituency of approximately 3.5 million (Brazil has 320,000 Baptists, 167,000 Presbyterians, 70,000 Missouri Synod Lutherans, 57,000 Methodists, and 13,000 Episcopalians). The Pentecostals have about 10,000 congregations. Manuel de Mello, leader of the Brazil for Christ movement, avoids playing the role of a politician himself but he does recommend certain candidates for public office whose sincerity and program he can endorse. The increased number of Pentecostal voters is becoming a key factor in Brazilian politics, and from the Christian standpoint this can be expected to have a favorable influence on the direction of national life. It is not without reason, therefore, that Armstrong states that Protestantism has no hope of staying alive in Brazil unless it is willing to learn from *Brasil para Cristo.*

The main problem in Latin American cities is not the indifference of the urbanites toward religion, but the indifference of many urban churches toward the masses. When churches care more for their traditional structures and practices than for their mission in the world, the advance of Christ's kingdom is stalemated. When church leaders look on the city and see only their own members scattered here and there in the vast sea of urban humanity, and church members in general have little concern for the multitudes around them, then the indifference on the part of outsiders to Christianity is simply a reflection of the indifference of Christians toward people and their needs.[36]

The emerging urban expression of the church is not the big expensive, red-brick-church-on-the-corner affair, but the small informal group, the house-church, gathered around the Bible, fused with spontaneous joy expressed in singing, testimony, and prayer, where monologue gives way to "every member" participation, and where the freedom of the Spirit is more honored than traditional structures.[37]

When this becomes more apparent the evangelical faith can spread like a flood through Latin America. The Catholic parish is no match for this kind of fellowship. The vastness, the anonymity of its membership, the scarcity of priests, and the indifference of

---

36. Takashi Yamada, "Studies in Extension Evangelism," Church Growth Pamphlet Series No. 3, trans. P. W. Boschman (Kobayashi City, Miyazaki, Japan: Kobayashi Kyodaisha, 1970), pp. 2-3.
37. See Arthur Glasser, "From Western Religion to Universal Faith," *World Vision Magazine,* April 1970, p. 22, for essentially the same thought.

many who hold that office prevent the kind of intimacy which characterizes the evangelical congregation. The urban expression of the evangelical church must be home and family centered. Neighborhood churches, living cells of the one body, meet the need better than any other structure. Here, in today's urban world, is the most authentic return to the primitive fellowship meeting of the New Testament church, with all the potential for empire-conquest that the early church possessed.

Beginning in 1968 and continuing over a span of two years, I interviewed fifty-eight persons in Mexico who had been converted to the evangelical faith during the decade between 1960 and 1970.[38]

TABLE 7

LARGE CHURCH VS. SMALL GROUP

Question 8: *Do you feel happier worshiping in a large church, or in a small group such as a mission?*

	Answers
Large church	9
Small group	20
No difference	29

They varied in age, though most were under twenty-five; and they were related to six different evangelical denominations. Ten key questions were asked during the interviews, and their answers were written down and tabulated. Figure 4 (p. 87) indicates the kind of response which was received about the factors that led to conversion. The Bible itself, church preaching, and the testimony of a relative figure highest among the factors leading to conversion. Within families women generally were the first to accept the evangelical faith, and the "bridges" pattern of conversion was plainly

---

38. See Appendix 1 for the questionnaire which was used in the interviews.

evident. Of particular importance at this point, however, was *the decided preference for small groups, over against large churches, as the place of worship.*

All fifty-eight persons interviewed in this survey were living in Mexico City, where they had access to a number of large congregations as well as to neighborhood churches (popularly called "missions") meeting in private homes. Not all of these fifty-eight people had been converted in the city, however; for many of them were immigrants from rural areas and small towns in other parts of Mexico. Their preference for small groups in the cities may reflect most of all their need for personal integration into the community, and the evangelical church has much to offer on that

---

TABLE 8

PLACE OF CONVERSION

Question 7: *Where were you converted?*

	Answers
In a large church	11
In a small group	44
Alone by myself	3

---

score. But their preference for small group services must be viewed also in the light of their answers as to *where they were converted:*

Apparently, whether in the city, the village, or the isolated rancho, the small cell group, gathered around the Bible with someone preaching or teaching the meaning of the gospel, with intimate testimonies, prayers, and simple, unadorned music and song, is the place where most people find the Christ as their Savior and make their decision to follow Him as their Lord. The beautiful custom in Latin America of calling every fellow believer *"hermano"* ("brother"), beginning from the time of his conversion, characterizes the face-to-face family relationship of the small church-in-the-house, which is far closer to the New Testament church than the stately structures called "churches" in Christendom today.

The Lay Apostolate

A renewed recognition of the apostolate of the laity is one of the greatest needs of the evangelical church in Latin America today. Strategies of church life and missions which are mere carry-overs from Roman Catholic clericalism must be discarded. The meaning of the priesthood of all believers must take on new significance. Nowhere does this fact become clearer than in the ministry of the small neighborhood church, the "covenant community" of local families who live in close proximity, worship together, and witness unitedly in both word and deed.[39] Ordained, seminary trained clergymen cannot be supplied to all these churches. Leadership must be in the hands of laymen, and more often than not, young people. They have the numbers and the zeal and they are "on location," permanently, in all parts of the city.

It is questionable whether many pastors will dare to let their laymen be free to evangelize, begin house-churches, and bring the gospel to bear on life in industry, business, and politics. But laymen should do it anyway. Laymen sometimes know more about the pain of the city than many ecclesiastical leaders do, and theirs is the responsibility to do something about it.

A positive program for Christian laymen in Latin America must begin with firsthand acquaintance with the real issues at stake in the city. A slum has been called a place where hope dies, where broken men and women, and children who never know what it means to be young, live out each day as a battle for survival.[40] Laymen from established churches should get to know what the slums are like. It will change their thinking. On several occasions, I purposely have taken influential laymen of Mexico City churches into the colonias where the masses of rural-urban immigrants live. In one instance, a high-level professional man became so upset by what he saw (and smelled) that he hurried back to the car and pleaded to be taken out of there. Another tall businessman swayed visibly on his heels as, for the first time in his life, he

39. Bruce Larson and Ralph Osborne, *The Emerging Church* (Waco, Tex.: Word Books, 1970), pp. 91-96.
40. Weldon Gaddy, *Urban Crisis,* a Resource Paper of the Christian Life Commission of the Southern Baptist Convention (Nashville: Christian Life Commission, n.d.), p. 2. It is an excellent paper, one that should be studied by every Christian in America, especially those in positions of influence.

caught sight of the inside of a four-story tenement located only a few blocks from the plush office building where he worked.

Slums are *part* of the city but they are not the whole of it, nor should Christian concern be limited to the slums alone. Christian voices should be heard in every dimension of urban life. Every level of society needs its Christian witness, and here laymen play the key roles. The apostolate of the laity is multidimensional. Its urban strategy includes the application of the Christian conscience, undergirded by Christian convictions, in matters of housing, education, commerce, and industry. Laymen can go and can speak influentially in areas where preachers never enter. Guided by the Spirit and fed by the Word, evangelical laymen should speak out for justice, equality, and the needs of the masses at all levels of life.

The oath of the ancient Athenian city-state read:

> We will ever strive for the ideals and sacred things of the city, both alone and with many;
> We will unceasingly seek to quicken the sense of public duty;
> We will revere and obey the city's laws;
> We will transmit this city not only not less, but greater, better, and more beautiful than it was transmitted to us.[41]

The Athenians had something there. They had a civic consciousness, a concern for the whole city, which not all evangelicals possess. "Christianity," says McGavran, "should be recognized as the religion which provides bedrock for urban civilization."[42] The multiplication of Christian churches will provide the basis for a new, egalitarian society in proportion to its vision and its concern for men and their needs.[43]

A Beautiful Example of a Fruitful Urban Church

Not all house-churches grow and develop into permanent institutions with their own buildings and full-time pastors. Their pur-

---

41. Ibid., citing Daniel P. Moynihan, "Toward a National Urban Policy," *Violent Crime: The Challenge of Our Cities* (New York: George Braziller, 1969), p. 40.
42. *Understanding Church Growth*, p. 295.
43. The Project of the Aztec Presbytery, an urban-industrial program being attempted in Mexico City by a group of Presbyterians headed by missionary John Hazelton, offers something unique in the area of educating pastors and lay leaders to the needs of urban workers. If it can maintain a conversion theology, and couple it with church-planting, the project will make a valuable contribution. "Proyecto del Presbiterio Azteca," Mexico City, 1970, pp. 1-3 (mimeographed).

pose is not to erect buildings, but to serve Christ and people here and now, whether that means continuing in a particular location for six months, six years, or until Christ returns.[44]

For that reason, no one should speak of "failure" when a house-church closes down due to circumstances beyond the control of the believers. When, for example, a landlord throws out the family that has invited the evangelicals to meet in their home, no one has failed, no one should be ashamed, nor should anyone hesitate to begin all over again at the next opportunity. Wherever people meet around the open Word, pray together, and sing, there Christ is with them (Matt. 18:20) and important things happen. People are saved, others are strengthened in their faith, weary souls find rest, and hopes revive even if the house-church lasts only a few months. The churches addressed by the Lord in the Apocalypse did not last forever either (Rev. 1—3).

Many house-churches, however, will become large and permanent institutions. Among the twenty-five churches in Mexico City, representing all the major evangelical denominations which I studied,[45] one church in particular stands out as a beautiful illustration of growth and multiplication in the city.

The church referred to is the *Iglesia "Resurreccion en Cristo"* (Church of the Resurrection in Christ), an independent Baptist church in the Colonia Industrial. Its present pastor is the Rev. David Bello, blind in both eyes but powerful in the pulpit and ably assisted in his pastoral work by his intelligent and attractive wife. The former pastor, the Rev. René Zapata, is a highly trained and articulate Mexican church leader.[46] Obviously, this Baptist church has been blessed by the ministries of two outstanding leaders. As will be seen, however, the capability of the pastors has not been the main secret of its ministry.

This church was founded in 1960, and by 1970 had 500 members. Church property is valued at 100,000 pesos; and the need for a larger auditorium is so urgent that the church is virtually divided into two congregations, one meeting in the morning and the other at night. Since the auditorium seats only 250, and there are always many visitors, a larger building or separation into two

---

44. For a good discussion of this principle applied to North American churches, see Ralph Neighbour, Jr., "Don't Let a Building Be a Burden," *Baptist Program*, July 1971, pp. 6-7.
45. See Appendix 2.
46. The information contained in the following paragraphs concerning the history and present state of the *Iglesia "Resurrección en Cristo"* is derived from the interview with David Bello, Mexico City, 12 April 1970, and the letter of René Zapata, 28 April 1970.

churches seem to be the only alternatives. Some 170,000 pesos have been raised so far, and present plans are to construct a new auditorium on the present site.

In this church young people and adult laymen have made the difference between stagnation and rapid growth. First of all, the Church of the Resurrection in Christ was started by young people. A group of young people from a downtown church began visiting house-to-house in the Colonia Industrial; and under the guidance of René Zapata, a church was established. In 1964, forty adult converts were received, plus the children who were regularly in attendance; in 1966, sixty converts were baptized, with many inquirers and unbaptized sympathizers attending all the services. By 1970, one hundred families were connected with the church. David Bello estimated that the main reason why more people did not become full members was because of the church's strong insistence on financial support. "We insist that to be a member, with voice and vote, one has to share the financial responsibility; and many of them don't want to do it," he said. The membership is strongly weighted on the side of youth: 60 percent of those who attend services are young people, though not all of them have so far requested baptism. Twenty percent of the full members work in factories, 15 percent are teachers, and about 30 percent are professionals and work in offices. When asked whether the church had problems holding on to its youth, Bello replied: "No, they attend!"

Not only do they attend, they evangelize. The most beautiful thing about the Church of the Resurrection in Christ is its history of church multiplication, and laymen and youth play the major role. Only ten years old, the church already has three grown "daughters" and four more on the way up. "Preaching centers," located in private homes, are established in Colonia Montezuma, Colonia Altavilla, Colonia Peruvilla, and Colonia Anahuac. Weekly services are conducted in each locale by youth groups, women, and laymen from the church. Besides, teams go out regularly to the prisons, hospitals, and parks of the city, preaching, testifying, and distributing tracts wherever they can, and evangelistic campaigns are held in the church.

The three daughter churches are lovely to describe. Consider these dates and the way in which the young churches began:

1960—Founding of the Church of the Resurrection in Christ, Colonia Industrial, by young people.

1963—Daughter Church No. 1, founded in Colonia Progreso Nacional, by young people.

1966—Daughter Church No. 2, founded in Colonia Viveros de Xalostoc, by a deacon.

1969—Daughter Church No. 3, founded in Colonia Oriental, by young people.

In all three instances, the colonias where new work was initiated were areas in which industrial workers, new migrants to the city, and many urban poor were located. The house-church, with laymen in charge of the services, was the universal pattern. Door-to-door visiting, a strong emphasis on the Bible and prayer, with plenty of singing at the services, were the common methods. When asked which was their particular method of evangelism, the reply was: "We use them all."

Daughter churches, like human offspring, are not born without pain. Zapata's letter tells of opposition, heartaches, and disappointments. But out of it new churches were born, agencies of God's redemptive operation in the city. What the Church of the Resurrection in Christ has done, other churches can do. "A sermon should not be preached in a church," said Martin Luther, "but in the city."[47] For churches already in the city, the importance of the task forbids further delay.

47. Cited by Martin E. Marty, *Second Chance for American Protestants* (New York: Harper & Row, Publishers, 1963), p. 164.

10

FOREIGN MISSIONARY AGENCIES

In the highly responsive areas of Latin America's great cities, foreign missionary agencies have an enormous responsibility to lead large segments of the population to personal faith in Jesus Christ. Missionary agencies can fail, however, if they persist in maintaining a number of wrong attitudes toward evangelism and social service. "What Christ demands is both service and mission in true proportion, remembering that this must be determined in the light of both the transient body and the eternal soul."[1] If one is substituted for the other, or emphasized at the expense of the other, the responsive urban world which God has prepared will not be evangelized as He expects.

The Shift to Urban-oriented Strategy

The first thing which must be done is a drastic shift from rural-oriented mission strategy to urban-based missions. Tomorrow's man is an urban man. This means that missionary strategy in Latin America (and everywhere else that this pattern holds true) must be urban oriented and geared to meet the needs of city people. Preoccupation with rural, small town, and preindustrial society does not fit the world of today, and even less the world of tomorrow.

Writing on the subject of strategic missionary planning, Stanley Mooneyham says:

We need to establish target areas to which we give priority,

---

1. McGavran, "Introduction," *Church Growth and Christian Mission,* p. 20.

so that we may use our limited financial and human resources to the maximum. By and large, we've evangelized on the shotgun principle, scattering the shot all over, when we ought to be using the rifle principle, singling out particular targets for Jesus Christ.

The big cities of the world ought to be at the top of the priority list. In Africa some 20 million young Africans are moving out of the bush and into the cities every year. The same thing is happening all over the world.

The churches are not equipped to enlist these young people for Christ. We do not have adequate ministries in these asphalt jungles to reach them.

Yet one mission board is currently considering whether it should invest more money and people and facilities in one small bush area which has a total population of 200,000 people when there are 100 cities in Africa with ten times that many people.[2]

Along this same line, Juan S. Boonstra, radio preacher on the *Hora de la Reforma* broadcast heard throughout Latin America, points out that while on the one hand urban populations are rapidly replacing rural in most parts of the hemisphere, mission work is still disproportionately rural. In the whole Amazon Basin, he observes, there are only 136,000 tribes people, mostly uncivilized and living in small tribes and speaking mutually unintelligible languages. Without question, they need to hear the gospel; and missionary effort must be put forth to reach them. But their evangelization must not be looked on as the main task of foreign missions, nor should the largest share of money and personnel be set aside for tribal work while in the meantime the far larger urban populations are neglected. In the Amazon Basin, Boonstra points out, 250 missionaries are working among these tribes people, which is more than the number working in the Brazilian states of Santa Catarina and Rio Grande do Sur, which have a combined population of over 9,000,000.[3]

Proper stewardship would indicate that the greatest effort should be placed where the most people are located, particularly when many of those people are receptive to the gospel. Why, therefore, are urban masses bypassed in favor of some far-off villagers? There is something exotic about the steaming jungles, the naked sav-

---

2. "Evangelical Changes in a World of Certainties," *World Vision Magazine,* April 1968, p. 5.
3. Juan S. Boonstra, "Statistics . . . More Statistics . . . And Some Questions," *Missionary Monthly,* January 1970, p. 14.

ages, and the distant mountains.[4] Savage Indians are much more photogenic for the home constituency than the cold, gray streets of the city. Prayer letters written from a grass hut, in which the missionary can talk about snakes, the burden of carrying water, and the problem of sleeping while natives beat their drums, bring much better response than letters typed in the city against the blare of car horns, the ringing of the telephone, and the hectic, unscheduled interruptions of urban life.

Is the soul of a savage worth more in God's sight than the soul of a university student, a slum-dweller, or a lonely teen-ager looking for a job in the unfriendly city?

> Take Bolivia for example. The university student population of 9000 is probably more than that of all the tribes combined. But where is our missionary effort directed? In comparison to only one evangelical couple dedicating full time to university student work, we have approximately 140 missionaries directly or indirectly involved in reaching the jungle Indians.
>
> When it is decided to fly missionary converts from Ecuador to the Berlin Congress, the choice is not a converted Communist in the University of Quito but the savage Auca Indians. A Latin American delegate to Berlin commented on this by exclaiming, "This Coney Islandish element makes me sick!"[5]

In 1971 one of these same Aucas was being paraded all across the United States as "Exhibit A" of mission work in Latin America. This is not meant to question the sincere motives of the organizations which sponsored these trips by the Aucas, nor discredit the possible impact these Indian believers can make on American churchmen. But the question must be raised: Is our overall missionary strategy properly balanced in view of the teeming unsaved millions in the great cities? Is the converted Auca the symbol of foreign missions' most urgent challenge and greatest success? I do not think so, and I believe that the foreign missionary enterprise as a whole is neglecting its God given responsibility by not placing greater emphasis on the cities in its missionary strategy.

In reading Latourette one observes that a great mistake in nineteenth century missionary strategy was that so much time and effort were spent on segments of the populations of India and China which were the least receptive to the gospel. They

---

4. C. Peter Wagner makes this point very forcibly in "Reshaping Missions," *World Vision Magazine,* May 1967, p. 14.
5. Ibid.

were the high castes, the intelligentsia, the respectable people. And they were, for the most part, inseparably attached to their traditional religions. Only later, and with reluctance, did Christian missionaries turn to the outcasts, the impoverished masses, and those who bore the brunt of the social system in which they were born. There the missionaries found open doors, and great numbers responded to the Christian message.[6]

The second mistake occurred when missionaries refused to accept the mass converts that came to their doorstep seeking baptism and membership in Christ's visible body. Both Anglican and Methodist missions, for example, turned away large numbers of low caste Hindus who wanted to become members of the Christian church during the great famine of 1876 in India. Feeling incapable of instructing such great numbers and doubting their sincerity, the missionaries let thousands turn away who might have been added to the church and instructed over a period of time. They were winnable at that moment, and never again did they show that same willingness to become Christians. Tragically, the Christian church and its missionary forces were unprepared for such an opportunity, and a great harvest was lost.[7]

A similar tragedy may occur in Latin America unless Christian missions turn their faces to the cities. The present period is one of rapid, unprecedented urbanization. Millions are moving from their *ranchos* and small villages to the big cities. Timely and urgent are the words of Read, Monterroso, and Johnson:

> The period during which the Evangelical Churches can grow in an immigrant situation is brief. Specific cases of urban church growth in Mexico City, Bogota, and Belo Horizonte indicate that it takes a rural migrant a decade or two to adjust to the new urban situation. During such a period of adjustment, he is responsive; we must act quickly if we are to act effectively.[8]

The Need for Urban Church Planting

The problem, says McGavran, is not to *reach* the cities, but to *multiply churches there*.[9] Missionaries in sizeable number have been living in the cities for decades, and they have been engaged

---

6. Kenneth Scott Latourette, *The Great Century in Northern Africa and in Asia,* Vol. 6 of *A History of the Expansion of Christianity* (New York: Harper & Brothers, Publishers, 1944), pp. 65-214, 253-369, *passim.* See p. 90 for a specific illustration of this predilection for the upper classes.
7. Ibid., p. 154.
8. *Latin American Church Growth,* p. 274.
9. "Urban Church Planting," *Church Growth Bulletin,* January 1970, p. 37.

in all kinds of church related activities. For the most part they have failed to establish sufficient numbers of churches in urban centers. "Only as that is done, only as thousands of churches are established in urban areas, will it become possible to influence individuals and societies in such a fashion that a just, merciful and peaceful society becomes somewhat more possible."[10]

Missionary executives can play a key role in guiding both missionaries and national leaders toward Biblical and adequate evangelistic strategies if they themselves have their priorities clearly defined. Right now, in the great cities of Latin America, the need and the opportunity is for church planting. National pastors and missionaries often are eager for help in defining their goals; and in the definition of these goals there ought to be the freest exchange of ideas between board secretaries, nationals, and missionaries.[11] When strategies are planned "up North," and relayed to the field as cut and dried decisions to be implemented by missionaries and nationals, the most foreign and inapplicable policies are put into effect. Schemes and ideas which may be feasible and right in one country are transferred abroad, with dire consequences on the expansion of the Christian church.

A classic example of this was the "Cincinnati Plan," drawn up in the city of Cincinnati in 1914 by executives from nine denominational boards. The plan divided Mexico among the various missions under a comity arrangement, which meant that churches and missions that had been begun by one mission suddenly were transferred to other administrations. Pastors and workers were uprooted and separated from their flocks, and congregations were cut off from the missionary organizations which had founded them. The evangelicals in Mexico termed it the "Assassination Plan" *(Plan de Asesinato)* because of the havoc it worked on the field. Five missions stayed out of the comity agreement, as did also the Mexican national churches and later missions from North America such as the Pentecostals and the Churches of God.[12]

---

10. Ibid.
11. Guy, "Directed Conservation," p. 198.
12. McGavran, Huegel, and Taylor, *Church Growth in Mexico,* p. 45, refer to the Cincinnati Plan as being "detrimental to the Protestant cause." The date 1917 which the authors give probably refers to one of the major stages in the plan's development. M. J. Penton, "Mexico's Reformation: A History of Mexican Protestantism from Its Inception to the Present" (unpublished Ph.D. dissertation, State University of Iowa, 1965), pp. 177-78, traces the plan from its inauguration in 1914 in Cincinnati, Ohio, to its ratification in Mexico City, in 1917. The plan is remembered with passionate disfavor to this day by many Mexican church leaders who feel that it represented the

The same kind of mistake can be repeated in the present period by the indiscriminate application of the European and North American industrial mission approach to the cities. In the writings of a man such as Henry D. Jones, for example, one finds a splendid sensitivity to both the strengths and the weaknesses of the industrial missions strategy in the Third World. "Surely, there is a place," he says, "for the social work approach in rapidly growing urban areas of Asia, Africa, and Latin America, but it does not seem to be the most creative approach when we face the over-all picture of these areas."[13] He cites Canon E. R. Wickham:

> The mission initiatives of the Church at home are rarely based upon ascertainable historical and sociological data. The Church thinks and plans within the context of the Church instead of setting her mission and her obedience within the given context of society and the world at large. And her "zeal without knowledge" is responsible for grossly inadequate expressions of mission. It is important to face the inescapable facts, to understand the process of history that has brought us to the present situation, that we may be delivered from superficial analysis and equipped for more soundly based missionary advance.... Mission planning in the Church must measure up to the realities of the situation.[14]

"The realities of the situation" must be the concern of missionary strategists. And these must be the realities of the Third World, not those which belong to Europe and North America where evangelical Christianity has been established for many generations and churches are numerous.

Some industrial mission leaders have called for church planting in the booming cities of the Third World.[15] Some industrial missionaries conduct churchlike services in industrial locations, where all the ingredients of a church are present without actually calling it so; and still others go a step further and reach out to working-class families, establishing churches in their homes and neighbor-

---

worst of foreign missionary paternalism and wrong strategy as far as missions is concerned. As for the deleterious effects of the plan, I have seen abandoned church buildings which once were the centers of worship for large village congregations, but which, due to comity reassignments, were completely disrupted.

13. Henry D. Jones, "Urban and Industrial Missions," *Occasional Bulletin* from the Missionary Research Library, 15 June 1959, p. 2.
14. Ibid., citing E. R. Wickham, *Church and People in an Industrial City* (London: Lutterworth Press, 1957), pp. 214-15.
15. Jones puts the establishment of new churches as a number one priority in his discussion of "New Planning," in "Urban and Industrial Missions," p. 4.

hoods.[16] Industrial missions have been particularly strong in the area of training lay workers for Christian witness, and the insistence of the movement on close contact between the church and industrial workers is a valid and much needed emphasis.[17]

However, the industrial mission approach as a whole has not evoked a great deal of confidence on the part of those who insist that what the cities of the Third World need most today is a strategy which aims at converting men to Jesus Christ, planting churches, and through the established church reaching out positively and dynamically to change society. This has led Donald McGavran, when confronted with the question whether industrial evangelism actually produces converts to the Christian faith, to reply:

> The answer is simple—because the industrial evangelism, so talked about today, does not convert. It does not propagate the faith. It does not add to existing churches or found new ones. It does not lead multitudes to put their faith in Jesus Christ and form living Christian communities, which enlist others. Industrial evangelism to date is an *exploratory Christian activity* which does not yet persuade many non-Christians to be baptized and live as committed Christians.[18]

The right strategy for Mexico City, Caracas, Bogotá, Sao Paulo, and Buenos Aires should fit the "realities of the situation" in which millions of urbanites know little or nothing about Biblical Christianity, are groping for a religious experience which is meaningful and true, and who today in the circumstances of urbanization are open to evangelism as never before. To apply to these areas an urban strategy which may or may not be effective in Europe and North America, but which at least appears relevant to conditions existing there, may be the height of folly for foreign missions. Latin American leaders sense that it is, and industrial missionaries do not find it easy to convince them that their approach is the

16. For example of this, see the article "How I Became an Industrial Pastor," by Aimei Kanai, *Church Labor Letter* (Kyoto, Japan), December 1965, pp. 2-11.
17. Ibid. Kanai's concluding sections, entitled "The Church and Workers" and "New Industrial Area and Labor Center," are excellent. They describe the outreach of house-churches in the Kansai area and call for a fresh study of the church's ministry in an industrialized society. The need for well-trained laymen who can witness relevantly in labor and industrial relations is underscored.
18. McGavran's statement was in answer to the question posed by Ronald Orchard, of the Division of Missionary Studies, World Council of Churches, Geneva, Switzerland, as reported in "Does 'Concern for Social Justice' Convert?", *Church Growth Bulletin*, January 1965, pp. 38-39.

right one. Latin American evangelicals are deeply concerned over the need for conversion-centered evangelism, and they do not readily accept the indirect approach of the industrial missionary.[19]

Who knows best what Latin Americans need? Who is ministering most effectively to industrial workers today? A strong case can be made for the Pentecostal churches in Latin America in their approach to industrial evangelism. They, not the traditional denominations, are the "churches of the laboring masses."[20] True, Pentecostals do not call what they are doing "industrial missions"; but that is what it is, and very effectively so. Working men feel at home in their churches. Pentecostal leaders are "horny-handed men accustomed to wield hammer and pickax."[21] And in true apostolic fashion, Pentecostal churches are multiplying among the common people, winning the industrial workers and laboring classes to faith in Jesus Christ. *This* is industrial evangelism at its best. Converting men and establishing churches, it offers every promise of producing an impact on society which will change the course of Latin American civilization and make life for the masses not only more "human" but most importantly, Christian.

Church Structures Which Promote Missions

It is very difficult for missionaries to understand that the patterns in which they themselves were trained at home are not necessarily the best in the countries in which they serve. National leaders, however, are recognizing that the uncritical and persistent importation of forms and structures of churches in other countries is greatly hindering the church and the gospel from becoming rooted in the soil of their own lands, with the result that growth is stalemated.[22] The "prison of previous patterns,"[23] composed of organization and methods, is one of the greatest hindrances to the expansion of the gospel in Latin American cities today. It is found in missionary policies, in missionary schools, and in the churches founded by foreign missionary organizations. If patterns of mission work, church organization, or anything else Christians seek to do to extend Christ's kingdom prove ineffective and actually hinder men from becoming members of Christ's church, those patterns should be

---

19. Interview with John Hazelton, urban-industrial missionary of the United Presbyterian Church, 3 June 1971.
20. McGavran, "Does 'Concern for Social Justice' Convert?", p. 38.
21. Ibid.
22. Takashi Yamada, "Studies in Extension Evangelism," trans. P. W. Boschman, Church Growth Pamphlet Series No. 3 (Kobayashi City, Miyazaki, Japan: Kobayashi Kyodaisha, 1870), p. 3. (English translation mimeographed).
23. The expression is found in McGavran, *How Churches Grow*, p. 108.

abandoned. The norm is the New Testament with its glorious liberty to adapt to the actualities of each situation, rather than to the prisonhouse of foreign tradition.

The city missionary who dares to enter the virgin territory of the great urban centers of Latin America will need courage, not only to face the flies, the mud, and the squalor, but also perhaps his fellow missionaries who do not share his vision or concern. But such men must be found.

> There must always be a man who breaks imprisoning patterns. Like Paul he usually has intense concern that men accept Christ as Saviour. This, not the accustomed way of doing things, the Church customs, the mission pattern, is of primary importance in his eyes.
>
> Like Paul on his first missionary journey, he makes a venture of faith: church growth is never a certainty. To break with imprisoning patterns before knowing that the opportunity will certainly yield new churches takes courage, imagination and faith. It involves loneliness and misunderstanding and many an hour of inner uncertainty when the man questions whether he is right. Yet it is the chief way in which new varieties of vigorous church growth begin.[24]

The foreign missionary's fascination with beautiful church buildings may be a very real obstacle in the way of urban church growth. The early church grew to power in the great cities of the Roman Empire—Jerusalem, Antioch, Alexandria, Ephesus, Corinth, Rome, Carthage—without such buildings. The custom, followed in Europe and North America, of building beautiful and expensive church edifices has proved difficult to reproduce in the towns and cities of the Third World.[25] Preoccupation with elaborate building facilities is a trap that should be avoided. People, not buildings, are important. Every church building that is erected should be the hub for a wide circle of house-churches which it serves as a center of instruction and inspiration. Periodically, large meetings should be held where the catholicity of the body of Christ is symbolized and demonstrated. But the neighborhood church, rather than the large centralized church, is the key to urban church growth in Latin America. It conforms more closely to the New Testament church and to the structure of the church when it conquered the Roman Empire. And it offers the greatest potential for rapid growth in Latin American cities.[26]

---

24. Ibid., p. 112.
25. McGavran, "Urban Church Planting," p. 37.
26. In Mexico, certain problems exist with respect to the neighborhood

Small groups and house-churches offer such amazing possibilities for the spread of the gospel in the cities. What a pity it will be if foreign missions place their weightiest efforts in methods and programs which do not proliferate churches. Standing, it appears, somewhat enviously on the outside looking in, Cecil Thompson writes about industrial evangelism:

> The groups that gain and hold the attendance and interest of the masses have certain characteristics which lay hold upon certain elemental desires or inclinations of human nature. They emphasize the Bible—whether with correct interpretation or not—which appeals to the working class of people. They have intense convictions, even though the convictions may be centered upon a narrow or distorted truth; they believe in their cause. They have an emotional content in their faith and preaching which lends warmth to their evangelism. Oftentimes there may be more heat than light, but at least they have the heat, which is often lacking in the more staid denominations. There is an esprit de corps and a spirit of fraternal purpose. The smaller sects often emphasize the necessity for separation from certain actions considered sinful, such as use of tobacco, cosmetics, movies, and other worldly things. Their religion costs something. Then again they often demand a definite system of tithing and stewardship—which secures the resources for buildings and radio programs.
>
> These groups, along with the Southern Baptists, oftentimes have uneducated pastors and preachers, but what is lost on the educational level is made up in the field of enthusiasm and evangelistic zeal. What is lacking in doctrinal and theological discernment is evidently made up by their common touch with the everyday lives of the people. Two things can happen, and perhaps both are slowly taking place. The small sects with their enthusiasm and missionary zeal are gradually taking on culture, polish, and acquiring a more educated leadership. They are building attractive churches and homes for their pastors. Will they lose their zeal as they

---

church meeting in private homes or rented buildings. Article 27 of the national Constitution requires that all property used for public worship be turned over to the government. This poses a problem for church planters who under normal circumstances would be able to use rented halls, theaters, or other building facilities. Because of the law, most new congregations in Mexico move directly from the church-in-the-house to a fixed building, which then is nationalized and becomes a permanent center of worship. In other Latin American countries, where such laws do not exist, it is advisable to consider carefully whether the permanent building is worth what it costs and whether some other alternative should be investigated.

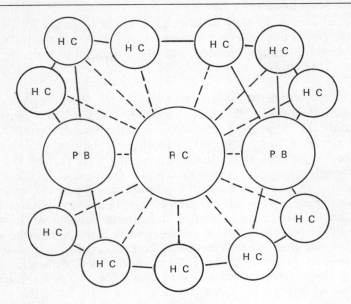

FIGURE 5

METROPOLITAN CHURCHES

H C HOUSE-CHURCHES, proliferating in every neighborhood of the city, serving as the primary locus of fellowship, witness, and Christian instruction.

P B PERMANENT-BUILDING CHURCHES, located in key areas of the city, emphasizing the training of laymen for their ministry elsewhere. Midweek classes and services every night conducted by gifted teachers of the Bible.

R C RALLY-CENTERS, for periodic conventions and campaigns, and the united witness to the catholicity of the evangelical faith. Public facilities generally can be obtained for such meetings.

gain these things? On the other hand, our more dignified and staid churches are beginning to realize they can give a better rounded and more positive message and method to the whole religious life of these communities. Each type of church must absorb some elements from the other.[27]

27. Cecil Thompson, "Industrial Evangelism," *Religion in Life* 21 (Summer

Social Responsibility in the City

Social action, properly understood, is not a substitute for preaching the gospel but rather a consequence of it.[28] Where the fullness of the gospel is being heralded and the life of the Spirit is continually replenished by rich, sound Biblical preaching, society is affected.

William Wonderly suggests that one of the three key areas for evangelical concern in Latin American cities is the matter of "relating the gospel to practical needs and physical health."[29] One does not have to be a liberal in theology to have a vital concern for men's physical and material needs, and it is part of the task of foreign missionary organizations to show *how* a conversion theology can be combined with a relevant meeting of the urbanite's physical needs. Tensions of priority are bound to develop here, but that is part of the challenge of authentic mission work. Without the verbal proclamation of the gospel there is no true compassion, for men need to be saved from their guilt and their sin. But neither is there authentic, Biblical mission work without a visible caring about men's needs here and now. The two are organically united. As Samuel M. Zwemer put it:

> All the older missionary heroes, Judson, Carey, Livingstone, Martyn, Hudson Taylor, lived for eternity and preached eternity, a Gospel that was other-worldly. They went out to save the lost. Yet . . . they had their schools, hospitals, and asylums; they were not unmindful of social evils and worked for social reform. But they considered all these as means to an end; these were only the scaffolding of the eternal palace. *That* consists of living stone, lives redeemed, character built up, souls won for glory.[30]

Evangelicals have often been charged with indifference to the social needs of the masses, and the church growth school of thought has been singled out in the public news media in Latin America as the prime perpetrator of this attitude. "Social revolution is the overwhelming fact in Latin America," wrote James E. Goff, in *The News,* Mexico City. "Church growth strategy seeks

1952): 363. Thompson is Professor of Evangelism and Church Extension at Columbia Theological Seminary, Decatur, Ga.
28. Stuart Barton Babbage, "Is There a Crisis in Preaching?", *Church Herald,* 17 May 1968, p. 5.
29. William L. Wonderly, "Urbanization: The Challenge of Latin America in Transition," *Practical Anthropology* 7 (September-October 1960): 208.
30. Cited in editorial, "The Urgency of Evangelism," *Christianity Today,* 15 January 1965, p. 26.

groups of people who are in need, not with the purpose of helping them in their struggle against dehumanizing forces but in order to make Church members of them."[31]

Nothing is further from the truth. If social action, on an individual basis or on the collective level, does not follow evangelism something is wrong. "A born-again believer," says Peter Wagner, "who does not feel a burden for the social well-being of his neighbor comes under the judgment of Scripture."[32] Admittedly, social action is an explosive subject in Latin America. But the Biblically aroused conscience cannot tolerate the continuation of injustice without compromising the faith it professes. United opposition, even violent opposition if necessary, is as legitimate for Americans south of the Rio Grande as it was for those Americans who gave the British the Boston Tea Party and stood their ground at Bunker Hill. With deep concern for the social injustices of Latin America, Wagner writes:

> In the developing nations social injustice is rampant and is the principal curse on society. . . . Becoming fully involved in eradicating social injustice is admittedly a risky business, much more so than handing out relief food and clothing. The Christian who runs the risk may find himself involved in politics, in revolution, even in violence. But once committed there is no turning back. Furthermore, his Church should not condemn him for it. God is not pleased when people are exploited like horses or cattle, and Christians must take practical action to testify to this truth. It may not be evangelism, but it is part of the well rounded Christian life.[33]

Missionary relief agencies can play an important role in Latin American cities, but not primarily by doling out charity. Training programs, especially for young people, are urgently needed in urban centers. The Chinese have a saying that to give a hungry man a fish is good, but to teach him how to catch fish is better. This principle should be applied to relief work in the cities. A job-training center for young men and women recently arrived from rural areas would be a very helpful program; a hostel for girls with a strongly Christian atmosphere, and an employment bureau to help them find work after their training is completed

---

31. James E. Goff, reviewing *Latin American Church Growth,* by William R. Read, Victor M. Monterroso, and Harmon A. Johnson, in *The News,* Mexico City, Sunday supplement, "Vistas," 1 March 1970, p. 8.

32. Peter Wagner, "Reshaping Missions," *World Vision Magazine,* May 1967, p. 14.

33. Ibid.

could mean a new life for countless numbers of young people.[34]

Alongside specific programs of urban relief, however, there is something else that must be worked at: helping Latin American evangelicals to think about their countries' social and political needs in Christian perspective. Evangelicals, for the most part, have no distinctively Christian point of view on the problems which vex their countries. They need to be taught how to view social justice and the needs of the masses, not in terms of the inflammatory slogans which the Marxists hurl so vociferously, but from the perspective of the Word of God. Sometimes the conclusions of the two parties—Marxist and Christian—may be the same on specific issues, but their frame of reference is entirely different, and the societies which they seek to build involve radically conflicting orientations.

Conscientizacion—the arousing of the Christian conscience to the fact of oppression and to the needs of the oppressed—is what evangelicals need. It represents a difficult problem, admittedly; for definitions of the gospel are involved, as well as the order of priorities for Christian mission. It is so easy to hurl accusations at one another—"Communist," "Marxist," "imperialist," and the like—without listening closely to what a man means and considering the issues with which he is wrestling.

But assistance in the development of a genuinely Christian conscience, and the struggle toward a viable approach to social renewal which evangelicals in Latin America can endorse are things the foreign missionary cannot avoid. The man who calls himself a Christian and at the same time can look at the poor, downtrodden, exploited masses of Latin America and feel nothing, say nothing, and *do* nothing to change the system which exploits them is a dastard and a hypocrite. The evangelical churches of Latin America need—and perhaps may soon have—their own special version of Camilo Torres Restrepo.[35] But when he appears will the evangelicals be prepared to follow him?

---

34. Says William L. Wonderly, "Urbanization: The Challenge of Latin America in Transition," p. 208: "Church-sponsored studies, of an intensive type comparable to that which Lewis has carried on, are called for if we are adequately to know what people's needs are and what aspects of the gospel are most relevant to those needs." This is an important observation and should open up new avenues of research for specialists in the area of mission related relief operations.

35. For Camilo Torres' recommendations for the cities, see *Revolutionary Priest: The Complete Writings and Messages of Camilo Torres,* chap. 10, "Urbanization and Urban Reform," particularly p. 186, where his recommendations are summarized. I would have no trouble endorsing the four propositions Torres puts forward.

11

MASS MEDIA

For Peru's twelve million inhabitants, there are more than six hundred radio stations. Costa Rican farmers, plowing behind oxen as their forefathers have done for generations, now exhibit a new feature: transistor radios swing from the horns of the bony animals. In Guatemala, six times as many people listen to radios as read newspapers; and in Mexico City, the "swingers" among boyfriends are those with transistor radios hanging from the handlebars of their bicycles.[1] All of this means that the potential of radio for Christian evangelism is enormous.

Evangelism by means of radio is one of the key methods of communication in Latin America. Besides local broadcasts, two of the world's largest Christian broadcasting centers are located in this region. Radio station HCJB of Ecuador, a long-time leader in the radio field, will soon begin a new television phase of its operations with a syndicated television program for evangelism. Television programs produced by the HCJB staff and other Christian groups will be duplicated on videotape and 16mm film for distribution to television stations throughout Latin America. On the Dutch island of Bonaire off the coast of Venezuela, the powerful new transmitters of Trans World Radio direct Christian programs to target areas all over the world. The Bonaire station combines a 260,000-watt and a 50,000-watt shortwave transmitter,

---

1. McGavran, "Radio and Church Growth," *Church Growth Bulletin,* November 1969, p. 17.

plus a 500,000-watt medium wave transmitter, to make it one of the world's most modern and efficient broadcasting centers. And all of it is dedicated to Christian evangelism.

Literacy is uniformly higher in the cities,[2] and this creates a large field for evangelical literature in the urban areas. This is especially true of the inhabitants of the really big cities over against the remainder of the urban population found in smaller towns and villages. The difference in literacy levels between rural and urban areas is greatest in countries whose average level of literacy is very low, such as in Guatemala, Peru, Haiti, and Honduras, and is least noteworthy in countries of higher literacy, such as Argentina, Chile, Cuba, and Costa Rica.[3] The potential for evangelism of the printed media, naturally, varies according to the level of literacy in each area.

Bible distribution plays a key role in the spread of evangelicalism in Latin America, and this is as true in the cities as in the rural areas.[4] The United Bible Societies have been distributing Scriptures in Latin America since 1821, when James Thomson, a Scot, entered South America as an agent of the British and Foreign Bible Society; and in the first flush of revolution after the expulsion of the Spanish, enjoyed amazing, though brief, success.[5]

The World Home Bible League is presently launched on an aggressive program in Latin America, offering Bibles and smaller portions of Scripture free or at highly subsidized prices as a direct evangelistic instrument. According to the League's director for Latin America, Chester M. Schemper, the World Home Bible League committed itself to supply seven million Scripture portions (including 200,000 complete Bibles and 350,000 New Testaments) for the Evangelism-in-Depth program in Mexico during 1971-72, and has chosen the major cities as specific target areas for distribution in a number of countries. In the Luis Palau evangelistic campaign in Guatemala City, for example, the World Home Bible League contributed 6,000 New Testaments for free distribution to inquirers.[6]

---

2. Hauser, *Urbanization in Latin America,* pp. 112-13.
3. Ibid., p. 112.
4. See Table 8, where the reading of the Bible is listed as the most frequently mentioned factor in the conversion of the persons interviewed.
5. Latourette, *The Great Century,* p. 109. The name United Bible Societies is a later designation and here refers to the British and American societies, with their affiliates throughout Latin America.
6. Information regarding the World Home Bible League's activities was derived from a personal interview with Chester M. Schemper, 17 May 1971, Fort Worth, Tex. The World Home Bible League is now working in coopera-

In addition to Scripture, many types of tracts and other printed materials are available. Evangelical bookstores are generally located in the key urban centers.[7] Bookmobiles and individual colporteurs can reach the isolated areas, but the cities call for well-supplied and attractive distribution points, where appeal is made to the wide range of tastes and characteristics of the urban populations—from students and intellectuals to the most humble inquirers about the evangelical faith.

Probably the most advanced and comprehensive use of the mass media by a missionary organization in a single Latin American country is located in the three-story building called *Centro Cultural, La Antorcha de México, A.C.,* in Mexico City.[8] Situated in the heart of the downtown area, just a few steps from one of the city's new metro stations, this mass communications center combines a daily Cine Club, where evangelical films are projected every afternoon and evening without charge to the public, a programming center for evangelical broadcasts heard on thirty-three stations throughout Mexico, an attractive Christian bookstore where everything from books to film-strip projectors and cassette tape recordings are available to pastors and missionaries, and a coffee bar for over-the-table conversations with inquirers. The World Home Bible League, Evangelism-in-Depth, and other evangelical agencies occupy space in the building; and one room is set up for journalism classes, special seminars, and strategy sessions.[9]

Fifteen thousand persons viewed evangelical films at the Cine Club between December 1970 and 30 May 1971.[10] After three and one-half hours of daily film projection, during which time most of the 160 seats are occupied, a 15- to 20-minute message is delivered in person by an evangelist on the staff, and an invitation

tion with the New York Bible Society in a program called Scriptures Unlimited, which reaches to all parts of Latin America and has committed itself to the publication of the dialect translations prepared by the Wycliffe Bible Translators organization.

7. The mission of the Christian Reformed Church in Mexico, for example, has established evangelical bookstores in the downtown areas of six key cities in Mexico—Mexico City (two stores), Acapulco, Mérida, Veracruz, Tijuana, and Tampico—and plans to continue until it has bookstores in all the major cities of Mexico.

8. The civil association *La Antorcha de México* is incorporated under Mexican law and is directed by an executive board.

9. Jack H. Roeda, *Mass Communication Center* (Grand Rapids: Christian Reformed Board of Foreign Missions, 1970), pp. 1-4.

10. Jack H. Roeda, personal interview, 3 June 1971, Mexico City. Information contained in this paragraph concerning the Cine Club and its ministry was provided by Roeda in this interview.

is extended for persons to believe the gospel. Follow-up is mainly through the Bible correspondence course which the center provides, and an average of seventy-five persons per week accept the course. Mexico City television stations have used evangelical films on loan from the Cine Club on a number of occasions and government schools have requested special programs featuring Moody Science films. The audiences at the Cine are a mixture of all the social classes, though students and young people predominate. The operation of the theater, the first of its kind in Latin America, is still a "research and development" project for evangelical missions.[11] It is a serious effort to coordinate in one program all the types of mass media used in the communication of the gospel. If successful, it could set the pattern for other metropolitan areas around the world.[12]

The Question of Effective Communications

Eugene Nida has strongly criticized much of the content which evangelicals use in mass media presentations, particularly radio. The sermons which are broadcast, he says, are often worse than nothing; and they may do more harm than good to the cause of the gospel. The music does not represent Latin American tastes in the least. Furthermore, the programming in general "does not speak to Latin life with Biblical realism."[13] Nida's basic and thought-provoking charge is that missionaries and evangelical broadcasters in general (and this would apply to those using the printed page as well as radio) are very un-Latin in their method of communication.

> Any attempt to produce programs which are fully meaningful to the Latin audience will also mean that programs sent out from the United States (which for the most part are "spiritually imperialistic" and often irrelevant in content) must be avoided. If they are merely useless, they would not be so bad, but the wrong approach can so inoculate a man against the real message that he is lost to the cause.[14]

Nida calls for a serious investigation as to which types of programs effectively communicate to Latin Americans, plus a thorough search for Latin Americans who can write, speak, and communicate the Christian message effectively to their fellow Latins. Time and money should be spent on this without delay by missionary

---

11. Roeda, personal letter, 24 January 1971.
12. Ibid.
13. Nida, "Communication of the Gospel to Latin America," p. 155.
14. Ibid.

organizations using the mass media. Only by training and using Latin personnel will culturally relevant and effective techniques of communication be discovered and put into operation.[15]

The UNESCO studies shed some valuable light on one of the areas in which Nida calls for more investigation; namely, the serial dramas heard on Latin American stations reflecting the cultural themes of vital interest to the masses. Not only the themes, but also the solutions which the dramas suggest are an indication of the ideas and values considered important in modern Latin American society. They do not decide the content of the message which evangelicals want to bring, but they are an important "diagnostic" technique to find out what Latin Americans are thinking.[16] In its study of recent rural-urban migrants in Brazil, the UNESCO report has this to say about radio (which ties in very closely to the earlier observations made in this study concerning the kinship ties in the city):

> The importance of radio is related to the exceptional predominance of the family and kin-group as the sanction group for the actions and opinions of its members, and therefore as the main arbiter of values, in comparison with other potential arbiters, such as associations, clubs, religious congregations and organizations, class or colour conscious groupings, etc. A radio programme is a common experience for some or all members of the family and its contents are therefore immediately subject to the evaluation of the family as a unit. The most widely listened-to programmes were (a) popular serials and (2) variety programmes with music, singers and humorists. Of the serials by far the most popular depicted a popular Robin Hood of the *sertuao* called Jeronimo, himself belonging to a family of landed property, but devoted to the interests of the poor and underprivileged share-cropper, squatter and petty proprietor, who is depicted as living in the interior at the mercy of the great landlords, beyond the effective protection of the law, or else subject to the injustices perpetrated by municipal law officers who are depicted as furthering the predatory interests of the harsh proprietor. The oppressed rural people are shown as quite unable to arrange effective resistance or to take any sort of initiative on their own, but in each episode they

15. Ibid., p. 156. A new agency, called Alfa Omega Publicidad, A.C., with its main office at Insurgentes Sur 1883-402, México 20, D.F., México, offers help to anyone needing technical or cultural assistance in the field of secular and religious communications.
16. Ibid.

are saved by the almost miraculous intervention of the justice-loving Jeronimo.[17]

This report goes on to say that the other programs which are the most popular are characterized by (a) the use of music of the popular regional traditions, and of the sambas and other types of songs which the urban populace has developed, and (b) the avid devotion to "star" singers, the best known of whom have risen to fame from humble origins.[18]

The studies, in general, showed that urban lower classes, and specifically the rural-urban immigrants, are deeply concerned over problems of social and economic security and hope desperately for some kind of hero-saint who will lead them out of their misery and upward to the Promised Land.[19] The basic rudiments of life are what concern them, not the sophisticated definitions with which the more privileged classes occupy their minds. The urban masses are looking for some ray of hope, some way of salvation from the wearying, burdensome existence that has enslaved them so long. From the soap operas they listen to, and the "star" singers they enjoy, the sensitive and attentive communicator of the gospel should be able to catch the rhythm of urban life and the pulse beat of Latin America's city populations, and from there move on to meeting their hopes and expectations with Biblical solutions. The sensitive structuring of evangelical communication to the nuances of Latin American life and thought is absolutely indispensable if the enormous potential of the mass media is to be realized.

The Question of Goals and Accomplishment

Many tools, says Calvin Guy, may be used to spread the Christian news; and today the media of mass communications are coming into prominence in strategy considerations. They all offer startling prospects *if church planting is their goal.*[20] Radio broadcasts, TV programs, newspaper evangelism, correspondence courses are all good if the churches are willing and ready to gather in those who are reached. It will all be like seed scattered to the wind unless the Christian community goes out to find each person who responds and ties together mass media evangelism with church-planting missionary strategy. The goal of the overall strategy is to place a church for fellowship, worship, and witness within reach of all those that are contacted.

---

17. Hauser, *Urbanization in Latin America,* p. 204.
18. Ibid.
19. Ibid., pp. 204-5.
20. "Directed Conservation," p. 212; emphasis mine.

To use these media without planting churches is to waste effort as did the men who planned the Tucker automobile; it was widely advertised immediately following World War II, and great interest was generated, but the car was never made available.[21]

It is so easy in mission work to be carried away by one's own promotional language and forget that all special ministries such as radio, literature, and correspondence courses must be integrated into the total evangelistic strategy. Each ministry in which missionary personnel are engaged and each item in the missionary budget must contribute discernibly to the fulfillment of the goals which have been agreed on. If a particular program does not make a measurable contribution toward the realization of those goals, it should be phased out, no matter how popular the program (or its supporters) may be.

In view of this, at least five observations should be made to evaluate the use of mass media in the cities:

First, mass communications must not become an escape from personal witnessing on the part of missionaries and national Christians. Says Don K. Smith, director of communications research for Daystar Communications:

> If Christian mass communications are to be effective, they must proceed from a basic one-to-one encounter with Jesus Christ, through one of his witnesses. Mass communications cannot be useful tools in Christian witness when they are consciously or unconsciously a substitute for a personal witness to individuals.
>
> Mass communications are useful tools of evangelism only when involvement is part of the process.[22]

The kind of urban strategy for Latin America that has been outlined in the preceding pages will not be accomplished by missionaries and national Christians who believe that they can sit back and let the mass media do the work for them. "Ground troops" are still needed—believers who are willing to walk the streets, knock on doors, and talk to people personally. Without that kind of person, missionary or national, mass communications media will not accomplish their goal.

Second, it must be recognized that mass communications generally do not convert unbelievers into disciples of the Lord Jesus

---

21. Ibid.
22. Don K. Smith, "No Magic in the Media," *World Vision Magazine,* May 1970, p. 9.

Christ, but rather strengthen the faith of those who are already believers. Mass communications, in other words, *reinforce* the attitudes and beliefs which the reader or listener already possesses; but only in rare instances do they result in a radical change in his attitudes.[23]

Illustrations of conversions through mass media can be produced, of course; and I myself can testify to having found a small mountain village in Mexico in which nearly every family was a believer and a lovely white church had been built as a result of an airdrop of Scripture portions from a missionary airplane.[24] But that is not the prevailing pattern. The mass media provide contacts, stimulate interest, and prepare the ground for evangelistic advance. But to assume that Christian truth is simply a set of facts which can be shipped across the world via the mass media with the expectation that large numbers will be converted, churches established, and the world changed after the pattern of the gospel, without the personal presence of human witnesses, is a serious mistake. The best media presentation cannot make this happen. Some Christian still must do the traditional man-to-man evangelism and plant churches in order for mass media to realize their full effectiveness. "Where there are no churches which listeners can find," says McGavran, "there gospel radio has to date little outcome in church growth."[25]

In areas of the world which are inaccessible to personal missionary outreach, radio and literature provide unique and invaluable instruments of communication, and by God's power they may be doing things beyond human measurement and expectation. But at the same time, a one-sided emphasis on the media can work great harm to the worldwide growth of the church if it becomes a substitute for man-to-man witnessing where this approach is possible.

Third, the ministry of the mass media is largely instructive; and here is found its unique and most valuable contribution. As the Argentine radio preacher Juan S. Boonstra has pointed out, the historic denominations are rendering invaluable service throughout Latin America by educating to deeper Christian maturity the Pentecostals who are multiplying so rapidly.[26]

---

23. Ibid., pp. 8-9.
24. The village is Ocotal, state of Mexico, about four hours by car west of Mexico City.
25. Donald A. McGavran, "Does Gospel Radio Grow Churches?", *Church Growth Bulletin,* September 1965, p. 11.
26. Juan S. Boonstra, "Impressions After Nine Years," *The Banner,* 23 October 1970, p. 15.

The obvious fact is that the Pentecostals are winning the urban masses, and the denominational missions are educating them in the deeper things of God's Word. "The highest percentage of customers in our seven bookstores," says Jack Roeda, "are Pentecostals."[27] Pentecostals in general lack theological acumen.

> But they reach deep into the masses, speak their language, and appeal to their hearts. The Bible becomes an incomparable book and its reading is required. Immorality is curbed and condemned. And they build "Protestant Cathedrals."
>
> But perhaps most moving of all is this: the moment they are converted, all Pentecostals become more than avid listeners to missionary radio stations. It is the means God has placed in our hands to reach them, teach them, and translate their energy into God-glorifying lives.[28]

This points to one of the greatest areas of service for foreign missionary organizations and national churches today. While God has given to the Pentecostals the special gift of soul winning, the older denominations can provide the literature, the instruction, and in many cases the educational facilities which the Pentecostals need for growth and maturity.

Fourth, strenuous effort must be put forth to make Christian communications culturally intelligible.[29] Probably the weakest area is that of evangelical literature. Those tracts which are so ardently distributed on the street may be doing more harm than good if they are culturally irrelevant on one hand, and produce unnecessary antagonism on the other. The naive bombardment of people with words may have the opposite effect from what is intended. Especially in the city where printed material is readily available, not everything that is read is believed. The Christian message poorly presented may make people more resistant than ever before to its basic thrust. In such cases, mass media can work at counter purposes in relation to primary goals of Christian missions.

This means, first of all, that the preparation of evangelical literature and the programming of radio and television broadcasts must be done *in* Latin America and *by* Latin Americans. Furthermore, wherever possible communication must be designed to fit

---

27. Roeda, interview, 5 June 1971.
28. Juan S. Boonstra, "Protestant Cathedrals," *Missionary Monthly,* October 1970, p. 270.
29. This point is stressed by both Nida, "Communication of the Gospel in Latin America," pp. 154-56, and by Smith, "No Magic in the Media," pp. 8-10.

particular local needs and not try to cover whole nations, or even an entire continent, with one identical format. If mass communications are going to be used most effectively to win men to Christ, they must be locally oriented, designed to speak effectively to definable groups in specific areas. The winning of a nation or a city to Christ, as Smith has pointed out, "is less dependent upon increased investment in the modern urbanized trappings of mass media than it is upon establishing locally-based media systems that are adjusted to their specific audience and to the existing national media."[30]

In other words, the programs that a church or mission broadcasts, the literature which it distributes, and whatever else it may do with the mass media which it has available must be consciously designed to communicate God's message to the groups within society which they are trying to reach. The target area must be clearly defined, the trajectory carefully planned, and the launching made as smoothly as possible or the mission of the mass media will fail.

Finally, more must be done to integrate the missionary use of mass communication into the overall strategy of urban evangelism. Everyone engaged in church planting and in mass communication should consciously and persistently strive to integrate all branches of ministry. Rather than ignoring one another, church-planting missionaries and mass media specialists should work together as a team.[31] The files of correspondence schools and of radio broadcasters should be used to make contacts with a view to establishing churches. Follow-up materials should be produced which instruct new converts in simple methods of church organization. In my opinion, the effectiveness of the mass media should be measured not simply by how many millions of potential listeners a program has, or how many tons of literature an agency distributes, but by the number of growing churches which have resulted. This is not an unreasonable demand if teamlike integration between church-planting missionaries and mass media specialists is put into effect.

An example of how this can be done comes from Tokyo, Japan, where one Christian radio program offers a New Testament, a Christian magazine, and a letter of introduction to the nearest church. A survey showed that 50 percent of those who receive the

30. Ibid., p. 10.
31. The plea for teamwork comes from McGavran, "Radio and Church Growth," p. 18.

letter actually attend church at least once, and 20 percent continue to attend.[32] That kind of coordination, applied to the responsive elements in Latin American cities, can bring some amazing results.

32. Mathew S. Ogawa and Vern Rossman, "Evangelism Through the Mass Media and Audio Visual Materials," *International Review of Missions* 50 (October 1961): 421. The same article states that "the Seventh-day Adventists report that eighty per cent of their baptisms come through their Bible correspondence course, some forty per cent of the contacts being through radio."

12

SEMINARIES AND BIBLE SCHOOLS

"The cities can best be reached," say Fife and Glasser, "not by a flood of foreign missionaries (a dim prospect anyhow) but by a missionary-minded, trained, and oriented native church, encouraged in its early stages by a missionary or national who is wholly bent on transmitting his vision of an expanding native church."[1] Seminaries and Bible schools aim to train leaders for such churches, and it is with the particular type of training necessary to reach the cities adequately and effectively that this chapter is concerned.

Indigenous churches in Latin America differ widely from the traditional denominations in the way they train their leaders. The leadership of the various indigenous movements tends to be composed largely of "laymen"—men who have worked their way up in the churches through an informal apprenticeship system.[2] They begin as youth leaders, ardent tract distributors, street preachers, Sunday school teachers, deacons and elders, assistant pastors in small, newly formed congregations; and finally, when they are forty or fifty years of age they may become full pastors of a church. Even while pastoring a large-size church, however, they may continue their secular employment in order to earn a living, while giving their spare time to the work of the ministry in the church.[3]

---

1. *Missions in Crisis,* p. 189.
2. Eugene A. Nida, "The Indigenous Churches in Latin America," *Practical Anthropology* 8 (May-June 1961): 99.
3. Ibid.

Two great advantages are enjoyed by this indigenous system of leadership training: by the time these men become pastors they are seasoned, mature men who have earned the confidence of the people they serve and have demonstrated the gifts of the Spirit which the ministry requires. And the financial burden of a formal school education for prospective leaders is avoided. Indigenous leaders must support themselves until they have gathered enough members to support them, which none but the gifted and dedicated worker can do.

Pentecostals, however, increasingly recognize the need for more highly trained leaders than their system generally produces.[4] A few decades ago, for example, the majority of Pentecostal pastors in Chile made it a rule to "let the Spirit speak" and considered it "carnal" to prepare sermons in advance. Today, however, advanced preparation, study, and the use of books is fairly common.[5] The lack of instruction on the part of many Latin American leaders accounts to some extent for a pattern of religious experimentation, a drift back and forth between various forms of religion.[6] The religious history of many people indicates that they have drifted from Folk Catholicism to the Jehovah's Witnesses, to Mormonism, to spiritism, and perhaps to several different evangelical denominations. They develop a certain attitude in which all existing religions are considered equally true, or at least potentially true; but they never really commit themselves fully to any one of them. Latin American cities are filled with such people, due largely to the weakness of the teaching ministry in all the religious bodies.

Two developments related to theological education are moving at cross-current to one another today. On the one hand, the indigenous, largely Pentecostal groups are moving toward more formal education for their pastors. On the other hand, the denominations are voicing dissatisfaction with their traditional training programs and are showing increasing interest in the decentralized approach to theological education represented by the Extension School movement.[7] As the two approaches to theological education draw closer

---

4. D'Epinay, *Haven of the Masses*, pp. 218-19.
5. Ibid., p. 219.
6. Willems, *Followers of the New Faith*, p. 258.
7. D'Epinay, *Haven of the Masses*, pp. 218-20, clearly shows the former; and *Theological Education by Extension*, ed. Ralph D. Winter (South Pasadena: William Carey Library, 1969), is replete with the latter. The table on p. 123 of Winter's book indicates that the big swing toward the Extension School approach occurred in 1967. According to a recent survey, at least 4,000 Latin Americans were taking theological studies by extension in 1971.

together some very good things are bound to happen. The indigenous churches are likely to receive a more trained and capable leadership that will meet the demands and warrant the respect of their more educated youth, and the denominations will progressively move away from the schoolboy type of seminarian toward the in-service training of more mature men who have demonstrated that they possess the necessary gifts and are personally dedicated to the work.

In evaluating the type of theological education best suited to the training of pastors and evangelists among the majority populations of the major cities, it must be borne in mind that Pentecostalism—judged by membership size and evangelistic zeal—has proved more adaptable to the aspirations and needs of the urban masses than any other form of evangelism.[8] To some extent, Pentecostalism's success is due to the fact that it represents a more radical reversal of the traditional social and religious order, namely, hierarchism.[9] The active role of the laity among Pentecostals, their emphasis on the priesthood of all believers, and the self-made leadership that is sanctioned not by academic diplomas and ecclesiastical courts but by the Holy Spirit and the people, represent massive reaction to Catholicism's hierarchy and specialized priesthood.

The historic denominations also believe in the priesthood of all believers but, unfortunately, they have developed their own kind of hierarchy. Academic degrees have come to mean more than the demonstration of the Spirit and of power in the actual ministry. On the other hand, Pentecostalism's traditional anti-intellectualism may prove to be self-defeating; for the masses also yearn for knowledge and their desire for better education is one of the primary reasons for migration to the cities. But the denominations must awaken to the fact that growth among the city masses requires a greater reliance on the laity and a practical implementation of the priesthood of all believers, avoiding the mistakes of Rome and putting into effect genuine New Testament Christianity. Consciously or unconsciously, large segments of the urban masses deeply resent Catholicism's hierarchy, and their pref-

---

This represented an increase of about 30 percent over 1970. Seventy-two percent of the extension students covered by the survey were studying at the certificate level (having less than a full primary school education) and 20 percent were studying at the diploma (full primary) level (*Latin American Pulse* 6, No. 4 (1971): 7.
8.   Willems, *Followers of the New Faith,* p. 249.
9.   Ibid.

erence for Pentecostalism, with its lay emphasis, is one of their ways of expressing it.[10]

One of the finest examples of a Pentecostal training school is the Bethel Bible Institute of the Assemblies of God in El Salvador. The fact that today this denomination has more churches and believers than any other evangelical group in El Salvador is due, principally, to the effectiveness of this school.[11]

The Bethel Bible Institute was founded forty years ago by Ralph Williams, and at that time it was the first Bible institute of the Assemblies of God in Central America. Today they have twenty-nine institutes throughout Latin America. Characteristic of their program is the indigenous approach to leadership training and church growth, and their concern that their graduates return to their own familiar locales, adequately and relevantly prepared to carry on a better ministry. El Salvador's population density is 350 people per square mile; the Assemblies of God has 330 churches, 651 preaching points, 11,220 church members, and 65,125 believers in this country, ample evidence of Bethel's extensive labors. The entire program of the school is designed to produce and foster church growth.

> A very significant factor in the student's acceptance is that he must have proved himself for six months as an "obrero local" (a lay worker or lay preacher). Every pastor makes a weekly visit to at least one preaching point. He should regularly be opening as many new works as he is able to and be finding obreros locales to care for them. The local church will choose obreros locales to make regular visits to

10. I was told of the daughter of a Pentecostal pastor in Mexico City who, as a student at the National University, passed herself off as a Presbyterian. Although she was active in her Pentecostal church, the stigma of anti-intellectualism associated with Pentecostalism influenced her to identify herself with the more intellectually respectable Presbyterians in the academic community. As increasing numbers of Pentecostal young people enter higher education, they will demand more education on the part of their pastors; and Pentecostal churches, if they are to hold these young people, will have to comply.
11. Data concerning the program of the Bethel Bible Institute and of the Assemblies of God in El Salvador is derived from Read, Monterroso, and Johnson, *Church Growth in Latin America,* pp. 150-53, and from Norman Chugg and Kenneth W. Larson, *Chugg-Larson Report to TEAM's 1970 Conference on Their Church Planting Study Trip to Central America,* Report to the Evangelical Alliance Mission, Wheaton, Ill., January 1970 (Instituto Bíblico, Ebenezer, San Cristóbal, Tachira, Venezuela, 1970), pp. 1-4. For the general principles of the Assembly of God mission, no better source can be found than Melvin L. Hodges, *On the Mission Field: The Indigenous Church* (Chicago: Moody Press, 1953).

the budding churches and later name the laymen to be in charge of them. As a nucleus of believers develops the mother church may ask the obrero local to be the pastor in charge of the growing daughter church. It is expected that the pastor will be weekly training his obreros locales to be more effective.[12]

Before enrolling a prospective student, the school requires that evidence be presented that he has been an effective *obrero local*. Questions are asked as to how many Sunday schools he has organized and what kind of ministry he has had as a layman. The institute offers a six-year course of study which is divided into two four-month periods each year. During the school terms students are assigned to specific places which local pastors believe are ripe for church planting. The institute pays the student's transportation to his assigned area, and his weekend room and board is the responsibility of the local group. At the close of the school year one of the church leaders visits the people who attend the services and asks them if they would be willing, not only to continue giving the student his room and board, but also tithe so as to support him for the next eight months. No student is allowed to return to the school until he has acceptably finished eight months of ministering in a church.

The ten nationals and seven missionary teachers spend much time each year recruiting young people to prepare themselves better for the ministry at the institute. They regard the institute as a key factor in the planting of new churches and the growth of the entire program of the Assemblies of God in El Salvador. The Chugg-Larson Report summarizes the success of the Assemblies of God in El Salvador as follows:

Every local church seems to be concerned with extending itself. Only proven lay workers, who therefore demonstrate high worker potential, even go to the Institute. Once in the Institute the student immediately is put to work on the weekends, no doubt in the same place where he will spend at least the next twelve months leading the work. To be able to continue his study the Institute requires that every student complete at least 8 months pastoring a church. For them a church is not a church unless it has a fulltime pastor. The whole Institute emphasis is really only to prepare pastors. The denominational emphasis is geared to, and organized for, lay worker participation with its "line upon line" and "how

12. *Chugg-Larson Report,* p. 2. *Obrero local* means a local lay worker engaged in church extension.

to do it" instruction. They emphasize strongly the Lord's provision in the ministry. The national workers seem to have a willing spirit to give of themselves sacrificially to the Lord's work in spite of economic needs.[13]

The Bethel Bible Institute is a beautiful example of a Pentecostal educational institution which combines an essentially indigenous approach to leadership development, cultural relevancy, and the kind of educational advancement which pastors need and want. The school is a vital part of the church-planting program of the Assemblies of God in El Salvador. The students who enroll are already experienced church planters, they practice and perfect their skills during academic training, and they eventually graduate into a ministry of church extension for which the program of the institute has directly prepared them. The entire program of both the school, church, and mission is geared for spiritual reproduction and the multiplication of converts and churches. The task, says McGavran (and he has mission, church, and school in mind), is to establish self-supporting churches in growing number:

> The missionary enthusiasm which drives the missionary must not die with him. It must be transmitted to the new churches. No question is of greater importance than getting a system of new congregations which slants everything in favor of reproduction. One reason the Assemblies have been so successful in Latin America is that their system of training ministers lets only those who have been successful in winning men and starting house churches become ministers. The educated lecturer on the Bible is not the minister. The man with twenty house churches to his credit is.[14]

The Purpose of Seminary and Bible School Training

This leads directly to the question of the purpose of the training given by Latin American seminaries and Bible schools. This question must be examined because there are reasons to believe that many, if not most, institutions are saying one thing and actually doing another. They aim to prepare effective pastors and evangelists for the cities and villages of Latin America, but the men whom they graduate are not eager or equipped to fulfill this task. They know much, but they do not function well. Something went wrong during their years of training which made them misfits even within the environment in which they were born and reared.

Probably no one knows more about this problem on a world-

---

13. Ibid., pp. 3-4.
14. Donald A. McGavran, personal letter, 28 April 1971.

wide scale than James F. Hopewell, associated as he was with the Theological Education Fund from its beginning in 1958, long before it had any formal connection with the World Council of Churches.[15] Hopewell visited hundreds of theological institutions around the world with the specific purpose of cutting through the outer, superficial appearances and getting at the core of their mission and ministry. Defining "mission" as the witness which Christians make outside the normal frontiers of the church, and "candidate" as the person being prepared by some theological institution for a career in Christian service, Hopewell says:

> The problem is that surprisingly few candidates are prepared to engage in that mission with any consistency or accuracy. And while this fault may be attributed to most any aspect of modern church structure, it seems particularly encouraged by the pattern of theological education now practiced in most seminaries around the world. . . .
> Now I would like to contend . . . that most of these factors that comprise our understanding of typical theological education have been unconsciously designed to avoid, and therefore to hinder, the basic Christian intention of mission. And I do not mean to beat the anti-intellectual drum against higher learning. What rather concerns an increasing number of critics is that the very tool of higher learning has been misappropriated to perform a third-rate job for a second-rate church structure. In a time when our understanding of the ministry more and more implies its dynamic, missionary function, we continue to rely upon a system of preparation which at its roots is essentially static and isolationist.[16]

Summing up what they found in their visits to various Bible schools and seminaries in Latin America, Chugg and Larson stated that "church planting seems to be the basic purpose of every group" which they visited. That is the stated purpose of most schools. But the question remains whether the "missionary" way of training, enrolling young and inexperienced men and women, following a curriculum which is little more than a direct translation of the curriculum in North American institutions,[17] and teaching students to depend on foreign funds to maintain themselves, is actually ac-

15. "The Worldwide Problem," in *Theological Education by Extension,* ed. R. D. Winter, p. 36.
16. James F. Hopewell, "Preparing the Candidate for Mission," in *Theological Education by Extension,* ed. R. D. Winter, pp. 38-39. The article appeared also in the *International Review of Missions* 56 (April 1966): 158-63.
17. McGavran, in *How Churches Grow,* p. 142, calls this the most damaging kind of "cultural overhang" that can be perpetrated on the younger churches.

complishing the purpose which school administrators give for their institutions.

Besides all this, there is reason to believe that the cultural orientation of most schools is wrong. As a result of their monumental survey of church growth throughout Central and South America, Read, Monterroso, and Johnson conclude:

> The Evangelical Churches of Latin America must seek to develop ministerial training programs within the numerous subcultures which are currently receptive and where churches are multiplying. What is at stake is not the prestige of the Evangelical Churches, but the very spiritual welfare of Latin America. . . . Evangelicals must end their slavery to an educational system designed to honor and glorify the culture of the classes presently in control. An education which emasculates the preacher and makes him ineffective among the common people cannot be described as education on a high level. "Lower standards" which, nevertheless, enable men to win others and shepherd the flock are a much more effective education. Therefore, theological training in Latin America must emphasize the *practical* aspects of the ministerial calling by means of a multi-level program.[18]

Theological educators in Latin America need to ask themselves seriously whether the education which they are imparting is specifically designed for the needs of Latin Americans, or is simply a carry-over from abroad. Most church members in Latin America are relatively new Christians. Doctrinally they are "babes in Christ." Does the curriculum in the average Bible institute or seminary reflect a conscious awareness and adaptation to the kind of ministry that most of the graduates will have? Unfortunately, this is not generally the case.

The purpose of a theological education is not to uproot the student socially and culturally, endowing him with values and ideals which economically he will never be in a position to enjoy. Yet this is what happens very often in mission schools. The frustration and dissatisfaction of so many graduates is probably due to the fact that the schools are culture-reorientation centers more than culturally relevant training institutions where men can come for training and later slip back into the environment from which they came, better prepared and not maladjusted.

The middle-class imprisonment of Christianity in Europe and America and its inability to reach the urban centers with their masses of the lower class must not be carried over to Latin American

---

18. *Church Growth in Latin America*, p. 231.

cities through the perpetuation of a middle-class mentality in the Bible schools and seminaries. There are many different levels of society, and each one has its own particular needs. The educational requirements of one single level should not be applied to all other levels. Nor should the full rights of the ministry be limited only to those who have achieved the academic standard which one segment of society considers necessary. To impose such a standard, or to universalize one level, is simply to brush aside the New Testament and to replace it with middle-class tradition.

The Need for City-oriented Bible Schools and Seminaries

Manuel J. Gaxiola, current bishop and president of the Apostolic Church of the Faith in Jesus Christ, in Mexico, a denomination which has grown from its inception in 1914 to nearly 15,000 members in 1970,[19] declares that with the present rate of urbanization, his denomination must swiftly move from a rural-based and -oriented church to one that is urban-oriented.[20]

> Up to now the attitude of the Church has been to work in the North, in the most sparsely populated part of the country. It is hard to bring those pastors to Mexico City, and they do not work out well here. We urgently need an urban training program.[21]

As president, Gaxiola has inaugurated a program which he calls *"Marcha al Centro"* ("March to the Center"). He means by it a shifting of evangelistic effort to the center of Mexico, particularly Mexico City in which the denomination already has five churches, and to other urban centers. The program calls for the placing of pastors in key cities—Querétaro and Leon, besides Mexico City and Puebla, which already have them, and Morelia, which is next on the list—with the expectation that they will work among the most rapidly increasing segments of the population with the purpose of planting churches.

These missionary pastors are salaried by the denomination whose

19. See Manuel J. Gaxiola, *La Serpiente y La Paloma* (South Pasadena, Calif.: William Carey Library, 1970), which is the history of his denomination, written under the direction of the School of World Missions, Pasadena, Calif., and particularly the graph on p. 140, showing the growth of the Apostolic Church since 1914. The denomination now includes 459 churches, 505 preaching points, and 1,176 ministers.
20. Read, Monterroso, and Johnson, *Latin American Church Growth,* p. 168; and Manuel J. Gaxiola, interview 9 June 1971, Mexico City.
21. Manuel J. Gaxiola, interview, 9 June 1971, Mexico City. Unless otherwise indicated, all information concerning the city program of the Iglesia Apostólica is derived from this interview.

National Evangelism Committee operates much like the mission boards of the traditional churches. Here is seen a shift from the spontaneous growth pattern which once saw the Apostolic Church increasing at a rate as high as 20 percent per year,[22] to the pattern of deliberate church planting with which other denominations are familiar. The slowing down of numerical increase to the present 10 percent per year, the rise of the educational level among the youth, the migration of many of its members to the city, and the drive for a better educated ministry are all characteristics of the present reorientation of the denomination. It is changing, consciously and unconsciously, to a modern, organized church, facing the same kinds of problems as their Baptist, Methodist, and Presbyterian brethren, but, thanks to leaders such as Manuel Gaxiola, with a bit more foresight than some of the others.

"Rural-trained pastors do not meet the needs of the city," says Gaxiola; "but unfortunately, many church leaders do not understand that." The Apostolic Church had a training school in Mexico City, but unsympathetic leaders moved it to Tepic. Most of the present pastors in Mexico City were trained at the school while it was still in Mexico City,[23] but after it was moved to Tepic there was nothing left by way of an urban training center. Gaxiola says that if plans to bring the school back to Mexico City are blocked, a new school for urban church planters will be established. "We need urban-oriented men," says Gaxiola, "and we can bring in sharp rural boys and after three years of training in the city they can be sent out to establish new city churches."

Gaxiola gives an illustration of how this works. He says that his church is now sending a pastor every weekend to the city of Puebla, a rapidly growing center less than two hours by bus from Mexico City. This pastor sustains himself by secular employment in Mexico City during the week; but on weekends, with the denomination paying his travel expenses, he goes to Puebla to engage in an evangelistic ministry. After the first two months of work, in mid-1971, he had a group of fifty members; and the early organization of a church was a live prospect.

The kind of school Gaxiola has in mind is precisely right. It is a school which has as its purpose not only to *inform* its students, and teach them to *interpret* the Bible relevantly to their situation, but also to *live* the gospel by sharing it. The seminary or Bible school that does not teach students how to win men to Christ—

---

22. Read, Monterroso, and Johnson refer to this training program in *Latin American Church Growth,* p. 168.
23. Ibid.

not just theoretically but *actually*—and how to plant churches when the crying need of the hour is for evangelical growth and expansion, is giving an inadequate training to its students, no matter how many other good things it may be doing. In a few very powerful words, McGavran sums it up:

> If the students master well New Testament material, but have not won a soul during the time of their studies, they ought to be failed. For they will have learned a falsehood, that the New Testament is simply knowledge and not a complete surrender to the saving activity of Christ.[24]

If school and mission administrators mean what they say when they insist that the purpose of their schools is to train the kind of leaders and evangelists that Latin America needs, then they will agree that the ultimate test of a school lies not in the classroom but in the *campo,* not in the final exams at the end of the semester but in the daily tests of the ministries of its graduates. Moreover, in this period of rapid urbanization, the test of evangelical effort in all its forms—educational, ecclesiastical, cultural, and evangelistic—lies in the city. For if evangelicals fail in the city, they will fail to win Latin America. The march of the masses is to the cities, and there lies the prime target for evangelical outreach for the remainder of this century.

The Program of City Oriented Bible Schools and Seminaries

In order for a school to train its students adequately in the urban situation three factors must be borne in mind:

1. *The location of the school.* The location of a school tells a great deal about its orientation.[25] Extension schools, for example, will be found located in a multitude of different places, for decentralization is the genius of the system and their purpose is to give in-the-field training to the real leaders of the churches. Schools of the ecumenical type, on the other hand, generally are located close together. "United Faculties" and "Theological Communities" are familiar names which tell their own story.

Far more common in Latin America is the isolationist type of school, which locates in some quiet, rural hamlet, perhaps in an old *hacienda,* reminding one of the old song about "a sweet little

---

24. Donald A. McGavran, letter to Peter Savage, published in *Boletín Informativo de CLATT,* ed. C. Peter Wagner, Cochabamba, Bolivia, January 1970.
25. Significantly, J. F. Hopewell mentions the question of the location of the school as the first question to be answered in analyzing a school's program and ministry. "The Worldwide Problem," p. 44.

nest, somewhere in the West, and let the rest of the world go by."
Urbanization does not disturb such schools. Let the masses go
to the city; that is not the school's concern.

"But *maestro,* we could pray better in the *campo.*" That was the
argument presented to me by my students in Mexico City when
the question was raised about locating the school outside the city.
The students were unanimous in their opinion that the countryside,
where they could be closer to nature and (presumably) closer to
God, was a much better location than the noisy, crowded, smog
filled inner city where the institute stood.[26]

But if the training of city pastors and urban evangelists is what
a school is primarily intended for, the heart of the city is the
proper location. Students who are led to think that they cannot
pray where "the noise of selfish strife" can never be completely
shut out, are not prepared for the ministry. If they cannot pray
amid the turmoil of the city during their student days, neither will
they be able to do it later on. Hard as it may be, one's praying—
and preaching—must continue despite the screeching of brakes,
the black soot of the busses, and the shouting of neighbors. The
city is the place where men must learn to minister, and the heart
of the city is where seminaries should be located.

2. *The atmosphere of the school.* Next to the location of the
school, and intimately related to it, is the matter of the prevailing
atmosphere of the institution. If Bible schools and seminaries are
to get out of the rut of being self-contained, academic institutions
and move toward becoming more vital participants in the total
mission of evangelicalism in Latin America, an "atmosphere of
perennial evangelism" must be maintained. This is A. Clark Scanlon's contention:

> To grow to their full stature as soul-winners, students must
> be taking courses and reading books and at the same time
> be at work in search for the lost. During vacation months
> students can help in or even lead evangelistic campaigns.
>
> Then too, throughout the year, students should be kept
> in an atmosphere of a perennial evangelism. In El Salvador
> the students of a Bible school carried out the Great Com-
> mission so well that the number of churches in the imme-
> diate area grew from 78 in 1954 to 210 in 1960. By the
> Spirit's help, perennial evangelism can produce the same type
> of results in other countries.[27]

---

26. Reference is to the *Instituto Cristiano Mexicano* (Mexican Christian
Institute), of which I was director from its founding in 1968 until June 1970.
27. *Church Growth Through Theological Education* (Guatemala City, Guat.:
El Faro, 1962), p. 60.

Where students are trained in an "atmosphere of perennial evangelism" everything that the school does—the materials which are studied, the prayers in chapel, and the faculty-student relations—is colored by the overriding concern of the institution: gaining converts and bearing evangelical witness to the world. The walls of the school are turned outward, so to speak. The "monastery" atmosphere is dispelled, and the school becomes a vital link in the chain of ministry and evangelism.

Because so many schools in the past did not possess this "atmosphere of perennial evangelism," many pastors, including city pastors, walk in a very narrow circle. They visit only the homes of their church members and never venture out into the *barrios* and *colonias de miseria* that encircle the city.

> The city pastor who frequents only the places of unimpeachable respectability can hardly expect the needy masses to throng to his church on Sunday morning. The battle is out there. The man of God, though not of this world, must surely be in it.
>
> The crushing anguish so present in our world is usually not apparent in a Sunday-morning or a Wednesday-evening congregation. Human distress ferments in the squalor of decaying tenement houses and at the back table of a gin mill on State Street, and boils in the core of a frenzied mob seeking vengeance on oppressors. As Nietzsche has written, "Great problems are in the street." So men and women of God must bring to the streets the message of deliverance for the victims of sin. And they must do so with holy indignation against the social, economic, and political abuses of the day.[28]

The schools which Latin America needs will offer, on the one hand, a solid Biblical and theological basis for missions. It will be one which sets everything the pastor and evangelist do within the framework of divine truth and divine action for man's redemption. Added to this will be a strong and continued emphasis on prayer, personal devotion and consecration, and the disciplined study habits apart from which only superficiality can result in the ministry. Finally, these schools will be filled with evangelistic zeal and a burden for the lost. "Evangelism" must not simply be a course in the curriculum, it must be the prevailing atmosphere of the school—something which faculty and students share as much as the air they breathe. Graduates of that kind of insti-

28. Gilbert James, "Reaching the 'Lonely Crowd,'" *Christianity Today,* 18 February 1966, p. 12.

tution will carry to their churches a vision and an enthusiasm which will turn them into God's missionary agents in the world. As Scanlon points out, institutes and seminaries cannot and should not usurp the place of local churches in carrying out the great commission; but there is no other way adequately to train evangelists apart from actual involvement in the work. "The lateness of the hour demands that theological institutions evangelize."[29] And in so doing, they will be in a better position to bring dormant churches back to life.

3. *The participation of the faculty in active evangelism.* "Seminary teachers," says R. Calvin Guy, "would do well to spend part of their time training their men by personal example."[30] The sad fact is that in many theological institutions students find it difficult to find personal models which they can accept for their own pastoral and missionary careers.[31] This weakness can appear in any kind of program, whether it be the traditional centralized school or the extension type program. Either type can produce—or it can fail to produce—church planters and church growth, depending largely on the kind of professors who are engaged. A professor who knows nothing about evangelism, church planting, and the application of God's Word to society at large from personal experience is nothing more than an academic mole forever buried in the world of books and institutions. He will be a failure in *any* kind of educational system, and he will produce a sizeable number of students just like himself.

But the teacher who in his own life combines academic acumen, Biblical perceptivity, devotion, and love for his fellow man with evangelistic involvement on weekends and during vacation periods, will form in his students' minds an image as to how they, too, can be faithful pastors and evangelists. They will learn from him how they can care for their flocks and still go out after the lost; how to study, grow, and teach God's people, while at the same time treading the city's streets in search of souls.

If traditional schools cannot produce effective church planters and pastor-evangelists they ought to be closed. Latin America does not need stuffy professionals, nor the influence of men whose lives and teaching have little relevance to the throbbing world outside the school walls. Each school and mission will have to examine for itself how well it performs. And the area for investigation must not be the school catalogue, nor the faculty minutes, but

29. *Church Growth Through Theological Education,* p. 35.
30. "Directed Conservation," p. 211.
31. "Memo to Seminary Professors," *Church Herald,* 29 December 1967, p. 3.

the ministry of the graduates. "We are not called on to create a static ministry for Churches content to remain at their present size in the midst of millions of the winnable," writes McGavran. "We are called to create a ministry which will keep growing Churches growing and start non-growing Churches on the road to great growth."[32] Very succinctly, that statement summarizes the task of the schools in urban Latin America.

---

32. McGavran, *How Churches Grow*, p. 142.

PART IV

URBAN STRATEGY TESTED
IN A LATIN AMERICAN CITY

13

MEXICO CITY: SETTING FOR A CASE STUDY

"No missionary, no church, no institution," says Calvin Guy, "will be automatically effective in church growth. Constant devising of ways and means to multiply churches is the hallmark of missions which are skilled in carrying out the Great Commission and reconciling men to God."[1]

Probably no better place could be found than Mexico City for testing the theories advanced in this study. The environment of Mexico City is reminiscent of the words of Martin E. Marty, for it is both beautiful and ugly:

> Some of the avenues of the world's cities are spectacular human creations. The cities are the home of most artists; here the symphonies and choral groups congregate. Acts of generosity in voluntary organizations and evidence of human greatness are the marks of beauty in the city. But if Abee Pierre is right: if in the sight of God and man the beauty of a city does not consist in its galleries but in the absence of slums and homeless people, then the postindustrial city is ugly. Two blocks from the spectacular avenues of the world are unspeakable slums where unwanted children are born to be chewed on by unwelcome rats and neglected by unheeding urbanites.[2]

---

1. "Directed Conservation," p. 213.
2. *Babylon by Choice: New Environment for Mission* (New York: Friendship Press, 1965), p. 57.

As an urban "laboratory" of missionary strategy, Mexico City has everything to offer. On the one hand, there are magnificent specimens of Latin American art and culture, even buildings and castles from the colonial era.[3] There are also all the signs of modern urbanization, with its problems, its slums, and its masses of people. Though more advanced than many parts of Latin America, the Mexican capital would appear to be as good a place as any to carry missionary theory outside the classroom, the textbook, and the missiologist's study, and put it to the test of actual practice.

The Socio-Economic Profile of Mexico City

How do you describe a city? How do you communicate its beauty and its horror, its grandeur and its wounds? The traveler to Mexico City, says George Kubler, or to Lima, Bogotá, Quito, Buenos Aires, or Rio de Janeiro can scarcely tell one commercial center or upper-class suburb or proletarian slum from another. There has occurred what he calls a "diminution in the cultural diversity of Latin American life," and it has produced a high degree of "typicalness" all across the Iberian urban world.[4]

The "typical" should not be allowed to deceive us, however; for beneath the uniformity of urban populations there is found a broad spectrum of diversity and individuality. The general population may be compared to a mosaic, in which each piece is a distinct social entity. Each unit of society has its own life style, its own standards and allegiances, its own self-image and character. Not to recognize these multiple, homogeneous units within urban society is to misunderstand the city altogether. For though the cities are great "melting pots," they are also, as close examination will reveal, composed of hundreds of separate social units, some as large as whole *colonias* and neighborhoods, others as small as

---

3. The pioneer in the rediscovery of colonial art and architecture in Latin America, and in Mexico City particularly, was Manuel Toussaint y Ritter (1895-1955), who founded the Instituto de Investigaciones Estéticas of the National University in Mexico City. In 1956, a valuable history of Mexico City, prepared by Toussaint, was published as the introduction to a book in honor of Alonso Garcia Bravo, under the title *Información de Méritos y Servicios de Alonso García Bravo: Alarife que Trazo la Ciudad de México* (México, D.F.: Imprenta Universitaria, 1956), pp. 7-23. Toussaint includes here a bibliography of the colonial period in Mexico and two maps of Mexico City in the sixteenth century, the first attributed to the Spanish conqueror Hernán Cortés and the second Toussaint's own interpretation of Cortés's map, in which he identifies the key areas of the city, most of which continue to this present day.

4. George A. Kubler, "Cities and Culture in the Colonial Period in Latin America," *Diogenes* 47 (Fall 1964): 53-62.

TABLE 9

MEXICO CITY POPULATION BY AGE GROUPS

Age	%	Male	Female	Total
	100.00	3,319,038	3,555,127	6,874,165
0 - 4	15.35	536,227	517,896	1,054,123
5 - 9	13.99	486,671	474,561	961,252
10 - 14	12.15	413,594	421,696	635,269
15 - 19	11.35	366,049	414,375	780,424
20 - 24	10.01	328,335	359,959	686,295
25 - 29	7.67	256,017	270,963	525,980
30 - 34	5.88	195,939	208,097	404,036
35 - 39	5.43	176,776	197,430	373,205
40 - 44	4.30	130,143	157,497	293,640
45 - 49	3.71	120,971	134,247	255,218
50 - 54	2.58	81,935	95,648	177,583
55 - 59	2.30	71,459	86,952	158,411
60 - 64	1.83	55,186	70,478	125,654
65 - 69	1.47	42,034	58,220	101,264
70 - 74	0.89	24,851	36,598	61,449
75 - 79	0.49	12,464	21,417	33,881
80 - 84	0.31	7,192	14,286	21,478
85 - above	0.29	6,194	13,808	20,002

Source: Census, 1970, p. 113.

a single *vecindad* or a small group of shanties huddled next door to a towering apartment complex. But each is an identifiable social unit, with its own place of residence, standards of conduct, and individual loyalties.[5]

The Mexican census of 1970 provides the statistical data for the broad profile of Mexico City.[6] Literacy, the census data reveals, is relatively high in the capital city, standing at 90.91 percent of the population.[7] Table 9 indicates that 62.85 percent of the urban population is under twenty-five years of age, and women outnumber men in all age categories except those under ten years of age.

Of the total working population above twelve years of age (4,520,374), the census indicates that only 2.41 percent is classified as "unemployed." This needs to be interpreted, however, in light of the fact that while relatively few people in Mexico City are entirely without work, their employment may not provide them with anything more than "hunger wages." The daily minimum wage in Mexico City is less than three dollars a day (32 pesos), but thousands actually receive less than this amount and the take-home pay of many manual laborers does not exceed one and a half dollars a day.[8] The principal occupations in Mexico City are shown in Table 12.

---

5. Donald A. McGavran, "Homogeneity and Church Growth," *Church Growth and Christian Mission,* p. 71.

6. Estados Unidos Mexicanos, Secretaría de Industria y Comercio, Dirección General de Estadísticas, *IX Censo General de Población, 1970* (Con Datos Sobre la Vivienda), 28 de Enero de 1970. Resumen de las Principales Características por Entidad Federativa (Mexico, D.F.: Secretaría de Industria y Comercio, 1970), hereafter cited as *Census, 1970.* By "Mexico City" is meant the Federal District unless otherwise indicated.

7. *Census, 1970,* p. 14. According to the census report, only 68,660 persons (1.18 percent) in Mexico City speak an Indian dialect and not Spanish; and only 67,213 (1.15 percent) admitted that, besides Spanish, they spoke an Indian dialect also. These figures, in my opinion, are open to serious question. From experience, it is my opinion that probably a large portion of the dialect speakers in the city are unwilling to admit that they spoke an Indian language; and since they spoke Spanish well enough to get by, they answered in the negative the census takers' question about the dialect. *Census, 1970,* p. 115.

8. Interviews with manual laborers in Mexico City indicate that construction "bosses" cut into the daily wages of the workers under them by demanding that they buy their noon lunches from certain women who show up to provide food to the entire construction crew, who in turn pay the bosses for assuring them business. Men have told me of some instances where even drinking water at the construction site was sold to the workers, leaving them only about half of their wages at the end of the day.

TABLE 10
PRINCIPAL OCCUPATIONS IN MEXICO CITY

Occupation	Percentage of Labor Force
Professionals and Technicians	10.95
Managers, directors, and administrators	5.41
Personnel administrators	16.65
Salesmen, venders	11.23
Drivers and service personnel	21.66
Agriculturalists	2.18
Manual laborers	29.14
Unspecified	2.78

Source: Census, 1970, p. 116.

It is very difficult to interpret employment figures such as these, or to ascertain precisely how well off the people in the various categories are. Drivers and service personnel are generally paid poorly, and manual laborers include most of those working at the daily minimum wage. On the other hand, by "technicians" is meant many who in other countries might be termed skilled industrial workers.

Of more value, perhaps, in deciphering the socio-economic picture in Mexico City is Table 11, which gives the monthly income of city workers.

This means that approximately 65 percent of the workers earn less than one hundred dollars per month, and 15 percent earn less than forty dollars per month. Family income, in many cases, is of course supplemented by the fact that several members of the family are employed. The husband may work in construction while the wife sells small items on the street, and one or two sons may be shoe polishers. Only in this way can the masses eke out a living.[9]

9. In *Five Families,* Lewis shows that upper income women who, in unexpected circumstances, are forced to seek sources of income apart from their

TABLE 11

MONTHLY INCOMES IN MEXICO CITY

From	To	Percentage
1	199 pesos	3.49
200	499 "	11.96
500	999 "	30.25
1,000	1,499 "	22.14
1,500	2,499 "	14.77
2,500	4,999 "	9.24
5,000	9,999 "	3.63
10,000 and above	"	1.61

Source: *Census, 1970,* p. 117. One dollar equals 12.49 pesos.

Housing conditions, as revealed by the 1970 Census, also fill in part of the profile of Mexico City. According to the census, 63.91 percent of the 1,219,419 homes have water piped into the house, 19.65 percent have water outside the house, 12.09 percent depend on public hydrants and faucets, and 4.35 percent have no water at all.[10] Table 12 gives an indication of the extent to which modern facilities are available in Mexico City homes. These housing conditions in Mexico City, when compared with the rest of the country, reveal a considerably higher standard of living in the capital city. The census covering the overall population of the country shows only 31.83 percent of the homes with bathrooms, 73.69 percent with kitchens, 58.85 percent with electricity, 45.33 percent with radio only, 1.85 percent with TV only, and 29.43 percent with both radio and TV.[11] In every category, Mexico

husbands' salaries, are in a much more difficult position than lower-class women who have been accustomed all along to finding some way to supplement the family income.
10. *Census, 1970,* p. 123.
11. Ibid., p. xxviii. Since Mexico City itself was included in the overall

TABLE 12

MEXICO CITY HOUSING

(Based on 1,219,419 homes, with 6,874,165 occupants)

Facilities	Percentage		Number of	
	Homes	Occupants	Homes	Occupants
BATHROOM	58.97	57.69	719,122	3,966,174
KITCHEN	82.21	82.99	1,002,498	5,704,369
ELECTRICITY	94.69	94.84	1,154,602	6,519,387
RADIO ONLY	23.22	21.28	283,173	1,462,966
TV ONLY	3.61	3.83	44,072	263,607
RADIO AND TV	66.71	61.50	813,492	4,777,385

Source: Census, 1970, p. 124.

City ranked considerably higher than the national average as far as home facilities were concerned.

One indicator of the socio-economic level of the city population is the frequency with which a family eats meat. The 1970 Census included a question which, based on the week previous to the census itself, aimed at finding out how often city dwellers could afford to add this item to the family menu. Table 15 shows the results.

The fact that one-fourth of the population of Mexico City cannot afford to eat meat more than twice a week gives some indication of the social and economic situation in which people live. This is revealed, too, by the fact that nearly one million people above the age of six (936,380) were listed by the census as being without any schooling whatsoever. Of the homes, 28.76 percent had only one room and 28.50 percent had two.[12] In other words, over

statistics, and therefore helped to raise the national average, areas outside the capital can be assumed to be on an even lower scale than these figures would seem to indicate.

12. Ibid., pp. 120, 117.

TABLE 13

FAMILY MEAT CONSUMPTION IN MEXICO CITY

Number of Days Each Week in Which Meat Is Eaten	Percentage of Population of the Federal District
0	4.13
1	7.13
2	14.58
3	20.21
4	10.12
5	5.79
6	6.53
7	31.51

Source: *Census, 1970,* p. 125.

50 percent of the population lives in houses of not more than two rooms.

Before turning to the religious scene in Mexico City two more tables must be examined. Table 14 reveals the percentage of in-migration during the decade between 1960—1970. This clearly shows that Mexico City is undergoing tremendous expansion at the present time, with 34 percent of the present population having migrated to the capital city and approximately half of that number within the past decade. Actually, however, this table does not by any means tell the whole story. While on the one hand, the Federal District, of which Mexico City is a part, grew at the rate of 43.84 percent in the decade between 1960—1970,[13] the greatest growth was in the "spill-over" areas, most of which lie in the state of Mexico, east of Mexico City. Table 15 makes this clear.

When one speaks of the skyrocketing growth of Mexico City,

13. Estados Unidos Mexicanos, Secretaría de Industria y Comercio, Dirección General de Estadística, *IX Censo General de Población, 1970,* 28 de Enero de 1970, Datos Preliminaries Subjetos a Rectificación (Mexico, D.F.: Secretaría de Industria y Comercio, May 1970), p. 17 (hereafter cited as *Census, 1970—Preliminary Data*).

TABLE 14

IN-MIGRATION, MEXICO CITY

Percentage of the population
which moved to Mexico City from
other parts of the country

Total	34.70
Less than one year ago	5.01
From 1 to 2 years ago	2.54
From 3 to 5 years ago	3.57
From 6 to 10 years ago	6.40
Ten or more years ago	15.94

Source: Census, 1970, p. 117.

included must be the fringe areas of Naucalpan, with its increase of 335 percent in a decade, and Tlalnepantla, with its increase of 254 percent. And then there is Netzahualcoyotl, bordering Mexico City on the east, which in the 1960 census was not even listed as having any population at all, but which in 1970 had 571,035 inhabitants. How does one calculate that kind of growth? Mexico City's population passed 345,000 in 1900, and one million in 1930.[14] In 1970, the metropolitan area contained between 8 and 10 million people, depending on how many of the "spill-overs" were included. This means that approximately 20 percent of the population of the entire country now lives in the Mexico City valley.

The Religious Profile of Mexico City

As far as the census statistics are concerned, the religious picture in Mexico City is not much different from that of the rest of the country. Evangelicals number 1.82 percent of the overall population of Mexico, and 1.63 percent of the population of the Federal District.[15] Clearly, the potential for evangelical growth which some

14. "Población y Urbanización en México," *Misión,* April 1971, p. 4.
15. *Census, 1970,* pp. xxviii and 118.

TABLE 15

MEXICO CITY "SPILL-OVER" GROWTH

	1960	1970	% of Growth	No. of Homes	No. of Inhabitants per Home
Naucalpan (State of Mexico)	85,828	373,425 Men:180,574 Women:192,851	335.09	57,934	6.45
Netzahualcoyotl (State of Mexico)		571,035 Men:284,248 Women:286,787	----	87,513	6.52
Tlalnepantla (State of Mexico)	105,447	372,657 Men:184,265 Women:188,392	254.36 253.41	61,185	6.11

Source: Census, 1970.

missionary leaders in the past have seen in this city so far has not been tapped.[16]

Mexico City has one feature which makes it stand out among the other urban centers of Latin America, and marks it as a

---

16. See McGavran, Huegel, and Taylor, *Church Growth in Mexico,* pp. 36, 65, 77, projecting the optimistic viewpoint as to what can be done in Mexico City. The problem has been that hopes and aspirations have not been matched by actions designed to win the urban masses and plant churches among them.

At the same time it should be pointed out that many evangelicals are hesitant about acknowledging their religious commitment for fear of reprisals of some sort from their neighbors or employers. This fear dates back to the rural situation where intimidation kept most people within the Roman Catholic fold. Even in the city, however, many are still afraid to acknowledge that they are evangelicals since census takers are usually from the immediate neighborhood and some chance of reprisal is feared when one admits to being an evangelical. At the time of the 1970 Census, evangelical pastors made a number of special announcements to their congregations, urging them to acknowledge openly their faith when the census takers came to their homes. It was hoped that this would have an effect and that the new census figures would show a sizeable increase in the percentage of evangelicals.

TABLE 16

RELIGIOUS ADHERENCE IN MEXICO CITY

Religion	Percentage	Total	Men	Women
Catholic	96.09	6,605,248	3,178,983	3,426,265
Protestant[a]	1.63	111,957	52,454	59,503
Jewish	0.37	25,191	12,724	12,467
Other	0.53	36,263	17,982	18,281
None	1.38	95,506	56,895	38,611

Source: Census, 1970.

[a]Includes such groups as the Jehovah's Witnesses, Mormons, and Spiritists as well as Evangelicals.

strongly Roman Catholic city. It is the presence of the Basilica of Guadalupe that makes the difference. The Basilica and the religious ritual connected to it probably do more than anything else to explain the fact that the Mexican peasant coming into the city finds it less difficult to let go of his adherence to rural-oriented Folk Catholicism and adjust religiously to the city. Loyalty to the Virgin lies at the heart of Latin American religion, both rural and urban;[17] and in Mexico particularly, "faith in the Virgin" and national patriotism are one and the same thing. The Basilica now standing in the center of Mexico City's teeming millions is where Mary appeared, according to Catholic belief, and where the only authentic picture of her in all the world can be seen.[18]

17. Eugene Nida, "Mariology in Latin America," *Practical Anthropology,* Supplement, 1960, p. 10.
18. Helen Behrens, *America's Treasure: The Virgin Mary of Guadalupe* (Mexico, D.F.: Editorial Progreso, S.A., 1964), pp. 9 ff. After appearing four times to Juan Diego, in 1531, the Virgin is believed to have given him the "sign" of her own divinely painted picture on the Indian's mantle. This he showed to his bishop, Friar Juan de Zumárraga, as proof that the Virgin had appeared to him and that she wanted a chapel built in her honor on the spot where she had appeared, where the Basilica now stands.

The worship of Guadalupe unites the nation ethnically and religiously, and is the principal reason why Roman Catholicism continues to be so strong, even among those who for various reasons resent the hierarchy or have given up traditional religious practices. Arnold Toynbee sheds light on this blending of the ethnic and religious elements in Guadalupan faith:

> The miraculous cures and rescues attributed to the Virgin of Guadalupe rival those attributed to the Virgin of Lourdes, and the primitiveness and sincerity of the naive pictures of the experiences, painted and dedicated by grateful beneficiaries, are deeply moving. At Guadalupe the Virgin has made secular history, as the Archangel has made it at Monte Sant'Angelo. A common devotion to the European goddess who made her epiphany to an Indian convert in Indian guise has fused together the European conquerors of Mexico and their native victims into a Mexican nation in which the differences of physical race have been transcended by intermarriage and, still more potently, by a union of hearts that has made intermarriage here psychologically acceptable. In Mexico, economic and social inequalities and the resulting political conflicts do not coincide with differences in physical race.[19]

The impact of the Virgin's image, and all the connotations of her worship, are difficult to overestimate. A city and a nation are built around them. Replicas of the Guadalupe image are found everywhere—from the dashboards of cars, buses, and taxis, to almost every room in every house, store, office, and factory in the city. Even evangelical missionaries sometimes find themselves living in rented houses or apartments which have replicas of the Virgin's image built into the edifices and therefore cannot be removed. As the dark-skinned image of the Virgin helped the Spanish conquerors and their Indian victims fuse their races and cultures during the colonial period, so now the influence continues as the Basilica and the worship surrounding it provide a religious and cultural continuum for the uprooted, rural masses moving to the city.

It is important that Protestant missionaries become more fully aware of the function which the worship of the Virgin serves in Mexico, for too often the missionaries' approach to the subject has been entirely from the theological viewpoint.[20] That is important, of course; but it is not the whole story. Millions of Mexicans cling

---

19. *Cities on the Move,* p. 162.
20. Nida, "Mariology in Latin America," p. 11.

to the Virgin because she represents their deepest emotional loyalties to the family, the race, and the nation. And for millions of slum dwellers, she is something they can hang onto which carries over from their rural past: one element of continuity which has not been broken by the city.[21]

In an evaluation such as this of the religious profile of the city, it is not without value, before launching into a description of one evangelical mission's attempt to evangelize the city, to take note of what a Roman Catholic writer has to say about Latin Catholicism and the city, and about evangelical mission work in the urban context. Writing in the Jesuit edited publication *America*, Jeffrey L. Klaiber has this to say:

> Most Latin Americans—from the masses living in squalid *barriadas* ringing most of the larger cities to the upper-class *hacienda* owners—are still living off the cultural "baggage" of folklore, myths, superstitions as well as authentic beliefs of the Catholic Christianity of the 16th century. On the other hand, most have yet to be exposed to the good news of salvation by a personal Saviour as a first-hand experience. . . .
>
> In this sense, Latin America is not much different from India so far as traditional mission concepts are concerned. It is a vast, underdeveloped continent largely indifferent or apathetic to the Christian message. One reason for this apathy is that it has not understood or even accepted the Word of God as preached to it. . . .
>
> It is usually held that the preaching of the Word should precede the celebration of a Word believed and received in faith. If this is so, perhaps the Protestant missionaries, by their concentration on preaching the Word, have better understood the real unevangelized state of Christianity in Latin America than their North American or Spanish Catholic counterparts. Christianity is definitely not an accomplished fact in Latin America; rather, it has yet to be preached. And the Protestant missionary is acutely aware of this fact. . . .
>
> This strong emphasis on witness in community and on the display of social fraternalism explains much of the magnetism that Protestantism exercises in the burgeoning *barriadas*. . . .

---

21. It must be recognized that the worship of the Virgin is not the same in all parts of Mexico. One of the problems facing Catholic priests in Mexico City is to convince their people that the different images of the Virgin which they have in their homes, villages, and everywhere else, are not distinct persons with different attributes but are all actually representations of the one and the same Virgin Mary. Cf. Wonderly, "The Indigenous Background of Religion in Latin America," p. 243.

The typical *barriada* dweller is a man bereft of the ancient values that once sustained him and his family in the rural community where he lived before he immigrated to the anonymous and depersonalizing city. He naturally looks forward to a religion in which he can either renew and relive his old values—something that many traditional Catholic churches still offer—or else he looks for a religion that will provide him with the strong sense of belonging or community that he so desperately needs. In many situations, it is the local Evangelical or Adventist church that best fulfills this longing among the uprooted *barriada* dwellers.[22]

The gospel and Christian fellowship—the two things urbanites need so desperately—are what evangelicals ought to be so anxious to share. Had the things which Klaiber says here been expressed by an evangelical missionary they might be brushed aside as religiously biased. But coming from a Roman Catholic they catch the evangelical by surprise, and they make him thankful not only for this opportunity to see his cause through another man's eyes, but also for the kindred spirit of the other man.

Jesuit Klaiber continues:

From a sociological point of view this [evangelical] movement could be described as a concerted effort to create a mutual participation, a true Gemeinschaft, in the midst of the squalid and depersonizing living conditions presently shared by millions of Latin Americans. . . . From a theological point of view, the movement signifies a return to the religion of the communal life as described in the Acts of the Apostles.[23]

It would indeed be one of the ironies of history if one of the greatest contributions of Latin American evangelicalism would be to awaken and revitalize a dormant Catholic church which, in rising from slumber, would not attack the evangelical movement as a hostile force as in the days of the Reformation, but would recognize the truth in what it teaches, and would reshape her own message and mission in line with it.[24]

---

22. "Pentecostal Breakthrough," *America*, 31 January 1970, pp. 99-101.
23. Ibid., p. 101.
24. Klaiber himself suggests something of this order in the closing lines of his article. Ibid., p. 102.

14

STRUCTURE OF AN URBAN MISSION

The Mexico City church-planting program of the Christian Reformed mission began December 1967, when the mission made two key decisions. For several years the mission had operated a bookstore in the city, and its seminary-Bible institute in the capital had more than forty students from all parts of the country. But the orientation of the mission was largely rural or small town, and every weekend professors and students alike traveled outside the city for their evangelistic work. Spotty attempts were made to begin city work, but without much success.

Then came the two key decisions on the part of the mission: first, to appoint one of its missionaries as director of Mexico City evangelism for the purpose of planting new churches, and second, to establish a school, later to be called the Mexican Christian Institute, for the purpose of training urban church planters.[1] Around these two decisions a new urban-oriented strategy began to take shape.

As it developed, this strategy for urban church planting included seven distinct elements, all of which contributed to the establishment—over the course of two and a half years—of twenty-

---

1. I was appointed by the mission to the dual position of director of the Mexico City evangelistic program and director of the Mexican Christian Institute, serving in this capacity until June 1970, when I was succeeded by the Rev. Larry Roberts.

five meeting places in Mexico City, of which the majority continue as recognizable house-churches.

1. *Training.* It was understood that evangelists need training in Scripture, in Christian doctrine, and in the methods of effective evangelism. This training can be received in a variety of ways and in a number of different places, but it must be obtained if prospective evangelists are to be prepared adequately. In the urban situation, the necessary training may be given by a local church, by a night school, or by a centralized Bible institute such as that which the Christian Reformed mission established. But, wherever it is given, it must prepare the student to communicate the gospel in a clear and simple way from Scripture and to defend it against the host of false teachings which circulate in the city.

2. *Motivation.* It takes a high degree of motivation to produce urban evangelists. Almost anything is more inviting than the streets of a slum or the endless stairways of apartment houses. In order to maintain a high level of spiritual morale and determination, and later pass it on to their churches, evangelists benefit tremendously from a year or more in an institution which lives in a continual atmosphere of evangelism. When teachers view their academic tasks, not as ends in themselves, but as preparing men and women to carry the gospel today, tomorrow, this coming weekend, and for years ahead to multiplied thousands of people; when everything from the prayer sessions in the chapel to the casual conversations between teachers and students is permeated by concern for church growth, attitudes are formed which produce an irresistible missionary energy. As the institute staff discovered time and again, when the evangelistic atmosphere became thin, motivation fell off and the growth of the young churches was affected immediately.

3. *Goal.* Many of the students trained by the institute had had previous experience in church work and evangelism. Few, however, had been led to think clearly about goals. Soul saving was their general aim, but the idea of not only making disciples but also of establishing churches in every neighborhood where there was no gospel witness was an entirely new thing for them. Strategy sessions at the institute were always directed toward planting new churches. Large city maps were located on the walls in the student lounge and in the director's home and office, and smaller maps were always close at hand. High-potential areas were circled, and new house-churches were marked. Every student understood at the outset that the goal of this urban program was the multiplication of city churches.

One of the methods employed at the institute to instill in the students an understanding of the meaning of church growth was the use of graphs and charts. Every house-church had its own graph which was updated each month, and these graphs were hung in the student lounge where everyone could examine them. In addition, a large wall chart showed both the exact weekly attendance and the amount of the offering of each congregation. It became a matter of deep pride and concern for the students that their entries for the week or month show upward progress. Some students actually broke down and cried when the graph of their particular house-church showed a decline.[2]

4. *House-to-house visitation.* Once an area of the city had been selected, the strategy of the institute was to visit every house, selling Bibles, distributing tracts, and making personal contacts. The aim was to find people who would open their homes for Bible study. Sometimes two or three such homes would be found in a single afternoon. The addresses were carefully noted and the families revisited, often by the director himself. In many cases, "old stock" evangelicals were found—people who were evangelical Christians from the village or from some other part of the city— who now were not attending any church at all. They would usually welcome the idea of beginning services in their home or would gladly attend meetings in some other home close by.

In three areas of the city the *paisano* approach was taken to initiate the work. In the colonias Rivera del Bosque, Agricola Oriental, and Hidalgo, relatives of some of the institute students were first contacted and their homes used for services. The work in these places was eventually discontinued, but not necessarily because of weaknesses inherent in the approach. Here also the house-to-house method of reaching new families was followed. It proved to be the most effective way of expanding the work.

5. *Verbal witness.* It was an underlying premise of the mission's Mexico City program that the gospel needs to be verbalized if men are to be won for Christ and churches established. Once the door-to-door evangelist had been invited into the home and had come to know the family personally, regular, planned instruction in the Scriptures was begun. Institute students were trained to

---

2. Says Donald McGavran: "All thinking about the Church should be done against the graph of growth, because when done without exact knowledge of how the Church has and has not grown, it is likely to find itself in error." National leaders as well as missionaries need to be trained to see the condition of both local churches and denominations in the light of graphs of growth. *Understanding Church Growth,* p. 109.

TABLE 17

ATTENDANCE AND OFFERINGS: MEXICO CITY HOUSE-CHURCHES, APRIL 15, 1970

(in order of the date of establishment)

Colonia	Date When Evangelism Began	Average Attendance Mar.-Apr. 1970	Average Offering Mar.-Apr. 1970 (pesos)	Total Offerings (pesos)
Ramos Millán	1964—discontinued. Feb. 20, 1968	35	9.17	737.85
San Francisco	Mar. 5, 1968	24	40.08	1,646.45
A. Lopez Mateos	Mar. 13, 1968	50	200.0 The congregation pays the rent	—
Valle de los Olivos	Mar. 18, 1968	54	Kept by the congregation	2,940.30
Cuchilla del Tesoro	Oct. 1, 1968	57	53.96	626.85
Isidro Fabela	Apr. 17, 1969	44	36.92	801.25
Sta. Cruz Atoyac	Sept. 15, 1969	16	—	—
Paraje San Juan	Sept. 25, 1969	32	8.26	156.95
Vergel de Guadalupe	Nov. 25, 1969	41	6.25	47.75
Arenal	Feb. 15, 1970	27	7.51	117.25
Providencia	Mar. 15, 1970	10	—	20.50
Puebla	June 18, 1970	17	15.13	69.90
Las Palmas	Begun by others	30	Kept by the congregation	—
Villa Coapa	Begun by others	25	Kept by the congregation	—
El Moral	Apr. 1, 1970	Just Beginning	—	—
Sta. Ursula	Apr. 5, 1970	Just beginning	—	—

TABLE 18

HOUSE-CHURCHES WHICH TERMINATED

Colonia	Date When Services Began	Avg. Attendance Normal Month	Total Offerings (pesos)	Date of Termination	Reason for Termination Key:
Sta. Cruz Meyehualco (1)	1/15/68	15	—	10/1/68	A
Tránsito	4/28/68	43	50.05	10/25/68	C
Sta. Cruz Atoyac ("Aurrerá")	11/15/65	23	609.00	1/15/70	B
Xoco	3/1/68	22	269.20	10/30/69	C
Ribera del Bosque	3/22/68	20	1,159.20	11/30/69	A
Agricola Oriental	4/1/69	25	—	8/5/69	C
Hidalgo	4/5/69	25	65.55	2/3/70	—
El Rodeo	9/30/69	12	—	2/15/70	D
Sta. Cruz Meyehualco (2)	4/11/70	6	—	3/21/71	D

A — The family in whose house services were held moved away and no other house was available.

B — The entire squatter settlement in which the house-church was located was leveled for the construction of a new building and the people were scattered.

C — The landlord refused to allow Evangelical services to continue.

D — Terminated due to poor attendance.

organize Bible study groups in as many houses as possible, and out of these more organized house-churches eventually came. The main emphasis was on the preaching and teaching of the Bible; and along with this, film strips, singing, personal testimonies, and intercessory prayers were made part of the program from the outset.

6. *Family centered.* Another of the basic principles on which the Mexico City program was based was the conviction that whole families build strong churches, and that family units can and should be reached in the context of the home. While it is true, of course, that urban society fragments human life to a great extent, men's deepest loyalties are still family centered, and that is the best place to reach them.

Institute students were trained to present the gospel relevantly to the whole family; and this required personal acquaintance with each member of the home, from the youngest child to the oldest grandparent. Large, extended families were often found in the *vecindades* and *barrios* of the city; and every problem known to man was represented. As the gospel began to exert a leavening influence within the home, relationships between members of the family improved and the social benefits of Christian moral standards soon appeared.

7. *Neighborhood churches.* Institute students were trained to establish neighborhood churches designed to meet the needs of the local people, rather than encouraging them to go a great distance to some larger church with more ample facilities. It was felt that face-to-face contact with concerned neighbors was what the people needed, and that both worship, witness, and service should be local and geared to the immediate neighborhood. Whether it was a tenement housing unit, a sprawling slum, or a modern condominium, the religious and social needs of the people could best be met close at home.

The problems related to politics and government, labor and economics, education and culture were not ignored in this strategy; but the attack on them was made primarily from the angle of the home. It was the presupposition of those involved that before anyone could capture the realms of culture for Christ he must first penetrate that most basic social unit, the family. In a city like the Mexican capital, families in great number needed to be brought to Christian discipleship. Churches built around entire families would have a greater social impact than those built around isolated individuals, providing, of course, the gospel which these churches preached was the full message of Christ as Savior and Lord.

In other words, the strategy of the institute was to get at the problems of society through the establishment of vital, living churches in which advancement in grace would be measured not only by evangelistic zeal but also by constructive action in all areas of life. The institute did not always succeed in passing this on to the students, and not all the house-churches caught the vision. But the attempt continued to be made and in some cases it brought results.

Abortive attempts to begin house-churches were numerous, especially in the beginning when the house-to-house approach was used in middle- and upper-class areas where it proved ineffective because of the barriers—walls, maids, and intercoms—which these classes have erected around themselves. Nevertheless, by following this strategy, the missionaries and students were able to establish twenty-five house-churches, most of which continued. Tables 17 and 18 give a profile picture of both the "successes" and the "failures." Table 18 indicates that the most frequent cause for the termination of services was the refusal of the landlords to allow evangelicals to hold meetings. This, of course, in Mexico is related to the legal strictures against worship services outside of federalized property. Even though the common interpretation of the law allows for house-churches to continue, the existence of the prohibition offers a pretext for those who want to oppose the meetings.

The importance not only of sizing up a responsive segment of the population, but also of judging correctly where a house-church can be established with the prospect of reasonable permanence is illustrated by the "Aurrerá" house-church in the Colonia Santa Cruz Atoyac. After a promising start, the entire squatter settlement was demolished when the owner of the land decided to erect a large new building. The people were scattered, untraceably, throughout the city. When people of this class move they leave so many debts behind that the worst thing that can happen to them is for someone to find out their new address. Bill collectors cannot find them in their new locations, but pastors and missionaries cannot find them either. One can only hope that they will find another house-church close by their new home.

The Chugg-Larson Report, which covered the Pentecostal work of the Assemblies of God in El Salvador, the International Baptists in that same country, and the Christian Reformed program in Mexico City, made specific reference to the more "uncommon details" which each program included.[3] Some of the details mentioned concerning the Mexico City work were the apparent synthesis on the part of the visitation teams of the methods of Campus Crusade and D. James Kennedy's Coral Ridge Program:[4] the strong emphasis on repeated home visits and the commencement of Bible classes as quickly as possible. The report also mentions that the Mexico City strategy called for offerings to be taken in most cases as soon as regular meetings were scheduled, and the funds were held by either the group or the school for the eventual

3. *Chugg-Larson Report,* p. 1. The summary of the Christian Reformed program is found on p. 4.
4. See D. James Kennedy, *Evangelism Explosion,* 4th ed. (Wheaton, Ill.: Tyndale House Publishers, 1970).

erection of church buildings. Careful records were kept of both the offerings and the attendance.

It was an observable fact that young people, especially boys, attended more regularly when services were held during the week rather than on Sundays. During the initial stages in many of the areas, services were conducted late in the evening so that the husbands and fathers who arrived home late from work could attend along with their families. This was particularly true in the Colonia A. Lopez Mateos, where the men usually did not arrive home until after eight o'clock in the evening.[5] Young people were attracted to these mid-week services, often because they had nothing else to do and the film strips which often accompanied the Bible lessons appeared new and interesting. When services were changed to Sunday, fewer young people attended. Sunday sports were the main thing that kept them away.

Kenneth Scott Latourette once observed that in Australia "the emphasis on sports detracted from attention to organized religion."[6] That certainly is true of Mexico City. In order to maintain the interest and loyalty of house-church youth, Abe Marcus, one of the Christian Reformed missionaries, has recently organized inter-church soccer teams, with colorful jerseys and good equipment. This has served to hold the young men in some of the churches, though the danger also exists that they will attend the services only to play on the team. Marcus is experimenting along this same line with sewing classes and vocational training for young women.

The Training of a Church Planter

For many people, the big problem in the city is property. Land costs are high and the believers are generally from the poorer classes, too financially hard-pressed themselves to give a great deal for church property. A foreign missionary organization can easily overcome this problem by buying land and erecting church buildings, and in some cases this may be the most feasible approach. At least, it is less likely to have a deleterious influence on the young church than the subsidizing of ministers' salaries.[7]

---

5. The history of the church in the Colonia A. López Mateos appears in my chapter dealing with modern urbanization and missions, in *Crucial Issues in Tomorrow's Missions,* ed. Donald A. McGavran, published by Moody Press, 1972.

6. *The Great Century,* p. 176.

7. Donald McGavran, in *Understanding Church Growth,* pp. 285-86 and 291-92, discusses the pros and cons of city church buildings and the various solutions which have been attempted. "Each scheme," he says, "has its draw-

The building bottleneck, however, is not the biggest problem. When Moisés Lopez threw up his hands and said, "I could open more fields if I only had good workers," he was expressing an opinion which has been borne out in the experience of the institute. The possibilities for church growth are limitless, and teams of trained workers can plant a new house-church on an average of one per month in an urban center like Mexico City. But such workers need training, motivation, and leadership. New groups must be taught, counseled, and encouraged to live out the Christian life in all its relationships. New believers generally have problems, and families come for counseling. Local leaders need instruction, and young people require attention. Other colonias beckon. New Christians tell of relatives living in other parts of the city who would like to be instructed in the Word of God. The harvest is plenteous, the laborers few, and the crying need of the hour is for trained and dedicated church planters.

The steps involved in training a young Christian to become an effective church planter are illustrated by the case study which follows. The young man is Sergio Morales, and the initial testing ground is the Colonia Isidro Fabela, a squatter settlement on the southern edge of Mexico City.[8] Much can be learned by following the sequence of events which led to the establishment not only of a new city church but also of a church in a remote rural area.

Sergio Morales enrolled in the Mexican Christian Institute in September 1968, at the age of nineteen. He came from the state of Oaxaca and was recommended to the institute for training by the Wycliffe Bible translator Searle Hoogshagen, who had been instrumental in his conversion. The Mixe dialect was Morales' mother tongue, and Spanish his second language. He spoke Spanish in a somewhat halting way and it was obvious that he was sometimes groping for the right Spanish word.

During his first semester at the institute, Morales received the usual Bible school course of instruction and was involved each weekend in one of the missions or house-churches which the school had begun. He learned how to use the Bible in personal work and how to conduct home visitation. His shyness gradually dis-

---

backs and solves the property problem only under special circumstances." The only real solution is rapid growth. The church which experiences rapid growth usually solves its own building problems.

8. The history of the establishment of the church in the Colonia Isidro Fabe'a (formerly called Pedregal Carrasco), and the role which Sergio Morales played, first appeared in my article entitled "Training Urban Church Planters in Latin America," *Church Growth Bulletin,* January 1970, pp. 38-43.

appeared as he became more involved in the practical work and gained a better command of Spanish.

In February 1969, Morales was among the group of institute students who set out to evangelize the Colonia Isidro Fabela. This is a low-income area not far from the Aztec Stadium which was built for the 1968 Olympics in Mexico City. Most of the men are unskilled industrial workers with monthly incomes between 400 and 700 pesos (32 to 57 dollars). Many men hold two jobs in order to make ends meet. They complain that not only are their wages below the monthly minimum set by the government but they also suffer because the short-term "contracts," by which their employers avoid the minimum wage law, leave them without any work every two or three months. They must then bribe some plant official in order to get a new contract.[9]

The goal, which every student clearly understood, was to plant an evangelical church in the colonia. The entire area was visited for three successive Sundays, and approximately three dozen Bibles and New Testaments were sold. By the third Sunday Bible classes had been started in three different homes. One of these homes, overrun with children, had to be abandoned when it was discovered to be the home of prostitutes and the neighboring families would not come near it. Nor would the other two homes allow these women and children to come for Bible study. The beginnings of that particular house-church had to be abandoned, therefore, for the sake of the wider neighborhood, though the students often talked about the attentiveness of those women as they listened to God's Word.

By April, the two continuing groups had been joined and a regular program of Sunday worship had been inaugurated. The first formal service was held on April 17. Because Morales had shown a particular amount of enthusiasm for this *colonia,* the usual policy of placing only second- or third-year students in charge of new churches was relaxed so that he could be given the main responsibility for this group. Most of the people with whom he had to deal were much older than he, but they had one thing in common: they were equally "lost" in the big city. Most of the residents of the area were relatively new in the city, but so was the pastor-evangelist, and there was an immediate empathy between them.

Morales' love for the Lord was warm and contagious, and he visited tirelessly, reading the Scriptures from house to house and

---

9. Personal interviews with workers and their families, Colonia Isidro Fabela, Mexico City, 1969-71.

praying for the sick. By the end of August, there was a simple stone chapel built on some donated land at the rear of one of the believer's homes. The floor was of dirt, but it was filled with people every Sunday. Except for ten crude church pews, a home-made pulpit, and a chalk board donated by the mission, the offerings and labor of the local people had done it all. Morales himself had made a most significant contribution: in three months he had worn out two pairs of shoes while visiting from house to house in the area.

There are things which can be better "caught" than taught, and the technique of church-planting evangelism is one of them. Once caught, however, it can be transmitted to other places. When Sergio Morales went back to his home in the village of Cuatlán during the following vacation period, he witnessed to his relatives and friends. Within a few days he had a group gathered to hear him preach and, despite the fact that the village was strongly Roman Catholic and had severely persecuted converts to evangelicalism in the past, a number of people publicly confessed faith in Jesus Christ, renounced their former Folk Catholicism, and requested baptism. At Christmas 1970, missionaries from Mexico City joined Wycliffe translator Searle Hoogshagen and Sergio Morales in the formal organization of the Cuatlán Presbyterian Church. The local consistory was composed of seven men. Morales and another man, who more recently received instruction at the institute, were chosen as the preachers. Among the first to be baptized was the town harlot, a sign to the village of the power of the gospel.[10]

Morales has subsequently finished the three-year course at the institute and is conducting an extension school in the village for a year before entering the seminary. If his facility in adapting the church-planting methods taught at the institute to the village situation is any indication of what can be expected in other areas, it can be assumed with a measure of confidence that graduates of the institute will, in the course of their lives, do a great deal of church planting in widely scattered parts of Mexico, some of it in densely populated urban areas and some of it also in the most primitive surroundings.

---

10. Information concerning the establishment of the evangelical church in Cuatlán, Oaxaca, was derived from personal letters from Searle Hoogshagen, 12 April 1970 and December 1970, and Chester Schemper, *The Birth of a Church: Only God Could Do It* (Grand Rapids: Board of Foreign Missions of the Christian Reformed Church, 1971). Promotional material.

15

URBAN STRATEGY CRITICALLY ANALYZED

Manuel Gaxiola points out in the last chapter of his history of the Apostolic Church that religious research, if it is to build men in the future and help them avoid past errors, must include critical analysis as well as historical accounting. "I see the church in its smallness and its greatness, in its weakness and its power," says Gaxiola, "and I know that there awaits her tomorrow something more glorious than either the present or the past."[1]

No strategy or plan can ever guarantee church growth.[2] The wind of the Spirit is beyond human comprehension or control (John 3:8). At the same time, the Spirit's movement in history follows certain discernible patterns. The expansion of the church can be studied, and from it valuable lessons can be learned. And today, the march of the masses to the city should be viewed as God's action, with vast significance for missions, and as providing this generation with unparalleled opportunity to disciple the nations for Christ.

The following critical analysis emerges out of a burden for the discipling of urban populations. I have faith in the essential correctness of the Mexico City strategy, but I also believe that it can be improved.

1. *Composition of house-church membership.* Figure 6 shows

---

1. *La Serpiente y la Paloma,* p. 149. Translation mine.
2. Harold R. Cook, *Historic Patterns of Church Growth: A Study of Five Churches* (Chicago: Moody Press, 1971), p. 117.

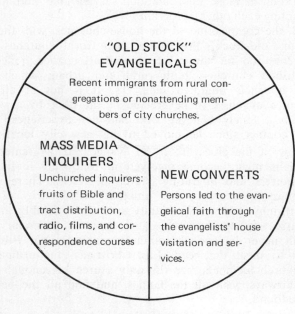

FIGURE 6

COMPOSITION OF A HOUSE-CHURCH

the three elements which make up the membership of the house-churches established by the institute in Mexico City. Proportions vary from place to place, but all groups have the same three elements. This says several things: first, more ought to be done to conserve the results of mass evangelism. Scattered here and there throughout the city are people who are reading the Bible, sometimes in secret, or are listening to an evangelical radio broadcast, or have taken a Bible correspondence course. More concerted efforts must be expended to locate them, instruct them—even by radio or by correspondence if they cannot be reached personally—so that they will not remain forever as scattered sheep with neither shepherd nor fold.

To be more specific, the church-planting program of the Mexican Christian Institute and the work of the Mass Communications

Center ought to have been drawn closer together. Located in the same city, these two branches of the same mission ought to have been working in close coordination, sharing one another's goals and promoting each other's program.

Second, the composition of the house-churches, with the sizeable element of "old-stock" Protestants from rural churches or from city churches too far away for regular attendance, reflects sadly on established churches, both rural and urban, which are not following up their migrated members. It is not at all unusual for student evangelists to be greeted at the door by a warm embrace from a lonely believer who had not experienced a single Christian contact since he moved to his new city location.

Somehow, if the cities are to be evangelized, a greater number of Christians must become involved in follow-up—both of mass media inquirers and migrating church members. There will have to be a massive return to the "amateur" missionaries of the first century, through whom Christianity spread so notably among the lower classes during the time of its greatest missionary power.[3] There will never be enough seminary graduates nor Bible school graduates to meet the need. Lay Christians, the ordinary rank-and-file church members, are the only source big enough to climb all the stairways, visit all the homes, and find all the people that need to be found.

2. *Local leadership.* One of the chief weaknesses of the institute's church-planting program in Mexico City has been its failure to raise up and train local leaders in the house-churches which it began. Students and faculty have monopolized the direction of the program and have been reluctant to turn over both the worship services and the control of the new groups to the local people.

Searle Hoogshagen, the Wycliffe Bible translator who was instrumental in the conversion of Sergio Morales, whose church-planting abilities were described in the previous chapter, sent the following criticism to me after reading an article which had been published about Morales' labors:

> I read your article in the *Church Growth Bulletin*. It was very interesting. . . . I am in wholehearted agreement with your thesis. However, I believe that there is one more step to go in the process of church planting, namely, training lay leadership. Sergio's church is a case in point. When he isn't there it tends to fold up.

---

3. Green, *Evangelism in the Early Church,* p. 173.

> I would agree that the first step is to teach the boys how
> to begin a church and the second step is to teach them
> how to teach lay leaders. The first step you are obviously
> doing very well. It is certainly something that you have
> taken a timid country boy like Sergio and developed him
> into a successful church planter in the city.[4]

Hoogshagen's observation is borne out in a number of places in the city, where everything seems to depend on the presence and leadership of the students. It has been observed that some students deeply resent and actively resist local initiative. Whether or not this reflects some unconscious influence of the missionaries is hard to determine, but surely it stifles spontaneous growth and witnessing on the part of the new Christians.

One Mexico City house-church which openly reacted against too close supervision by the institute and the constant participation of the students in its services was the Valle de los Olivos congregation on the extreme southeast corner of the city, where local leadership appeared in the person of Alberto Bello. Bello requested that the institute begin evangelistic work in this colonia, and offered his own home for services. As the group grew the meetings were moved from around the kitchen table (March-April 1968) to a covered porch (May 1968), to a new front room facing the street (May 1969), to an attractive church building (May 1970) erected almost entirely from the offerings of the group itself.

One problem connected with this particular church was that students did not care to go there. The reason was that Bello criticized their preaching, took over the service himself, and his authority carried more weight with the congregation than did that of the visiting students. The offerings, for example, were not sent to the school with regularity nor in their entirety, which embarrassed the students and made their entry on the wall chart at the school appear lower than it really was. Another source of friction was Bello's practice of inviting outside preachers, some of whose doctrine was not very Presbyterian. Bello, in fact, let it be known that he found Presbyterianism too restrictive; and he felt the local church should be free to invite whomever they chose, regardless of denominational affiliation.

These differences came to a head on 11 April 1970, when it was mutually agreed that hereafter (1) offerings would be kept and used by the local congregation; (2) no student leader would be appointed to this group on weekends and first-year students would

---

4. Searle Hoogshagen, personal letter, 12 April 1970.

be sent only as helpers to Bello; (3) no student would be assigned during the summer months, and if there was a need for guest preachers the group should appeal to a nearby Presbyterian church; and (4) the 3,000 pesos which the congregation had deposited with the school would be invested immediately in their building project. Besides this, the institute agreed to donate new benches for the new chapel building under construction.

For all practical purposes, therefore, the young church in the Colonia Valle de los Olivos was now independent of the institute which had founded it. Whatever help was still given was by invitation, and the direction of all local affairs was in the hands of the group itself. The climax came at the dedication of the new church building on 17 May 1970, to which Bello invited the president of the Mexico City ministerial association and guests from various denominations. To the surprise of the missionaries, Bello produced a carefully prepared document which everyone present was asked to sign, declaring that the church was now independent and that he himself was its pastor. It appeared to be the will of the congregation, so the missionaries joined in signing it. Some missionaries later expressed their grave disappointment over the matter, but nothing could be done about it. It appeared that this church was "lost" as far as the Presbyterians were concerned.

But it did not turn out that way. Once the autonomy of the local group was asserted, and Bello was recognized as the pastor of the group, relations with the institute improved. Bello even directed the missionaries to the home of a friend in an unevangelized *colonia* where within a few weeks another house-church was established. Bello had taught the institute and the missionaries a valuable lesson; namely, if evangelistic enthusiasm and administration are not to come and go with the missionary, local leaders should be trusted and responsibility turned over to them as soon as possible. The struggle over leadership in the services, preaching, and offerings should not have occurred. Bello was the God-given leader the new church needed; and the missionaries should have guided the students in recognizing that, despite the fact that Bello lacked formal theological training. He conducted himself in a Christian manner, preached with power, and showed all the qualities of a born leader. Instead of complaining that Bello was usurping their place at the head of the congregation, the students should have rejoiced that local leadership was taking over.

The fact is that despite Bello's unpredictable and independent ways (which missionaries especially find hard to take), he and his church have done more than any of the other young churches connected with the institute to fulfill two ideals set before them. First, they have made a social contribution to their community by setting up a medical and dental clinic next door to the church, where an evangelical lady doctor comes each Sunday to serve without charge the people of the area. Second, they have sparked a new mission program in another *colonia*. That record is hard to beat, especially because it has been carried out with missionary assistance but without missionary control. Much more of this kind of independence should be taught and encouraged. Missionaries and students alike should be busy training local leaders to take charge of the local churches as quickly as possible.

3. *Ecclesiastical structure.* Beyerhaus and Lefever point out that one of the signs of greatness in Roland Allen was the fact that, devoted Anglo-Catholic that he was, he was willing to modify his episcopal views in the light of the needs of the young church and his confidence in the guidance and power of the Holy Spirit. Though an Anglican by denomination, Allen came close to Congregationalism in missionary practice because he was willing to bow to the leading of the Spirit in the concrete missionary situation.[5] This is an observation for missionary strategists to keep in mind. When an ecclesiastical system is translated from one country to another without change or modification, something is almost bound to be wrong.[6]

Traditional ecclesiastical structures will require some reshaping if the cities are to be discipled and "churched." The house-church, which will probably be the organizational form in which Christianity most often appears in the Third World for the remainder of this century, does not easily fit the laws and structures of most denominations. For this reason the majority of the house-churches founded by the institute still lack official recognition as Presbyterian churches, and many of them would have trouble fitting into almost any definition of a church as traditionally conceived. This leads to misunderstanding, frustration, and stunted development.

House-churches, by their very nature, are highly flexible organizations. Some of them in a short time can develop into the kind of institutions which presbyteries and conferences readily acknowledge as churches. But for most of them this is a long process, and may never be realized. And, in the meantime, these groups hover

---

5. Peter Beyerhaus and Henry Lefever, *The Responsible Church and the Foreign Mission* (Grand Rapids: Eerdmans Publishing Co., 1965), pp. 56 ff. 1965), pp. 56 ff.
6. Bengt Sundkler, *The World of Mission* (Grand Rapids: Eerdmans Publishing Co., 1965), pp. 56 ff.

between the status of church and nonchurch, being local assemblies of Christians meeting regularly for worship, fellowship, and service, but lacking certain characteristics which denominationally defined churchhood requires.

For example, some house-churches lack male members with any leadership potential at all; while the women, young people, and children make up a vigorous, enthusiastic congregation. Husbands and fathers may be absent for a number of reasons. Oscar Lewis found, for example, that 46 percent of the marriages in the *vecindad* in Mexico City were of the common-law type;[7] and families of this sort are not known for their stability. What does one do, therefore, with a congregation composed mainly of unwed mothers and their numerous children, some of them already teen-agers, a sprinkling of men, none of whom lead the kind of lives that would justify appointing them as office-bearers, and perhaps a few old people, both men and women? Must such a group forever stay in the limbo between church and nonchurch?

Table 17 indicates that the financial resources of the Mexico City house-churches varied greatly. And as the church in the Colonia Ribera del Bosque demonstrated (Table 18), even the financial status of a group was not a true indicator of its strength or permanence. In this instance a house-church that had a sizeable amount of offering money in the bank shut down when the principal family moved away from the neighborhood.

In my opinion, the multiplication of house-churches in the city calls for a new type of metropolitan church organization of the kind which on the one hand will avoid the un-Biblical concept of a "chapel," and on the other hand will allow each congregation meeting for worship, witness, and service to be just as much a "church" as any other group, even if there are no office-bearers or substantial financial resources in that particular group.[8]

Under such an arrangement, resources, both human and material,

---

7. Lewis, *Five Families,* p. 27.
8. This idea of a new type of metropolitan church organization is drawn from Norman Shepherd, "What Church Does Dr. Van Til Belong To?" *Presbyterian Guardian,* May 1971, p. 71. The concept is similar to the Collegiate System of church organization and ministry followed by the Dutch Reformed Church in the cities of the Netherlands. I served under this system as a missionary-pastor of the Dutch Reformed Church in Ceylon, and I am fully aware of both its strengths and weaknesses. In Ceylon, as well as in the Netherlands, it is currently applied to churches whose strength would more than justify greater independence from one another. But in the urban house-church situation in Latin America, the system might serve a particular end.

would be shared. The metropolitan church would include a number of house-churches scattered about the city, each of them duly recognized local members of the body of Christ, but linked together because they need one another in special ways. One would speak, therefore, of the Church of Netzahualcoyotl, even though that church met for Sunday worship in a number of different homes scattered throughout the vast urban area. Its youth organization might serve many or all of the local house-churches, and its office-bearers drawn from Netzahualcoyotl as a whole. Ministers would be expected to serve a number of house-churches, and be supported, if at all, by the groups together.

Under this arrangement, the erection of permanent buildings in each location might be postponed indefinitely, though auditoriums placed in key centers undoubtedly would prove beneficial. Each particular house-church would be free to move in whatever direction it would choose, and mutual help might be given to those that had financial problems. But the main thing in any such arrangement is that the erection of buildings must not be allowed to slow down the proliferation of local assemblies of believers or their dignity as churches of Christ. Second-rate ecclesiastical status, like second-rate citizenship, stultifies initiative and reduces every kind of growth. Nothing as extraneous as a building should be allowed to affect a church's dignity or status. Nor should the members of a house-church be neglected ministerially simply because their resources and facilities are limited. The reality of house-churches on the growing edge of the evangelical movement in the cities must be recognized, and the necessary adjustments must be made in ecclesiastical structure so that this new (and probably permanent) form of organization does not remain forever in an ecclesiastical limbo, while its members suffer spiritually and psychologically from their nonchurch status.

4. *Apartment house evangelism.* The strategy of the institute in Mexico City scored approximately "zero" in the apartment houses; and since apartments and condominiums comprise an increasing proportion of home construction, the inability to reach apartment residents is a major concern. Between January 1968 and June 1970, institute students and missionaries conducted door-to-door visitation in five large apartment complexes: the mammoth multifamiliar "Miguel Aleman" was covered three times; the twenty-five three-story buildings of the Unidad "Presidente Kennedy" were visited for two months; a five-unit apartment house in the Colonia San Francisco was systematically visited (and an enclave of Jehovah's Witnesses was discovered living there). In the downtown

tenement, "Edificio Colonial," in the Colonia Transito, where 300 families are crowded into apartments designed to accommodate 103 families, services were held for six months with good attendance; but the work was forcefully terminated (see Table 18).

Only in the large and modern Villa Caopa, on the southeast edge of the city, was a congregation established; and that was through the "unorthodox" approach of Ciro Morales. A graduate of the Seminario Juan Calvino, he used his lay profession as a book salesman to gain entrance to the apartments; and after giving people his regular sales pitch, would tell them about the gospel. In the spring of 1970, Morales turned over the group he had organized to the Christian Reformed mission; and missionaries began visiting the area.

E. N. Poulson of the Singapore Bible College has written about the church-planting program which the faculty and students of his school have initiated among the 600,000 people whom the Singapore government has resettled—not always by their own choice—from their former slum dwellings and squatters' shacks to a series of clean and inexpensive apartments. Poulson describes the new flat-dwellers as multiracial, multilingual, multireligious, lonely, and highly "winnable." The established churches in Singapore would welcome the opportunity which the apartment houses offer if they were not "overcome by cultural inertia." Locked in their Western style edifices and financially unable to buy land and erect new buildings near each housing development area, the churches remain "content to draw a few inhabitants across town to the old sanctuaries."[9]

The Singapore Bible College, however, convinced that a church could be planted in each highrise building with its 1,200 occupants, launched a door-to-door evangelism program which bore fruit.

> *More than half a dozen such churches have emerged as a result of intensive door-to-door evangelism within each building.* In some instances services have been held in the flat of a believer. At least three worshipping groups are housed in a ground-floor shop. During the week the "church" is used as a kindergarten, the fees of which pay the rent. Other congregations have been helped in the initial stages, by an older sponsoring church or by a group of concerned individuals.[10]

---

9. E. N. Poulson, "Every Thirteen Story Building Is a Parish," *Church Growth Bulletin,* January 1970, pp. 45-46. All quotations from Poulson in this paragraph and information about the Singapore program are drawn from this article.

10. Ibid., p. 56; emphasis is Poulson's.

On the basis of his experience in the Singapore apartments, Poulson concluded that "with determination and faith an indigenous church can be planted in every building with minimum expense and maximum contact with the population."[11]

Here Poulson makes several important points, and particularly the last one—maximum contact with the population—is relevant to the problems in Mexico City. *Accessibility of the family* was the key to the Mexico City strategy of planting house-churches. The question "Who comes to the door?" became, through experience, the thumbnail rule for deciding whether a neighborhood offered likely prospects.

Because both upper-class and apartment people were largely inaccessible, the institute teams turned to the sprawling lower-class districts of the city, where there were no sidewalks, but instead an abundance of flies, open drains, dense population, and crude housing construction. In those homes, however, the men and women themselves answered the door. They were open to visitors' ideas and generally were responsive to the gospel.

Some types of apartment buildings, particularly those which house "family" people, probably offer as much opportunity as do the lower-class neighborhoods as far as responsiveness is concerned. The institute's experience in the tenement "Edificio Colonial" proved that. But where overcrowding is severe, the problem remains as to where to hold meetings. It is a relatively simple matter for shanty-dwellers to add an extra room or build a small chapel on the edge of their land. Even squatters are in a better position— at least until they are evicted—than the family on the fifth floor of an apartment building. In order to assemble a congregation, even a small one, space is required; and if all the individual apartments are crowded to capacity with beds, tables, and people, and the renting of a separate apartment for religious purposes is impossible,[12] then the only alternative seems to be to work with the families one by one in their private dwellings, assembling them for congregational worship in the closest place available outside the apartment complex.

Richard E. Moore and Duane L. Day suggest that the "unique challenge of high-rise living to the Church is one clear example of the inadequacy of pure congregationalism in the total ministry to metropolis." They suggest that "an effective strategy for high rise must be developed and executed on a broader basis than that

---

11. Ibid.
12. This is the problem in Mexico City, where the use of apartments for religious purposes is forbidden.

of the local church."[13] They recognize two important factors in appraising apartment house evangelism, the first being the fact that apartment houses represent a different *style* of life, and the second, that different types of apartments appeal to people in different *stages* of life. If the strategy of the missionary is basically "family" centered, as that of the institute was, then the type of apartments which appeal to unmarried people or to couples in the prechild and postchild periods of maturity and retirement is not fertile ground for evangelism.

It so happens that this type of apartment building is not as common in the Third World as it is in the United States; but nevertheless, apartment houses everywhere tend to attract the kind of people who do not want to be bothered either by callers or their neighbors. "Attempts to form apartment-house churches have not been statistically successful," write Moore and Day.

> Is this because the denominations have not really put their resources behind new Church developments designed exclusively for high-rise dwellers, or is it rather that the apartment dwellers are reluctant to involve themselves in the lives of neighbors with whom they share little beyond proximity?[14]

Perhaps Ciro Morales will find the answer in Mexico City when he takes up residence in the Villa Coapa. The important thing to keep in mind, as Moore and Day have pointed out, is not the kind of *building* but the sort of *people* who live in it: their needs and concerns.[15] Each apartment house, tenement, and condominium should be studied by itself; for it has its own character which the evangelist must come to know. And perhaps here was one of the weaknesses of the institute's approach: it was too swift, too barnstorming, for the subtle, sophisticated barricades around many Mexico City apartments.

5. *Advance with tensions.* Pastors and evangelists, says R. Calvin Guy, should be equipped like the Roman legions—lightly, so as to be able to make free and complete use of the essential equipment they carry. Too much equipment in the form of abstruse theological material slows down the rate of march. It is what Caesar called *impedimenta*.[16] Most teachers and administrators probably would agree with this, but immediately the question arises:

---

13. *Urban Church Breakthrough* (New York: Harper & Row, Publishers, 1966), p. 57.
14. Ibid., p. 58.
15. Ibid., p. 59.
16. "Theological Foundations," *Church Growth and Christian Mission*, p. 45.

which part is superfluous? Some say that Greek, and even Hebrew, are necessary parts of the evangelist's equipment. They point out that education in the cities is on a high level and the evangelist never knows whom he will meet in the course of his work. When I was director of the Mexican Christian Institute, English was obligatory for all upperclassmen. Few things are more symbolic of upper-class status than English; and I admit (shamefacedly) that often English was taught to students who hardly knew Spanish.

Tensions between what middle-class teachers think is necessary and what the masses really need, between what some regard as essential and others consider *impedimenta,* are unavoidable. At the institute, the faculty walked the tightrope between the traditional academic approach to Bible school training and a completely mission oriented program which put the welfare of the young churches above all other considerations. One teacher or administrator may lean to one side, and another person to the other side; but perfect balance will never be found. The tension remains.

The thing to be avoided, however, is the cultural dislocation of the students. The students themselves may want to make a cultural jump through education, and they may be disappointed in the school which consciously avoids allowing them to make it. I was often disturbed by a question asked by seminarians and Bible school students of Christian young people whom they hoped to enroll in one of the theological schools of the mission: *"¿No quiere estudiar?"* ("Don't you want to study?") That was not the right question. The particular calling of a seminarian is not simply to study and by that means improve himself socially and intellectually. Any school can do that for him, but seminaries and Bible schools are different. They intend to train Christians to minister more effectively in the church and in the world. *Don't you want to serve the Lord better? That* is the question which ought to be asked of prospective students. The other question— Don't you want to study?—serves simply to shed light on the cultural and religious tensions in the mind of the students who ask it. The theological school, for some, is the only means of escape from the monotony and futility of their lower-class status. It means going to the city and, hopefully, securing a job. The desire to serve the Lord is present in most cases, but the motives are confused. This tension between Christian vocation and middle-class status stays with them, sometimes for life.

Bible school education, like basic training in military service, is a "must" for all who can acquire it. Untrained leaders, just like guerrillas in the hills, may be effective in their field; but the

Lord's regular army needs classroom instruction, supervised drilling, and experienced leadership. What the school does to the student makes all the difference. Whether he goes on to become a pastor, teacher, evangelist, or lay leader in the local church, he will carry with him the imprint of the school in which he has been trained. If he has been trained in an atmosphere of perennial evangelism and has learned to see every apartment building, every slum, and every area of the city as a field for church-planting, and if he knows *how* to evangelize the receptive segments of the urban population, then the school which trained him will have fulfilled its purpose. It will have supplied the student with the necessary tools—theological, sociological, evangelistic—and it is up to him to use them.

And many *will* use them. The hunger shown by evangelical young people for the simple evangelistic methods of Campus Crusade and the continentwide interest in programs like Evangelism-in-Depth, plus a growing concern for social justice for all Latin Americans, indicate a deep spiritual awakening and the dawn of a new day. If revitalized churches whose leaders have been trained in church growth-oriented schools can be turned loose in the burgeoning cities, then a multiplication of churches will occur such as the world has not seen since the first century. And then the present pace of urbanization, with all its change and turmoil, will be viewed unhesitatingly as God's choicest gift to Christian missions. "Disciplining urban populations," says McGavran, "is perhaps the most urgent task confronting the Church. Bright hope gleams that now is precisely the time to learn how it may be done and to surge forward actually doing it."[17]

---

17. *Understanding Church Growth,* p. 295.

APPENDIX 1

SURVEY OF NEW CONVERTS TO THE
EVANGELICAL FAITH
QUESTIONNAIRE USED IN THE INTERVIEWS

1. Name ....

2. Denomination ....

3. Church Address ....
   ....
        Street   Colonia   City or Town

4. In which year did you accept Christ as your Saviour? ......

5. Were you converted (if 2 or 3 of these factors entered in
   your conversion, indicate which they were)
   By a sermon in a church? ....
   In an evangelistic campaign? ....
   By a tract? ....
   By reading the Bible? ....
   By the testimony of a family member? ....
   By the testimony of a friend? ....
   By the testimony of a pastor? ....
   By a radio program? ....
   By a Christian film? ....
   In another way? ....

6. Are other members of your family evangelicals? ....
   Who were the first, second, and third converted to the Gospel
   in your family?

237

Father	Brother	Husband ....
Mother	Sister	Wife ....
Grandfather ...	Aunt or Uncle	Son ....
Grandmother ..	Other	Daughter ....

7. Where were you converted?
   In a large church? ....
   In a small group? ....
   Alone by yourself? ....

8. Do you feel happier worshipping in a large church or in a small group such as a mission? ....

9. Were you a member of a sect before you were converted to the Gospel? ....
   Which was it: Jehovah's Witnesses? ....
   Mormons? ....
   Spiritists? ....

10. Tell some things that have been changed in your life since your conversion:

APPENDIX 2

SURVEY ON THE GROWTH OF
EVANGELICAL CHURCHES IN MEXICO
QUESTIONNAIRE USED IN THE INTERVIEWS

1. What is the name of your church? ....
2. What is the name of your pastor? ....
3. What is the name of the denomination? ....
4. What is the address of your church? ....
                    Colonia .... Postal Zone ......

HISTORY OF THE CHURCH

1. When was it founded? ....
2. When did the work begin here? ....
3. In which decade did the church grow most rapidly? ....
   To what is this attributed? ....
4. In which period did the church remain static in growth? ....
   .... How do you account for this? ....
   ....
5. How many members in full communion have been received
   into the church by means of conversion in the last five years?
   1964.... 1965.... 1966.... 1967.... 1968.... 1969....
6. How many years have you had a church building? ....
   How much is the building and the land worth? ....
   How much did the construction cost? ....
   How did you finance the construction? ....

7. In what way is the pastor supported? . . . .
   Which pastors work in something else? . . . .

8. How many members has the church lost to the sects? . . . .
   To which sects? . . . .

9. What has the church done to educate the members in the er-
   rors of the sects? . . . .

10. How many members in full communion were there in 1900?
    . . . . in 1910. . . . in 1920. . . . in 1930. . . . in 1940. . . .
    in 1950. . . . in 1960. . . . in 1970. . . .

11. How many members were received in the church during this
    last year? . . . . . . How many of them were converts from
    the world? . . . . . . How many by transfer? . . . . . .
    How many were children of Evangelicals? . . . .
    How many by transfer from other denominations? . . . .

THE ACTUAL MEMBERSHIP OF THE CHURCH

1. Attendance Average   How many are:

Children (1-14)	Unmarried (15-25)	Unmarried (25-45)	Unmarried (46-)
	Married (15-25)	Married (25-45)	Married (46-)

2. How many full members are there? . . . .

3. How many attend the services but are not members? . . . .
   What are their reasons for not becoming members? . . . .
   . . . .

4. In how many families are both the mother and the father
   converted? . . . .

5. In how many just the father? . . . .
   In how many just the mother? . . . .

6. How many members have been added through marriage with
   Catholics in the last five years? . . . .
   How many have been lost through marriage with Catholics?
   . . . .

7. In mixed marriages, is it easier to win the unconverted wife
   or the husband? . . . .

8. Analysis of the occupations of the members: . . . .

Unskilled laborer . . . .   Student . . . .
Housewife . . . .   Professional . . . .
Factory Worker . . . .   Office Worker . . . .
Construction Worker . . . . .   Government Employee . . . . .
Businessman . . . .   Teacher . . . .
Unemployed . . . .

9. Which are the most difficult problems of your church?
. . . .

10. Do you have problems in keeping the youth in the church?
If you have, explain them . . . .

11. Which societies of the church meet weekdays for:
Women . . . .   Men . . . .
Young people . . . .   Married couples . . . .

12. Do you have Christian doctrine classes for:
New converts? . . . .   Children and young people? . . . .

13. In your opinion, which aspect of the ministry of the church
should receive the most attention of the pastor (in order of
importance)?
. . . . . .   Preparation of sermons and preaching
. . . . . .   Visiting in the homes of members and sick
. . . . . .   Evangelistic work
. . . . . .   Social work

THE EVANGELISTIC PROGRAM OF THE CHURCH

1. How many missions does the church have?
In the Federal District? . . . .
Outside the Federal District? . . . .
Where are they located? . . . .
. . . .

2. When were they begun? . . . .
How were they begun? . . . .
In the city . . . .
In the village and rural areas . . . .

3. How many members has the church won from the sects?
From the Jehovah's Witnesses . . . . How? . . . .
From the Mormons . . . . How? . . . .
From the Spiritists . . . . How? . . . .
From the Seventh-day Adventists . . . . . . How? . . . .

4. Who are in charge of the missions? Laymen . . . .
Pastors . . . . Others . . . .

5. How many missions have become churches? . . . .
Where are they? . . . .
. When were they organized as churches? . . . .

6. What evangelistic projects does the church have? . . . .
. . . .

7. Which group in the church is the most active in evangelism?
. . . . . . the official leaders, elders, deacons, etc.
. . . . . . the young people
. . . . . . the women
. . . . . . the men

8. Do you consider the Sunday School effective in the conversion
of new members? . . . .

9. Do you allow persons not civilly married to be baptized in
the church? . . . .

10. In your experience, which is the best way to evangelize?
(in order of effectiveness)
. . . . House to house   . . . . Correspondence courses
. . . . Preaching campaigns   . . . . Testimony by a layman to
. . . . Bible distribution   his friends and
. . . . Radio programs   acquaintances
. . . . Tract distribution   . . . . Others

11. How many members have been won through listening to
Evangelical radio programs? . . . . Which program? . . . .

12. In your opinion, what is the task of the pastor in the evangelistic program of the church? . . . .

13. In your experience, are the foreign missions a help or an im-
pediment in the development of the church in Mexico today?
. . . . Why? . . . .

14. How can the missionaries improve their services to the church
in Mexico? . . . .

15. Does your denomination have foreign missionaries? . . . .
Where? . . . .

16. Do you have plans to send missionaries to other countries?
. . . . . Where? . . . .

17. What ought to be done so that the Evangelical movement will increase in our country? ....

Observations:
This survey was prepared by ....
By a personal interview with ....
By mail .... Date ....

BIBLIOGRAPHY

Books

Abell, Aaron Ignatius. *The Urban Impact on American Protestantism, 1865-1900.* Cambridge: Harvard University Press, 1943.

Abrecht, Paul. *The Churches and Rapid Social Change.* New York: Doubleday & Company, 1961.

Adams, Richard N.; Gillin, John P.; Holmberg, Allan R.; Lewis, Oscar; Patch, Richard W.; and Wagley, Charles. *Social Change in Latin America Today: Its Implications for United States Policy.* New York: Vintage Books, 1960.

Adams, Robert McC. *The Evolution of Urban Society: Early Mesopotamia and Prehistoric Mexico.* Chicago: Aldine Publishing Co., 1966.

Alexander, Robert Jackson. *Today's Latin America.* New York: Praeger, 1968.

Allen, Roland. *Educational Principles and Missionary Methods: The Application of Educational Principles to Missionary Evangelism.* Library of Historic Theology Series. Edited by William C. Piercy. London: Robert Scott Roxburghe House, 1919.

————. *Missionary Methods: St. Paul's or Ours?* 3rd ed. London: World Dominion Press, 1953.

————. *The Spontaneous Expansion of the Church; And the Causes Which Hinder It.* London: World Dominion Press, 1956.

————. *Missionary Principles.* London: World Dominion Press, 1964.

Alves, Ruben A. *Religion: ¿Opio o Instrumento de Liberación?* Montevideo: Tierra Nueva, 1968.

————. *A Theology of Human Hope.* New York: Corpus Books, 1971.

Anderson, Gerald H., ed. *The Theology of the Christian Mission.* New York: McGraw-Hill Book Co., 1961.

Anderson, Nels. *Sociología de la Comunidad Urbana; Una Perspectiva Mundial.* Mexico City: Fondo de Cultura Ecónomica, 1965.

245

————, ed. *Urbanism and Urbanization*. Vol. II of *International Studies in Sociology and Social Anthropology*. Edited by K. Ishwaran. Leiden: E. J. Brill, 1964.

Angell, James W. *Put Your Arms Around the City*. Old Tappan, N.J.: Fleming H. Revell Co., 1970.

Arango, Jorge. *The Urbanization of the Earth*. Boston: Beacon Press, 1970.

Arciniegas, Germán. *Latin America: A Cultural History*. Translated by Joan MacLean. New York: Knopf, 1967.

Bailey, Wilfred M., and McElvaney, William K. *Christ's Suburban Body*. Nashville: Abingdon Press, 1970.

Baird, William. *The Corinthian Church: A Biblical Approach to Urban Culture*. New York: Abingdon Press, 1964.

Barbieri, Sante Uberto. *Land of Eldorado*. New York: Friendship Press, 1961.

Bavinck, J. H. *The Impact of Christianity on the Non-Christian World*. Grand Rapids: Eerdmans Publishing Co., 1949.

————. *An Introduction to the Science of Missions*. Grand Rapids: Baker Book House, 1960.

Bazzanella, Waldemiro. *Problemas de Urbanizacao: fontes bibliográficas*. Rio de Janeiro: Centro Latinoamericano de Pesquisa en Ciencias sociais, 1960.

Beaver, R. Pierce. *The Christian World Mission: A Reconsideration*. Calcutta: Baptist Mission Press, 1958.

————. *The Missionary Between the Times*. Garden City, N.Y.: Doubleday & Co., 1968.

————, ed. *To Advance the Gospel: Selections from the Writings of Rufus Anderson*. Grand Rapids: Eerdmans Publishing Co., 1967.

Behrens, Helen. *America's Treasure: The Virgin Mary of Guadalupe*. 7th revised ed. Mexico, D.F.: Editorial Progreso, S.A., 1964.

Benítez Zenteno, Raul. *Analisis Demográfico de México*. Biblioteca de Ensayos Sociológicos. Mexico City: Instituto de Investigaciones Sociales de la Universidad Nacional Autónoma de México, 1961.

Berkouwer, Gerrit C. *Conflict with Rome*. Translated under supervision of David H. Freeman. Grand Rapids: Baker Book House, 1958.

Beyer, Glen H., ed. *The Urban Explosion in Latin America: A Continent in Process of Modernization*. Ithaca, N.Y.: Cornell University Press, 1967.

Beyerhaus, Peter, and Hallencreutz, Carl F., eds. *The Church Crossing Frontiers*. Essays on the nature of mission in honour of Bengt Sundkler. Vol. 11 of Studia Missionalia Upsaliensia. Uppsala, Sweden: Gleerup, 1969.

Beyerhaus, Peter, and Lefever, Henry. *The Responsible Church and the Foreign Mission*. Grand Rapids: Eerdmans Publishing Co., 1964.

Biddle, William W., and Biddle, Loureide J. *The Community Development Process: The Rediscovery of Local Initiative*. New York: Rinehart and Winston, 1965.

Bieder, Werner. *Das Mysterium Christi und Die Mission,* Elin Beitrag Zur Sakramentsgestalt Der Kirche. Zurch: Evangelische Verlag, 1964.

Blanco, Roberto Moheno. *Tlatelolco: Historia de una Infamia.* Mexico, D.F.: Editorial Diana, 1969.

Blauw, Johannes. *The Missionary Nature of the Church: A Survey of the Biblical Theology of Mission.* New York: McGraw-Hill Book Co., 1962.

Boer, Harry R. *Pentecost and Missions.* Grand Rapids: Eerdmans Publishing Co., 1961.

Bornkamm, Gunther. *Paul.* Translated by G. M. D. Stalker. New York: Harper & Row, Publishers, 1971.

Braun, Neil. *Laity Mobilized.* Grand Rapids: Eerdmans Publishing Co., 1971.

Braun, Neil, Boschman, Paul W.; and Yamada, Takashi. *Experiments in Church Growth: Japan.* Kobayashi City, Japan: Japan Church Growth Research Association, [1969].

Breese, Gerald. *The City in Newly Developing Countries: Readings on Urbanism and Urbanization.* Modernization of Traditional Societies Series. Englewood Cliffs, N.J.: Prentice-Hall, 1969.

Brookings Institution, Washington, D.C., Advanced Study Program. *The Premises of Urban Policy; Selected Readings in the Fundamentals of Urbanism.* A Multidisciplinary Seminar in the Study of Urbanization. Prepared by the Advanced Study Program, the Brookings Institution, Washington, D.C., in association with Texas Christian University (n.p., 1966-67).

Brunner, Emil. *The Misunderstanding of the Church.* Philadelphia: Westminster Press, 1953.

Campbell, Robert E., ed. *The Church in Mission.* Maryknoll, N.Y.: Maryknoll Publications, 1965.

Carter, Lawrence. *Can't You Hear Me Calling?* New York: Seabury Press, 1969.

Chang, Lit-sen. *Strategy of Missions in the Orient.* Philadelphia: Presbyterian and Reformed Publishing Co., 1970.

Chavero, Alfredo. *Los Azteca o Mexica. Fundación de Mexico Tenochtitlan.* Mexico, D.F.: Biblioteca Mínima Mexicana, 1955.

Clark, Dennis. *Cities in Crisis.* New York: Sheed & Ward, 1959.
————. *The Third World and Mission.* Waco, Tex.: Word, 1971.

Clark, S. D., ed. *Urbanism and the Changing Canadian Society.* Toronto: University of Toronto Press, 1961.

Coleman, Robert E. *The Master Plan of Evangelism.* Westwood, N.J.: Fleming H. Revell Co., 1963.

Coleman, William J. *Latin-American Catholicism: A Self-Evaluation.* Maryknoll, N.Y.: World Horizon Reports, Maryknoll Publications, 1958.

Comhaire, Jean, and Cahnman, Werner J. *How Cities Grew.* Madison, N.J.: Florham Park Press, 1959.

Conant, J. E. *Every-Member Evangelism*. New York: Harper & Row, Publishers, 1922.

Congreso Continental de Estudios. *La Naturaleza de la Iglesia y Su Misión en Latinoamérica*. 1-8 December 1963. Bogotá Colombia: Publicaciones del Comité de Cooperación Presbiteriana de América Latina, 1964.

Considine, John J., ed. *The Religious Dimension in the New Latin America*. Notre Dame, Ind.: Fides Publishers, 1966.

Consulta Latinoamericana de Iglesia y Sociedad. El Tabo, Chile, 1966. *Social Justice and the Latin Churches*. Translated by Jorge Lara-Braud. Richmond: John Knox Press, 1969.

Cook, Harold R. *Strategy of Missions: An Evangelical View*. Chicago: Moody Press, 1963.

————. *Historic Patterns of Church Growth: A Study of Five Churches*. Chicago: Moody Press, 1971.

Cook, Robert, and Mitchell, Gordon. *Urban America: Dilemma and Opportunity*. New York: Macmillan Co., 1965.

Cox, Harvey. *The Secular City: Secularization and Urbanization in Theological Perspective*. Rev. ed. Toronto, Ontario: Macmillan Co., 1966.

Cross, Robert D., ed. *The Church and the City, 1865-1910*. Indianapolis and New York: Bobbs-Merrill Company, 1967.

Cullmann, Oscar. *Message to Catholics and Protestants*. Translated by Joseph A. Burgess. Grand Rapids: Eerdmans Publishing Co., 1959.

Cully, Kendig Brubaker, and Harper, F. Nile. *Will the Church Lose in the City?* New York: World Publishing Co., 1969.

Damboriena, Prudencio. *El Protestantismo en América Latina*. Vol. II. *Estudios Socio-Religiosos Latino-Americanos*, Vol. 13. Madrid: Sucesores de Rivadeneyra, S.A., 1962.

Danker, William J. *Two Worlds or None*. St. Louis: Concordia Publishing House, 1964.

Danker, William J., and Kang, Wi Jo. *The Future of the Christian World Mission: Studies in Honor of R. Pierce Beaver*. Grand Rapids: Eerdmans Publishing Co., 1971.

D'Antonio, William V., and Pike, Frederick B., eds. *Religion, Revolution, and Reform: New Forces for Change in Latin America*. New York: Frederick A. Praeger, Publishers, 1964.

Davis, J. Merle. *How the Church Grows in Brazil*. A Study of the Economic and Social Basis of the Evangelical Church in Brazil. New York: Department of Social and Economic Research and Counsel, International Missionary Council, 1943.

De Acosta, Joseph. *Vida Religiosa y Civil de los Indios*. Historia Natural y Moral de las Indias. Biblioteca del Estudiante Universitario, 83. Mexico City: Universidad Nacional Autónoma de México, 1963.

DeKoster, Lester. *Communism and Christian Faith*. Grand Rapids: Eerdmans Publishing Co., 1956.

————. *Vocabulary of Communism*. Grand Rapids: Eerdmans Publishing Co., 1964.

D'Epinay, Christian Lalive. *Haven of the Masses: A Study of the Pentecostal Movement in Chile.* Translated by Marjorie Sandle. London: Lutterworth Press, 1969.

De Ridder, Richard Ralph. *The Dispersion of the People of God.* The Covenant Basis of Matthew 28:18-20 against the Background of Jewish, Pre-Christian Proselyting and Diaspora, and the Apostleship of Jesus Christ. Kampen, Netherlands: J. H. Kok Co., 1971.

Desintegración Familiar. 2nd ed. Mexico, D.F.: Obra Nacional de La Buena Prensa, A.C., 1967.

De Vries, Egbert. *El Hombre en los Rápidos Cambios Sociales.* Mexico, D.F.: Casa Unida de Publicaciones, 1962.

Díaz del Castillo, Bernal. *The Conquest of New Spain.* Translated by J. M. Cohen. Harmondsworth, England: Penguin Books, 1963.

Dietrich, Suzanne de. *The Witnessing Community: The Biblical Record of God's Purpose.* Philadelphia: Westminster Press, 1958.

Dimont, Max I. *Jews, God, and History.* New York: Signet Books, pub. by New American Library, 1962.

Documentos Pontificios. Decreto del Concilio Vaticano II. *Ad Gentes: Sobre la Actividad Misionera de la Iglesia.* Mexico, D.F.: Ediciones Paulinas, S.A., 1966.

Douglass, Harlan Paul. *How to Study the City Church.* Garden City, N.Y.: Doubleday, Doran, & Co., 1928.

Doxiadis, Constantinos A., and Douglass, Truman B. *The New World of Urban Man.* Philadelphia: United Church Press, 1965.

Dufty, N. F., ed. *The Sociology of the Blue-Collar Worker,* Vol. 9 of *International Studies in Sociology and Social Anthropology.* Leiden: E. J. Brill, 1969.

Duhl, Leonard P., ed. *The Urban Condition: People and Policy in the Metropolis.* New York: Basic Books, 1963.

Edwards, Fred E. *The Role of the Faith Mission: A Brazilian Case Study.* South Pasadena, Calif.: William Carey Library, 1971.

Eells, Richard, and Walton, Clarence, eds. *Man in the City of the Future; A Symposium of Urban Philosophers.* London: Macmillan & Co., 1968.

Elias, C. E., Jr.; Gillies, James; and Riemer, Svend. *Metropolis: Values in Conflict.* Belmont, Calif.: Wadsworth Publication Co., 1964.

Ellul, Jacques. *The Meaning of the City.* Grand Rapids: Eerdmans Publishing Co., 1970.

Ericksen, E. Gordon. *Urban Behavior.* New York: Macmillan Co., 1954.

Fava, Sylvia Fleis, ed. *Urbanism in World Perspective: A Reader.* New York: Thomas Y. Crowell Co., 1968.

Fife, Eric S., and Glasser, Arthur F. *Missions in Crisis: Rethinking Missionary Strategy.* Chicago: Inter-Varsity Press, 1961.

Finegan, Jack. *Light from the Ancient Past.* The Archeological Background of the Hebrew-Christian Religion. Princeton: At the University Press, 1946.

Fisher, R. M. *The Metropolis in Modern Life*. Garden City, N.Y.: Doubleday, 1955.

Forman, Charles W., ed. *Christianity in the Non-Western World*. Englewood Cliffs, N.J.: Prentice-Hall, 1967.

Freire, Paulo. *Pedagogy of the Oppressed*. [New York:] Herder and Herder, [1970].

Freyre, Gilberto. *The Mansions and the Shanties: The Making of Modern Brazil*. Translated by Harriet de Onis. New York: Alfred A. Knopf, Borzoi Book, 1966.

Gaddy, Welton. *Urban Crisis*. A Christian Life Commission Resource Paper. Nashville: Christian Life Commission of the Southern Baptist Convention, 1971.

Garcia Loya, Diego. *Mosaic of Mexican History*. Mexico City: Editorial Cultura, T.G., S.A., 1958.

Gaxiola, Manuel. *La Serpiente y la Paloma*. South Pasadena, Calif.: William Carey Library, 1970.

Gerassi, John, ed. *Revolutionary Priest: The Complete Writings and Messages of Camilo Torres*. New York: Random House, Vintage Books edition, 1971.

Geyer, Georgie Anne. *The New Latins: Fateful Change in South and Central America*. Garden City, N.Y.: Doubleday & Co., 1970.

Gibbs, Jack P., ed. *Urban Research Methods*. Princeton, N.J.: D. Van Nostrand, 1961.

Giese, Vincent J. *Revolution in the City*. Notre Dame, Ind.: Fides Publishers, 1961.

Glazer, Nathan, and Moynihan, Daniel Patrick. *Beyond the Melting Pot: The Negroes, Puerto Ricans, Jews, Italians, and Irish of New York City*. Cambridge, Mass.: M.I.T. Press and Harvard University Press, 1963.

González, Justo L. *The Development of Christianity in the Latin Caribbean*. Grand Rapids: Eerdmans Publishing Co., 1969.

Goodall, Norman. *The Local Church: Its Resources and Responsibilities*. London: Hodder and Stoughton, 1967.

Graham, W. Fred. *The Constructive Revolutionary: John Calvin and His Socio-Economic Impact*. Richmond: John Knox Press, 1971.

Grandenburg, Frank R. *The Making of Modern Mexico*. Englewood Cliffs, N.J.: Prentice-Hall, 1964.

Grassi, Joseph A. *A World to Win: The Missionary Methods of Paul the Apostle*. Maryknoll, N.Y.: Maryknoll Publications, 1965.

Green, Michael. *Evangelism in the Early Church*. Grand Rapids: Eerdmans Publishing Co., 1970.

Greer, Scott. *The Emerging City: Myth and Reality*. Glencoe, Ill.: Free Press, 1962.

Greer, Scott; McElrath, Dennis L.; Minar, David W.; and Orleans, Peter. *The New Urbanization*. New York: St. Martin's Press, 1968.

Gunther, John. *Inside South America*. New York: Pocket Books, 1968.

Guy, Robert Calvin. "Directed Conservation." *Church Growth and Chris-*

tian Mission. Edited by Donald Anderson McGavran. New York: Harper & Row, Publishers, 1965.

Hahn, Ferdinand. *Mission in the New Testament.* Studies in Biblical Theology, No. 47. Naperville, Ill.: Alec R. Allenson, 1965.

Hanke, Lewis. *Modern Latin America: Continent in Ferment.* 2nd rev. ed. Princeton: Van Nostrand, 1967.

————, ed. *History of Latin American Civilization: Sources and Interpretations.* 2 vols. Boston: Little, Brown, and Co., 1967.

Hatt, Paul K., and Reiss, Albert J., Jr., eds. *Cities and Society: The Revised Reader in Urban Sociology.* Glencoe, Ill.: Free Press, 1957.

Hauser, Philip M., ed. *Urbanization in Latin America.* Seminar on Urbanization Problems in Latin America, Santiago, Chile, 6-18 July 1959. New York: International Documents Service, Columbia University Press, for United Nations Educational, Scientific, and Cultural Organization, 1961.

Heath, Dwight B., and Adams, Richard N. *Contemporary Cultures and Societies of Latin America.* A Reader in the Sociological Anthropology of Middle and South America and the Caribbean. New York: Random House, 1965.

Herrick, Bruce H. *Urban Migration and Economic Development in Chile.* Cambridge: The M.I.T. Press, 1965.

Herring, Hubert. *A History of Latin America from the Beginnings to the Present.* New York: Alfred A. Knopf, 1962.

Hocking, Michael. *The Parish Seeks the Way: A Strategy for a Working-Class Parish.* London: Mowbray, 1960.

Hodges, Melvin L. *On the Mission Field: The Indigenous Church.* Chicago: Moody Press, 1953.

Hoekendijk, J. C. *The Church Inside Out.* Philadelphia: Westminster Press, 1964.

Horner, Norman A. *Cross and Crucifix in Mission.* A Comparison of Protestant-Roman Catholic Missionary Strategy. New York: Abingdon Press, 1965.

Houtart, Francois, and Pin, Emile. *The Church and the Latin American Revolution.* Translated by Gilbert Barth. New York: Sheed and Ward, 1965.

Howard, George P. *Religious Liberty in Latin America?* Philadelphia: Westminster Press, 1944.

Howes, Robert G. *Steeples in Metropolis.* Dayton: Pflaum Press, 1969.

International Missionary Council Meeting at Tambaram, Madras, 12-29 December 1938. *The Growing Church.* Vol. 2 of *The Tambaram Series.* London: Oxford University Press, 1939.

International Missionary Council Meeting at Tambaram, Madras, 12-29 December 1938. *Evangelism.* Vol. 3 of *The Tambaram Series.* London: Oxford University Press, 1939.

International Missionary Council Meeting at Tambaram, Madras, 12-29

December 1938. *The Life of the Church.* Vol. 4 of *The Tambaram Series.* London: Oxford University Press, 1939.

Isais, Juan M. *El Otro Lado de la Moneda.* San José, Costa Rica: Fraternidad de Servicio Cristiano, 1966. Distributed by Editorial Caribe; copyrighted by Eerdmans Publishnig Co.

————. *The Other Revolution.* Waco, Tex.: Word Books, 1970.

Iturriaga, Jose E. *La Estructura Social y Cultural de México.* No. II de Coleccion Estructura Económica y Social de México. Mexico-Buenos Aires: Fundo de Cultura Económica, 1951.

Janssen, Lawrence H. *These Cities Glorious.* New York: Friendship Press, 1963.

Jastrow, Morris, Jr. *The Civilization of Ancient Babylonia and Assyria.* Its Remains, Language, History, Religion, Commerce, Law, Art, and Literature. Philadelphia: J. P. Lippincott Co., 1915.

Jiménez, Wigberto Moreno; Miranda, José; and Fernández, María Teresa. *Historia de México.* Mexico City: Editorial Porrúa, S.A., 1963.

Johnson, Harvey L., and Weeks, Richard V. *Contemporary Latin America.* A Selection of Papers Presented at the Second Annual Conference on Latin America, 27-29 April 1967. Houston, Tex.: At the University, Office of International Affairs, 1968.

Judge, E. A. *The Social Pattern of Christian Groups in the First Century.* London: Tyndale Press, 1960.

Kahl, Joseph A., ed. *La Industrialización en América Latina.* Mexico City: Fondo de Cultura Económico, 1965.

Keen, Benjamin. *Readings in Latin-American Civilization, 1492 to the Present.* 2d ed. Boston: Houghton-Mifflin, 1967.

Kennedy, D. James. *Evangelism Explosion.* 4th ed. Wheaton, Ill.: Tyndale House Publishers, 1970.

Kenrick, Bruce. *Come Out the Wilderness.* The Story of East Harlem Protestant Parish. New York: Harper & Row, Publishers, 1962.

Kessler, J. B. A., Jr. *A Study of the Older Protestant Missions and Churches in Peru and Chile.* With Special Reference to the Problems of Division, Nationalism, and Native Ministry. Goes, Neth.: Oosterbaan and le Cointre N.V., 1967.

Koninklijk Instituut voor de Tropen. *The Indonesian Town:* Studies in Urban Sociology. The Hague, Neth.: W. Van Hoeve, 1958.

Kraemer, Hendrik. *A Theology of the Laity.* London: Lutterworth Press, 1958.

————. *World Cultures and World Religions: The Coming Dialogue.* London: Lutterworth Press, 1960.

Kromminga, Carl Gerhard. *The Communication of the Gospel Through Neighboring.* A Study of the Basis and Practice of Lay Witnessing Through Neighborly Relationships. Franeker, Neth.: T. Wever, 1964.

Kuiper, R. B. *God-Centered Evangelism.* A Presentation of the Scriptural Theology of Evangelism. Grand Rapids: Baker Book House, 1963.

La Ciudad. Acta Sociológica I. Facultad de Ciencias Políticas y Sociales, Centro de Estudios del Desarrollo, Universidad Nacional Autónoma de México, Mexico City, 1969.

Lambert, Jacques. *Latin America: Social Structure and Political Institutions.* Translated by Helen Katel. Berkeley: University of California Press, 1967.

Lamott, Willis Church. *Revolution in Missions.* From Foreign Missions to the World Mission of the Church. New York: Macmillan Co., 1958.

Larson, Bruce, and Osborne, Ralph. *The Emerging Church.* Waco, Tex.: Word Books, 1970.

Latourette, Kenneth Scott. *The Great Century in the Americas, Austral-Asia, and Africa.* Vol. 5 of *A History of the Expansion of Christianity.* New York: Harper & Brothers, Publishers, 1943.

————. *Advance Through Storm.* Vol. 7 of *A History of the Expansion of Christianity.* New York: Harper & Row, Publishers, 1945.

————. *Desafío a los Protestantes.* Buenos Aires: Editorial "La Aurora," 1957.

Law, Howard W. *Winning a Hearing.* An Introduction to Missionary Anthropology and Linguistics. Grand Rapids: Eerdmans Publishing Co., 1968.

Lebret, Louis-Joseph. *The Last Revolution.* The Destiny of Over-and-Underdeveloped Nations. New York: Sheed and Ward, 1965.

Lee, Robert. *Cities and Churches.* Readings on the Urban Church. Philadelphia: Westminster Press, 1962.

————. *The Church and the Exploding Metropolis.* Richmond: John Knox Press, 1967.

Lee, Rose Hum. *The City: Urbanism and Urbanization in Major World Regions.* Chicago: J. B. Lippincott Co., 1955.

Lenski, Gerhard. *The Religious Factor: A Sociological Study of Religion's Impact on Politics, Economics, and Family Life.* Garden City, N.Y.: Doubleday and Co., 1961.

Lewis, Oscar. *Five Families: Mexican Case Studies in the Culture of Poverty.* New York: Basic Books, 1959.

————. *Tepoztlan: Village in Mexico.* Case Studies in Cultural Anthropology. Edited by George Spindler and Louise Spindler. New York: Holt, Rinehart, and Winston, 1960.

————. *Children of Sanchez: Autobiography of a Mexican Family.* New York: Random House, 1961.

————. *La Vida.* London: Panther Books, 1968.

Lindsell, Harold. *An Evangelical Theology of Missions.* Grand Rapids: Zondervan Publishing House, 1970. Originally published as *A Christian Philosophy of Missions* by Van Kampen Press, 1949.

————, ed. *The Church's Worldwide Mission.* Proceedings of the Congress on the Church's Worldwide Mission, 9-16 April 1966, at Wheaton College. Waco, Tex.: Word Books, 1966.

Linz, Mandred. *Anwalt der Welt: Zur Theologie der Mission.* Stuttgart: Kreuz-Verlag, 1964.

Lipset, Seymour Martin, and Solari, Aldo, eds. *Elites in Latin America.* New York: Oxford University Press, 1967.

Little, Kenneth. *West African Urbanization.* A Study of Voluntary Associations in Social Change. London: Cambridge University Press, 1965.

Long, Luman H., ed. *The World Almanac and Book of Facts, 1971 Edition.* New York: Newspaper Enterprise Association, 1970.

Lopetegui, Leon. *Historia de la Iglesia en la América Española, desde el Descubrimiento hasta Comienzos del Siglo XIX.* Madrid: Editorial Católica, 1965-66.

Loprete, Carlos A., and McMahon, Dorothy. *Iberoamérica: Sintesis de su Civilización.* New York: Charles Scribner's Sons, 1965.

MacEoin, Gary. *Revolution Next Door: Latin America in the 1970s.* New York: Holt, Rinehart, and Winston, 1971.

McGavran, Donald A. *Bridges of God: A Study in the Strategy of Missions.* New York: World Dominion Press, 1955.

———. *The Bridges of God: A Study in the Strategy of Missions.* New York: Friendship Press, 1955.

———. *How Churches Grow: The New Frontiers of Mission.* London: World Dominion Press, 1959.

———. *Church Growth in Jamaica. A Preview of Things to Come in Many Lands.* Lucknow, India: Lucknow Publishing House, 1962.

———. *Understanding Church Growth.* Grand Rapids: Eerdmans Publishing Co., 1970.

McGavran, Donald A.; Huegel, John; and Taylor, Jack. *Church Growth in Mexico.* Grand Rapids: Eerdmans Publishing Co., 1963.

McGavran, Donald Anderson, ed.; Guy, Robert Calvin; Hodges, Melvin L.; and Nida, Eugene A. *Church Growth and Christian Mission.* New York: Harper & Row, Publishers, 1965.

Macin, Raul A. *Teología de la Vergüenza de Dios.* Monterrey: Editorial ISAL—Mexico, 1970.

Mackay, John A. *The Other Spanish Christ.* London: Student Christian Movement Press, 1932.

McKelvey, Blake. *The Urbanization of America.* New Brunswick, N.J.: Rutgers University Press, 1963.

McKenna, David, ed. *The Urban Crisis.* Grand Rapids: Zondervan Publishing House, 1969.

McNeil, Jesse Jai. *Mission in Metropolis.* Grand Rapids: Eerdmans Publishing Co., 1965.

MacQueen, James G. *Babylon.* New York: Frederick A. Praeger, Publishers, 1965.

Madsen, William. *The Virgin's Children: Life in an Aztec Village Today.* Austin: University of Texas Press, 1960.

Mander, John. *The Unrevolutionary Society: The Power of Latin American Conservatism in a Changing World.* New York: Alfred A. Knopf, 1969.

Mangin, William, ed. *Peasants in Cities: Readings in Urban Anthro-*

pology. Resources for the Study of Anthropology Series. Boston: Houghton-Mifflin Co., 1970.

Mardock, Marvin. *By All Means: Trends in World Evangelism Today.* Minneapolis: Bethany Fellowship, 1969.

Marty, Martin E. *The New Shape of American Religion.* New York: Harper & Brothers, Publishers, 1958.

————. *The Improper Opinion: Mass Media and the Christian Faith.* Philadelphia: Westminster Press, 1961.

————. *Second Chance for American Protestants.* New York: Harper & Row, Publishers, 1963.

————. *Babylon by Choice: New Environment for Mission.* New York: Friendship Press, 1965.

Meadows, Paul, and Mizruchi, Ephraim H., eds. *Urbanism, Urbanization, and Change: Comparative Perspectives.* Reading, Mass.: Addison-Wesley Publishing Co., 1969.

Michonneau, Abbe G. *Revolution in a City Parish.* Westminster, Md.: Newman Press, 1956.

Miller, Donald G. *The Nature and Mission of the Church.* Richmond: John Knox Press, 1957.

Milone, Pauline Dublin. *Urban Areas in Indonesia.* Administrative and Census Concepts. Berkeley: Institute of International Studies, University of California, 1966.

Miner, Horace. *The Primitive City of Timbuctoo.* Rev. ed. Garden City, N.Y.: Doubleday and Co., 1965.

Mook, Vianna. *Bandeirantes e Pioneiros: Paralelo entre Duas Culturas.* 4th ed. Rio de Janeiro: Editora Globo, 1957.

Moore, Paul, Jr. *The Church Reclaims the City.* New York: Seabury Press, 1964.

Moore, Richard E., and Day, Duane L. *Urban Church Breakthrough.* New York: Harper & Row, Publishers, 1966.

Moore, Robert Cecil. *Los Evangélicos en Marcha en América Latina.* El Paso, Tex.: Casa Bautista de Publicaciones, 1959.

Moynihan, Daniel Patrick, ed. *On Understanding Poverty: Perspectives from the Social Sciences.* Vol. 1 in the American Academy of Arts and Sciences Library. New York: Basic Books, Publishers, 1968.

————. *Toward a National Urban Policy.* New York: Basic Books, Publishers, 1970.

Mumford, Lewis. *The Culture of Cities.* New York: Harcourt, Brace, and Co., 1938.

————. *The City in History: Its Origins, Its Transformations, and Its Prospects.* A Harbinger Book. New York: Harcourt, Brace, & World, 1961.

————. *The Urban Prospect.* New York: Harcourt, Brace, & World, 1968.

Murray, Ralph L. *Christ and the City.* Nashville: Broadman Press, 1970.

Nederhood, Joel H. *The Church's Mission to the Educated American.* Grand Rapids: Eerdmans Publishing Co., 1960.

Neill, Stephen. *The Unfinished Task*. London: Edinburgh House Press, 1957.

Nevius, John L. *The Planting and Development of Missionary Churches*. 4th ed. Philadelphia: Reformed and Presbyterian Publishing Co., 1958.

Newbigin, Lesslie. *The Household of God*. Lectures on the Nature of the Church. New York: Friendship Press, 1953.

Nichol, John Thomas. *Pentecostalism*. New York: Harper & Row, Publishers, 1966.

Nida, Eugene A. *Message & Mission: The Communication of the Christian Faith*. New York: Harper & Row, Publishers, 1960.

————. "Dynamics of Church Growth." *Church Growth and Christian Missions*. Edited by Donald A. McGavran. New York: Harper & Row, Publishers, 1965.

————. *Religion Across Cultures*. A Study of the Communication of the Christian Faith. New York: Harper & Row, Publishers, 1968.

Niebuhr, H. Richard, and Williams, Daniel D., eds. *The Ministry in Historical Perspective*. New York: Harper & Row, Publishers, 1956.

Noyce, G. B. *The Church Is Not Expendable*. Philadelphia: Westminster Press, 1970.

O'Brien, Jose P. *"Lo Que No se Ha Dicho"* (Acerca de los Peregaminos del Mar Muerto). Monterrey: Ediciones ISAL-Mexico, n.d.

Oppenheimer, Martin. *The Urban Guerrilla*. Chicago: Quadrangle Books, 1969.

Othon, Miguel de; Otero, Mariano; Molina, Andres Enríquez; Whetten, Nathan L.; Plerm, Angel Vich; Stavenhagen, Rodolfo; and González, Pablo Casanova. *Ensayos sobre las Clases Sociales en México*. Mexico City: Editorial Nuestro Tiempo, S.A., 1968.

Packer, J. I. *Evangelism and the Sovereignty of God*. Chicago: Inter-Varsity Press, 1961.

Pahl, R. E. *Readings in Urban Sociology*. London: Pergamon Press, 1968.

Paradise, Scott. *Detroit Industrial Mission*. A Personal Narrative. New York: Harper & Row, Publishers, 1968.

Paton, David M., ed. *The Ministry of the Spirit: Selected Writings of Roland Allen*. With a Memoir by Alexander McLeish. Grand Rapids: Eerdmans Publishing Co., 1960.

Paz, Octavio. *The Labryrinth of Solitude: Life and Thought in Mexico*. Translated by Lysander Kemp. New York: Grove Press, 1961.

Percy, J. O., comp. *Facing the Unfinished Task*. *Messages Delivered at the Congress on World Mission*. Grand Rapids: Zondervan Publishing House, 1961.

Peters, George W. *Saturation Evangelism*. Grand Rapids: Zondervan Publishing House, 1970.

Pickett, J. Waskom. *The Dynamics of Church Growth*. New York: Abingdon Press, 1963.

Pickett, J. W.; Warnhuis, A. L.; Singh, G. H.; and McGavran, D. A.

Church Growth and Group Conversion. Lucknow, India: Lucknow Publishing House, 1962.

Picon-Salas, Mariano. *A Cultural History of Spanish America: From Conquest to Independence.* Translated by Irving A. Leonard. Berkeley: University of California Press, 1963.

Piddington, Ralph, ed. *Kinship and Geographical Mobility.* Vol. 3 of *International Studies in Sociology and Social Anthropology.* Edited by K. Ishwaran. Leiden: E. J. Brill, 1965.

Piet, John H. *The Road Ahead: A Theology for the Church in Mission.* Grand Rapids: Eerdmans Publishing Co., 1970.

Pike, Fredrick B. *The Conflict Between Church and State in Latin America.* New York: Alfred A. Knopf, 1964.

Poulat, Emile. *Naissance des Prêtres Ouvriers.* Paris: Casterman, 1965.

Rainwater, Lee, and Yancey, William L. *The Moynihan Report and the Politics of Controversy.* A Trans-action Social Science and Public Policy Report. Including the full text of *The Negro Family: The Case for National Action,* by Daniel Patrick Moynihan. Cambridge: The M.I.T. Press, 1967.

Ramsay, Wm. M. *The Cities of St. Paul: Their Influence on His Life and Thought.* Reprinted from the 1907 edition by Hodder and Stoughton, London. Grand Rapids: Baker Book House, 1960.

Read, William R. *New Patterns of Church Growth in Brazil.* Grand Rapids: Eerdmans Publishing Co., 1965.

Read, William R.; Monterroso, Victor M.; and Johnson, Harmon A. *Latin American Church Growth.* Grand Rapids: Eerdmans Publishing Co., 1969.

Reformed Ecumenical Synod Baarn Missions Conference, 1968. Conference Papers. *The Christian Message to a Changing World.* Published in *International Reformed Bulletin,* October 1968.

Reindorp, Reginald Carl. *Spanish American Customs, Culture, and Personality.* Macon, Ga.: Department of Foreign Languages, Wesleyan College, 1968.

Report of a Survey of Theological Education in the Evangelical Churches Undertaken February-May 1961, on Behalf of the International Missionary Council. The Christian Ministry in Latin America and the Caribbean. B. Foster Stockwell, chairman. Geneva: Commission on World Mission and Evangelism, World Council of Churches, 1962.

Ricard, Robert. *La Conquista Espiritual de México.* Mexico City: Editorial Jus. Editorial Polis, 1947.

Richards, Lawrence O. *A New Face for the Church.* Grand Rapids: Zondervan Publishing House, 1970.

Richardson, William J., ed. *The Modern Mission Apostolate: A Symposium.* Maryknoll, N.Y.: Maryknoll Publishers, 1965.

————. *Revolution in Missionary Thinking: A Symposium.* Maryknoll, N.Y.: Maryknoll Publishers, 1966.

Riesman, David; Glazer, Nathan; and Denney, Reuel. *The Lonely Crowd.* Abr. ed. New Haven: Yale University Press, 1961.

Rippy, James Fred. *Latin America: A Modern History.* Rev. ed. Ann Arbor: University of Michigan Press, 1968.

Rivera, Pedro R. *Protestantismo Mexicano: Su Desarrollo y Estado Actual.* 3d ed. Mexico City: Editorial Jus, 1961.

Roberts, C. Paul. *Statistical Abstract of Latin America, 1968.* 12th ed. Los Angeles: Latin American Center, University of California, 1969.

Roberts, W. Dayton. *Revolution in Evangelism: The Story of Evangelism in Depth in Latin America.* Chicago: Moody Press, 1967.

Robertson, A. T. *Types of Preachers in the New Testament.* New York: George H. Doran Co., 1922.

Roels, Edwin Dale. *God's Mission.* The Epistle to the Ephesians in Mission Perspective. Grand Rapids: Eerdmans Publishing Co., 1962.

Rubble, Kenneth, and Hamour, Mukhtar. *Statistical Abstract of Latin America, 1969.* Los Angeles: Latin American Center, University of California, 1970.

Rubingh, Eugene. *Sons of Tiv.* A Study of the Rise of the Church Among the Tiv of Central Nigeria. Grand Rapids: Baker Book House, 1969.

Rycroft, W. Stanley. *Religion and Faith in Latin America.* Philadelphia: Westminster Press, 1958.

Rycroft, W. Stanley, and Clemmer, Myrtle M. *A Study of Urbanization in Latin America.* Rev. ed. New York: Commission on Ecumenical Mission and Relations, The United Presbyterian Church in the U.S.A., 1963.

St. Clair, David, trans. *Child of the Dark: The Diary of Carolina María de Jesús.* New York: E. P. Dutton & Co., 1962.

Salem, Luis D. *Francisco G. Penzotti: Apostel de la Libertad y de la Verdad.* Mexico City: Sociedades Bíblicas en América Latina, 1963.

Santos, Ángel Hernández. *Misionología: Problemas Introductorios y Ciencias Auxiliares.* Santander, Spain: Editorial "Sal Terrae," 1961.

Scanlon, A. Clark. *Church Growth Through Theological Education (in Guatemala)* Guatemala City: Impreso El Faro, 1962.

Schaller, Lyle E. *Planning for Protestantism in Urban America.* Nashville: Abingdon Press, [1965].

Scharpff, Paulus. *History of Evangelism.* Grand Rapids: Eerdmans Publishing Co., 1964.

Scherer, James A. *Missionary, Go Home!* A Reappraisal of the Christian World Mission. Englewood Cliffs, N.J.: Prentice-Hall, 1964.

Schlesinger, Arthur Meier. *The Rise of the City, 1878-1898.* Vol. 10 of *A History of American Life.* Edited by Arthur M. Schlesinger and Dixon R. Fox. 12 vols. New York: Macmillan Co., 1933.

Schuller, David S. *The New Urban Society.* The Christian *Encounter Series.* St. Louis: Concordia Publishing House, 1966.

Scopes, Wilfred, ed. *The Christian Ministry in Latin America and the Caribbean.* New York: Commission on World Mission and Evangelism, World Council of Churches, 1962.

Seamands, John T. *The Supreme Task of the Church*. Sermons on the Mission of the Church. Grand Rapids: Eerdmans Publishing Co., 1964.

Seminar on Urbanization Problems in Latin America, Santiago de Chile, 1959. *Urbanization in Latin America: Proceedings*. Edited by Philip M. Hauser. Technology and Society Series. New York: International Documents Service, c. 1961.

Sennett, Richard, ed. *Classic Essays on the Culture of Cities*. New York: Appleton-Century-Crofts, 1969.

Se Vive Como Se Puede. Montevideo: Tierra Nueva, 1970.

Sjoberg, Gideon. *The Preindustrial City: Past and Present*. New York: Free Press, 1960.

Soltau, T. Stanley. *Missions at the Crossroads: The Indigenous Church—A Solution for the Unfinished Task*. Grand Rapids: Baker Book House, 1955.

Sosa, Adam F. "Latin America." *World Christian Handbook*, 1962 ed. Edited by H. Wakelin Coxill and Kenneth Grubb. London: World Dominion Press, 1962.

Stagg, Paul L. *The Converted Church: From Escape to Engagement*. Valley Forge, Pa.: Judson Press, 1967.

Stott, John R. W. *One People*. Downers Grove, Ill.: Inter-Varsity Press, 1968.

Sundkler, Bengt. *The World of Mission*. Grand Rapids: Eerdmans Publishing Co., 1965.

Symanowski, Horst. *The Christian Witness in an Industrial Society*. Philadelphia: Westminster Press, 1964.

Syrdal, Rolf A. *To the End of the Earth: Mission Concept in Principle and Practice*. Minneapolis: Augsburg House, 1967.

Tannenbaum, Frank. *Ten Keys to Latin America*. Vintage Book. New York: Random House, 1960.

Taylor, Clyde W., and Coggins, Wade T., eds. *Protestant Missions in Latin America: A Statistical Survey*. Washington, D.C.: Evangelical Foreign Missions Association, 1961.

Taylor, Jack E. *God's Messengers to Mexico's Masses*. Eugene, Ore.: Institute of Church Growth, 1962.

Taylor, Lee, and Jones, Arthur R., Jr. *Rural Life and Urbanized Society*. New York: Oxford University Press, 1964.

Tenney, Merrill C. *New Testament Survey*. Grand Rapids: Eerdmans Publishing Co., 1961.

Teran, Fernando de. *Ciudad y Urbanización en el Mundo Actual*. Madrid: Editorial Blume, 1969.

Tippett, Allen R. *Church Growth and the Word of God: The Biblical Basis of the Church Growth Viewpoint*. Grand Rapids: Eerdmans Publishing Co., 1970.

Torney, George A. *Toward a Creative Urban Strategy*. Waco, Tex.: Word Books, 1970.

Toynbee, Arnold. *Cities on the Move.* New York: Oxford University Press, 1970.

Tuggy, Arthur L. *The Philippine Church: Growth in a Changing Society.* Grand Rapids: Eerdmans Publishing Co., 1970.

United Nations. Department of Economic and Social Affairs. *Urbanization: Development Policies and Planning.* International Social Development Review, No. 1. New York, 1968.

United Nations. Economic and Social Council. *Population Trends and Policy Alternatives in Latin America.* (E/CN.12/874), 8 Feb. 1971.

United Nations. Economic and Social Council. *Preliminary Study of the Demographic Situation in Latin America.* (E/CN.12/604), 23 April 1961.

Van Leeuwen, Arend Theodoor. *Christianity in World History.* New York: Charles Scribner's Sons, 1964.

Vasconcelos, José. *Breve Historia de México.* 5th ed. Mexico, D.F.: Ediciones Botas, 1944.

Vergara, Ignacio. *El Protestantismo en Chile.* Santiago, Chile: Editorial del Pacifico, S.A., 1962.

Verkuyl, J. *De Taak der Missiologie en der Missionaire Methodiek in Het Tijdperk Van Saecularisatie en Saecularisme.* Kampen, Neth.: J. H. Kok, 1965.

Verney, Stephen. *People and Cities.* Westwood, N.J.: Fleming H. Revell Co., 1969.

Vicedom, Georg F. *The Mission of God: An Introduction to a Theology of Mission.* Translated by Gilbert A. Thiele and Dennis Hilgendorf. St. Louis: Concordia Publishing House, 1965.

Villagrana, Bernardo Castro; Labastida, Horacio; Garcia, J. Jesus; Rondero, Javier; Flores, Victor Olea; Lenkersdorf, Karl; Lage, Francisco Pessoa; Condal, Elias; Allaz, Tomas G.; and Mendez, Sergio Arceo. *La Iglesia, el Subdesarrollo y la Revolucion.* Mexico City: Editorial Nuestro Tiempo, 1968.

Visser 't Hooft, W. A. *No Other Name.* The Choice Between Syncretism and Christian Universalism. Philadelphia: Westminster Press, 1963.

Vitalis, Hellmut Gnadt. *The Significance of Change in Latin American Catholicism Since Chimbote 1953.* Cuernavaca, Mexico: Centro Intercultural de Documentacion, 1969.

Vos, Gerhardus. *The Kingdom and the Church.* Grand Rapids: Eerdmans Publishing Co., 1958.

Wagner, Pedro. *Teología Latinoamericana: ¿Izquierdista o evangélica?* La Lucha por la Fe en una Iglesia Creciente. Miami, Fla.: Editorial Vida, 1969.

Warren, Max. *The Christian Imperative.* New York: Charles Scribner's Sons, 1955.

Webber, George W. *God's Colony in Man's World*. New York: Abingdon Press, 1960.

——. *The Congregation in Mission*. Emerging Structures for the Church in an Urban Society. New York: Abingdon Press, 1964.

Weber, Max. *The City*. Translated and edited by Don Martindale and Gertrud Neuwirth. Glencoe, Ill.: Free Press, 1958.

——. *The Protestant Ethic and the Spirit of Capitalism*. New York: Scribner's, 1958.

——. *The Sociology of Religion*. Boston: Beacon Press, 1963.

West, Charles C. *Communism and the Theologians: Study of an Encounter*. Philadelphia: Westminster Press, 1958.

West, Charles C., and Paton, David M., eds. *The Missionary Church in East and West*. London: SCM Press, 1959.

Whiteford, Andrew H. *Two Cities of Latin America*. Anchor Book. Garden City, N.Y.: Doubleday & Co., 1964.

Wickham, E. R. *Church and People in an Industrial City*. London: Lutterworth Press, 1957.

——. *Encounter with Modern Society*. New York: Seabury Press, 1964.

Willems, Emilio. *Followers of the New Faith: Culture Change and the Rise of Protestantism in Brazil and Chile*. Nashville: Vanderbilt University Press, 1967.

Willey, Gordon R., ed. *Prehistoric Settlement Patterns in the New World*. Viking Fund Publications in Anthropology, No. 23. New York: Wenner-Gren Foundation for Anthropological Research, 1955.

Windass, Stanley. *Chronicle of Worker Priests*. London: Merlin Press, 1967.

Winter, Gibson. *The New Creation as Metropolis*. New York: Macmillan Co., 1963.

Winter, Ralph D. *Theological Education by Extension*. South Pasadena, Calif.: William Carey Library, 1969.

Wirt, Sherwood Eliot. *The Social Conscience of the Evangelical*. New York: Harper & Row, Publishers, 1968.

Wonderly, William L., and Lara-Braud, Jorge. *¿Los Evangélicos Somos Asi?* Mexico City: Casa Unida de Publicaciones, S.A., 1964.

Wood, Robert. *Missionary Crisis and Challenge in Latin America*. St. Louis: B. Herder Book Co., 1964.

Worcester, Donald E., and Schaeffer, Wendell G. *The Growth and Culture of Latin America*. New York: Oxford University Press, 1956.

Yamada, Takashi. *Studies in Extension Evangelism*. Translated by P. W. Boschman. Church Growth Pamphlet Series, No. 3. Kobayashi City, Miyazaki, Japan: Kobayashi Kyodaisha, 1970. (English translation mimeographed.)

Zamora, Nestor Paz. *Cartas de un Guerrillero* (a Dios y a su Esposa). Monterrey: Ediciones ISAL-Mexico, [1971].

Articles

Adams, Robert McC. "Urban Revolution: Introduction." *International Encyclopedia of the Social Sciences.* Vol. 16. Edited by David L. Sills. New York: Macmillan Co. and Free Press, 1968.

Alsop, Stewart. "The Cities Are Finished." *Newsweek,* 5 April 1971, p. 100.

Armillas, Pedro. "The Concept of Civilization." *International Encyclopedia of the Social Sciences.* Vol. 16. Edited by David L. Sills. New York: Macmillan Co. and Free Press, 1968.

Armstrong, James. " 'The People Are Doing . . . Badly' in Brazil." *Christian Century,* 6 January 1971, pp. 14-16.

Babbage, Stuart Barton. "Is There a Crisis in Preaching?" *Church Herald,* 17 May 1968, pp. 5-7.

Báez-Camargo, G. "Protestantism in Latin America: Mexico." *Religion in Life* 27 (Winter 1957-58): 35-44.

————. "The Missionary Task of the Church in Mexico and Central America." *International Review of Missions* 36 (April 1947): 163-74.

Bishop, Jordan. "Numerical Growth—An Adequate Criterion of Mission?" *International Review of Missions* 57 (July 1968): 284-90.

Boer, Harry R. "Some Suggestions for a Theology of African Rural Development." *Reformed Journal,* April 1966, pp. 6-8.

Boonstra, Juan S. "Impressions After Nine Years." *The Banner,* 23 October 1970, pp. 14-15.

————. "Latin America—What's Happening." *The Banner,* 6 March 1970, pp. 10-12.

————. "Protestant Cathedrals." *Missionary Monthly,* October 1970, pp. 270-72.

————. "Statistics . . . Statistics . . . and Some Questions." *Missionary Monthly,* January 1970, pp. 13-14.

Borda, Orlando Fals. "Una Estrategia para la Iglesia en la Transformación de América Latina." *Cristianismo y Sociedad,* II, No. 3 (1964): 31-39.

Bridges, Julian C. "Census Data and Estimating Church Growth." *Church Growth Bulletin,* May 1971, pp. 143-44.

Browning, Harley L. "Recent Trends in Latin American Urbanization." *Annals of the American Academy of Political and Social Science,* 316 (March 1958): 111-20.

Budd, Jim. "Mexican Scene: Changing Tactics." *The News,* Mexico City, 22 December 1969.

Butterworth, Douglas S. "A Study of the Urbanization Process Among Mixtec Migrants from Tilaltongo in Mexico City." *America Indigena* 22 (July 1962): 257-74.

Bystrom, Kenneth N. "God's Word for Latin America: An Imaginative Approach." *Latin America Evangelist,* January-February 1967, pp. 8-10.

Castro, Emilio. "Christian Response to the Latin American Revolution." *Christianity and Crisis,* 16 September 1963, pp. 160-63.

————. "Evangelism in Latin America." *International Review of Missions* 53 (October 1964): 452-56.

Chandler, Douglas R. "John Wesley and His Preachers." *Religion in Life* 24 (Spring 1955): 241-48.

Chartier, R. A.; Nilius, L.; and Sabanes, C. M. "Missionary Structures and Training for Mission." *International Review of Missions* 57 (April 1968): 217-25.

Clark, Dennis. "The University and the City." *America,* 5 March 1966, pp. 324-26.

————. "A Virile Freedom in the Younger Churches." *World Vision Magazine,* April 1970, pp. 12-15.

Cleal, C. H. "The Work of Industrial Chaplains." *World Dominion* 33 (March-April 1955): 110-14.

Clowney, Edmund P. "The Theology of Evangelism." *Christianity Today,* 29 April 1966, pp. 5-8.

Coppens, Betty. "Social Work in Urban Areas, with Special Reference to Family Life." *International Review of Missions* 41 (October 1952): 464-70.

Couch, Ricardo. "La Responsabilidad del Cristiano y de la Iglesia." *Iglesia y Sociedad en América Latina,* January 1960, pp. 1-9.

Cox, Harvey. "Mission in a World of Cities." *International Review of Missions* 55 (July 1966): 273-81.

Dale, John T. "Evangelismo Práctico en el Campo Rural." *Promotor de Evangelización,* December 1965, pp. 1-2.

————. "The Home as an Evangelizing Agent." *Practical Anthropology* 13 (May-June 1966): 122-28.

Davies, J. G. "Church Growth: A Critique." *International Review of Missions* 57 (July 1968): 291-97.

Davis, Donald R. "Baptist Principles of Action for Work in the Inner City." *Reformed Journal,* December 1968, pp. 15-16.

Davis, Kingsley. "Recent Population Trends in the New World." *Annals of the American Academy of Political and Social Science* 316 (March 1958): 1-10.

Dayton, Edward R., and Klebe, John. "Newest Tool for Missions." *World Vision Magazine,* October 1966, pp. 10-11.

De Alvarez, Leo Paul. "Imperialism: The Threat to Existence." *Intercollegiate Review* 2 (March-April 1966): 311-22.

Denton, Charles F. "Latin America in Transition: Social Implications for the Missionary." *World Vision Magazine,* March 1970, pp. 11-12.

————. "Protestantism and the Latin American Middle Class." *Practical Anthropology* 18 (January-February 1971): 24-28.

D'Epinay, Christian Lalive. "Training of Pastors and Theological Education: The Case of Chile." *International Review of Missions* 56 (April 1967): 185-92.

Division of Overseas Ministries, National Council of Churches. "An

Analysis of the Context of World Mission Today." *Occasional Bulletin,* Missionary Research Library, September 1966, pp. 1-9.

Drummond, L. "What Is the Goal of Industrial Mission?" *Baptist Quarterly* 23 (July 1969): 104-10.

Dykstra, D. Ivan. "Evangelical Christianity and Social Concern." *Religion in Life* 24 (Spring 1955): 269-77.

Editorial. "Humanism and the Churches." *Christianity Today,* 10 April 1970, pp. 32-33.

Editorial. *Church Herald,* 14 February 1969, pp. 6-7.

Editorial. "The Urgency of Evangelism." *Christianity Today,* 15 January 1965, pp. 26-27.

Epps, Dwain C. "Una Nueva Forma de Ministerio Cristiano; Algunas Reflexiones sobre la Misión Urbana de la Iglesia." *Cristianismo y Sociedad* 8, No. 2 (1970): 5-22.

Escobar, Samuel. "A Look Ahead." *World Vision Magazine,* May 1971, pp. 11-13.

———. "The Social Responsibility of the Church in Latin America." *Evangelical Missions Quarterly* 6 (Spring 1970): 129-51.

Estep, W. R., Jr. "Church and Culture in Latin America." *Southwestern Journal of Theology* 4 (April 1962): 24-47.

Fager, Charles. "Experimenting with a Simpler Life Style: An Interview with Harvey Cox." *Christian Century,* 6 January 1971, pp. 9-13.

Farrell, Frank E. "Mission Trends in the 70's: Today and Tomorrow." *World Vision Magazine,* April 1970, pp. 34-38.

Fish, John H. "A New Role for the Church in the Urban Ghetto." *Lutheran Quarterly* 19 (October-December 1967): 385-96.

Fitzpatrick, Joseph P. "What Is He Getting At?" *America,* 25 March 1967, pp. 444-49.

Flatt, Donald C. "In Search of God's Bride for Mission: A Critique of the Church Growth Philosophy." *World Vision Magazine,* January 1970, pp. 18-20.

Ford, Leighton. "Evangelism in a Day of Revolution." *Christianity Today,* 24 October 1969, pp. 6-12.

Gerber, Vergil. "How Churches Grow." *World Vision Magazine,* May 1971, pp. 17-19.

Glasser, Arthur F. "Theology of Mission in the 70's: From Western Religion to Universal Faith." *World Vision Magazine,* April 1970, pp. 22-27.

———. "Theology: With or Without the Bible." *Church Growth Bulletin,* January 1971, pp. 111-14.

"Globe at a Glance." *World Vision Magazine,* May 1971, p. 20.

Goff, James E. "Latin American Church Growth." *The News,* Mexico City, Sunday Supplement, *Vistas,* 1 March 1970.

Goshko, John. "Uruguay's Tupamaros Turning Terroristic." *The News,* Mexico City, 17 December 1969.

Gouzee, C. "Counterpoint." *International Review of Missions* 57 (July 1968): 318-25.

Greenway, Roger S. "A Church-planting Method That Works in Urban Areas." *Evangelical Missions Quarterly* 6 (Spring 1970): 152-57.

————. "Ecology and Missions." *Missionary Monthly*, January 1971, pp. 26-27.

————. "Folk-Catholicism vs. Historic Christianity in Mexico." *The Banner*, 13 March 1970, pp. 4-6.

————. "Foreign Missions and Diaconal Aid." *International Reformed Bulletin*, Winter 1970, pp. 15-21.

————. "A House Divided." *The Banner*, 6 February 1970, pp. 4-6.

————. "Training Urban Church Planters in Latin America." *Church Growth Bulletin*, January 1970, pp. 38-43.

Gutiérrez, Gustavo Merino. "Apuntes para una Teología de la Liberación." *Cristianismo y Sociedad* 8, Nos. 3 and 4 (1970): 6-22.

Guy, Robert Calvin. "A Strategy for World Mission." *Southwestern Journal of Theology* 4 (April 1962): 9-26.

Hard, Theodore. "The Religious Aspects of Myth." *Reformed Bulletin of Missions*, July 1966, pp. 1-14.

Haroutunian, Joseph. "Missions and the New Hope." *Occasional Bulletin* from the Missionary Research Library, August 1963, pp. 1-8.

Harrod, Howard L. "Formation of Ministers for Urban Society." *Encounter* 29 (Autumn 1968): 348-54.

Hayward, Victor E. W. "Call to Witness—But What Kind of Witness?" *International Review of Missions* 53 (April 1964): 209-18.

Hazelton, John S. "La Comunicación del Evangelio en el Ambiente Urbano." *Noticiero*, No. 12, n.d.

Heise, David R. "Prefatory Findings in the Sociology of Missions." *Journal for the Scientific Study of Religion* 6 (Spring 1967): 49-58.

Henry, Carl F. "Strategy for World Evangelism: Are We Too Late?" *World Vision Magazine*, February 1970, pp. 6-8.

Hess, Margaret Johnston. "Weekday Bible Classes: A Way to Reach Women." *Christianity Today*, 25 November 1966, pp. 14-16.

Highbaugh, Irma. "The Family Life Programme Evangelizes." *International Review of Missions* 40 (October 1951): 426-34.

Hodges, Melvin L. "A Pentecostal's View of Mission Strategy." *International Review of Missions* 57 (July 1968): 304-10.

————. "Surmounting Seven Obstacles to Church Growth." *Church Growth Bulletin*, January 1970, pp. 43-45.

Hoekendijk, J. C. "The Call to Evangelism." *Occasional Papers*, Department of Missionary Studies, World Council of Churches, Series II, No. 7 (July 1963): 1-12.

Hopewell, J. F. "Training a Tent-Making Ministry in Latin America." *International Review of Missions* 55 (July 1966): 332-39.

Howard, Thomas. "Sodom and the City of God." *Christianity Today*, 31 January 1969, pp. 384-86.

Hubbard, David Allan. "The Church: God's Risk, Our Pledge." *World Vision Magazine,* September 1969, p. 7.

Hyslop, Ralph D. "Missions and the Missionary: A Study by the Ecumenical Fellows of the Program of Advanced Religious Studies, Union Theological Seminary, New York." *International Review of Missions* 53 (October 1964) : 459-66.

Illich, Ivan. "The Seamy Side of Charity." *America,* 21 January 1967, pp. 88-91.

Jackson, Herbert C. "The Missionary Obligation of Theology." *Occasional Bulletin* from the Missionary Research Library, January 1964, pp. 1-6.

James, Gilbert. "Reaching the 'Lonely Crowd.' " *Christianity Today,* 18 February 1966, pp. 12-13.

John, Matthew P. "Evangelism and the Growth of the Church." *International Review of Missions* 57 (July 1968) : 278-83.

Jones, Henry D. "Christian Approaches to Labour in Latin America." *International Review of Missions* 40 (October 1951): 435-43.

Jones, Henry P. "Urban and Industrial Missions." *Occasional Bulletin* from the Missionary Research Library, 15 June 1959, pp. 1-7.

Jones, Richard G. "Towards a New Theology of Mission?" *London Quarterly and Holbein Review* 192, 6th Series, 35 (January 1967): 53-63.

Kessler, J. B. A., Jr. "Hindrances to Church Growth." *International Review of Missions* 57 (July 1968) : 298-303.

Kietzman, Dale W. "Conversion and Culture Change." *Practical Anthropology* 5 (September-December 1958): 203-10.

Kitchen, L. Clayton. "Discussion on Evangelism." *Occasional Papers,* Department of Missionary Studies, World Council of Churches, Series III, No. 6, September 1965, pp. 1-5.

Klaiber, Jeffrey L. "Pentecostal Breakthrough." *America,* 31 January 1970, pp. 99-102.

Koops, Hugh A. "Toward the Holy City." Parts I and III. *Reformed Journal,* October 1966, pp. 8-12, and December 1966, pp. 16-21.

Krass, A. C. "A Case Study in Effective Evangelism in West Africa." *Church Growth Bulletin,* September 1967, pp. 1-4.

Kubler, George A. "Cities and Culture in the Colonial Period in Latin America." *Diogenes* 18 (Fall 1964) : 53-62.

"Latin America: The Urban Guerrilla." *Time,* 19 September 1969.

Lewis, Oscar. "La Cultura de Vecindad en la Ciudad de México." *Ciencias Políticas y Sociales.* Revista de la Escuela Nacional de Ciencias Políticas y Sociales. Universidad Nacional Autónoma de México, V (July-September 1959), 349-64.

Lindsell, Harold. "The Crisis of the Church." *Christianity Today,* 11 September 1970, pp. 4-6.

Lleras, Alberto. "El Monstruo de la Urbanización." *Visión*, 11 April 1969, p. 19.

Lores, Ruben. "A New Day." *World Vision Magazine*, May 1971, pp. 8-10.

Luzbetak, Louis J. "Christo-Paganism." *Practical Anthropology* 13 (May-June 1966): 115-21, 128.

Lyall, Leslie T. "Missionary Strategy in the Twentieth Century." *Evangelical Missions Quarterly* 2 (Winter 1966): 65-79.

MacDonald, Gordon. "What Mission Strategy Is and Does." *Evangelical Missions Quarterly* 8 (Fall 1971): 1-6.

MacEoin, Gary. "Neocolonialism in Latin America." *Christian Century*, 2 June 1971, pp. 685-97.

McGavran, Donald A. "Bring in the Vacuum Cleaner: The Right Way to Say It." *Church Growth Bulletin*, May 1971, pp. 147-48.

————. "Church Growth Strategy Continued." *International Review of Missions* 57 (July 1968): 335-43.

————. "Comments." *Church Growth Bulletin*, September 1967, pp. 5-6.

————. "Does Gospel Radio Grow Churches?" *Church Growth Bulletin*, September 1965, pp. 10-11.

————. "Essential Evangelism—An Open Letter to Dr. J. C. Hoekendijk." *Occasional Papers*, Department of Missionary Studies, World Council of Churches, Series III, No. 2, June 1964, pp. 1-10.

————. "One Goal or Many?" *World Vision Magazine*, October 1966, pp. 9, 28.

————. "Radio and Church Growth." *Church Growth Bulletin*, November 1969, pp. 17-18.

————. "Urban Church Planting." *Church Growth Bulletin*, January 1970, pp. 37-38.

————. "Urban Church Planting and Evangelical Theology." *Church Growth Bulletin*, January 1970, p. 47.

————. "What Can Christians Do About It?" *Church Growth Bulletin*, May 1971, pp. 137-38.

————. "Wrong Strategy: The Real Crisis in Missions." *International Review of Missions* 57 (October 1968): 451-61.

MacKay, John A. "Life's Chief Discoveries." *Christianity Today*, 2 January 1970, pp. 3-5.

Mallon, Vincent T. "Medellin Guidelines." *America*, 31 January 1970, pp. 92-95.

Mangin, William P. "The Role of Regional Association in the Adaptation of Rural Population in Peru." *Sociologus* 9 (1959): 23-35.

Martin, Marie-Louise. "Does the World Need Fantastically Growing Churches?" *International Review of Missions* 57 (July 1968): 311-17.

Michalson, Carl. "Protestant Missionary Obligation at the End of Our Time." *Occasional Bulletin* from the Missionary Research Library, XIV, No. 6 (June 1963): 1-6.

Miller, Donald G. "Toward a Theology of Evangelism," Part II. *Christianity Today,* 27 May 1970, pp. 9-12.

Millon, Rene. "Early Civilizations of the New World." *International Encyclopedia of the Social Sciences.* Edited by David L. Sills. New York: Macmillan Co. and Free Press, 1968. Vol. 16.

Mintz, Sidney. "The Folk-Urban Continuum and the Rural Proletarian Community." *American Journal of Sociology* 61 (September 1953): 136-43.

Moffett, Samuel H. "Self-Containment: A Hindrance to Evangelism in the Church." *Latin America Evangelist,* May-June 1967, pp. 13-14.

————. "What Is Evangelism?" Parts I and II. *Christianity Today,* 22 August 1969, pp. 3-5, and 12 September 1969, pp. 13-14.

Moltmann, Jurgen. "Hacia una Hermeneutica Política del Evangelio." *Cristianismo y Sociedad* 8, Nos. 2 and 3 (1970): 23-42.

Money, Herbert. "Protestantism in Latin America: Peru." *Religion in Life* 27 (Winter 1957-58): 24-34.

Monsma, Timothy M. "Is Reformed Christianity Relevant in West Africa?" *The Outlook,* June 1971, pp. 6-10.

Mooneyham, Stanley. "Evangelical Changes in a World of Certainties." *World Vision Magazine,* April 1968, p. 5.

Moraes, Benjamin. "Giant Steps in Brazil." *World Vision Magazine,* May 1971, pp. 14-16.

Morse, Richard M. "Recent Research on Latin American Urbanization: A Selective Survey with Commentary." *Latin American Research Review* 1 (Fall 1965): 35-74.

Murray, J. S. "What We Can Learn from the Pentecostal Churches." *Christianity Today,* 9 June 1967, pp. 10-12.

Negen, Gordon. "Reformed Strategy for Ministry in the Inner City." *Reformed Journal,* December 1968, pp. 16-17.

Neighbour, Ralph, Jr. "Don't Let a Building Be a Burden." *Baptist Program,* July 1971, pp. 6-7.

Neill, Stephen. "Conversion." *Church Growth Bulletin,* May 1971, p. 145.

Neiswender, Don. "Scripture and Culture in the Early Church." *Christianity Today,* 10 November 1967, pp. 7-8.

"News of Religion: Graham Suggests Extraordinary Steps." *Presbyterian Journal,* 5 May 1971, pp. 4-5.

Nida, Eugene A. "African Influence in the Religious Life of Latin America." *Practical Anthropology* 13 (July-August 1966): 133-38.

————. "Christo-Paganism." *Practical Anthropology* 8 (January-February 1961): 1-14.

————. "Communication of the Gospel to Latin Americans." *Practical Anthropology* 8 (July-August 1961): 145-56.

————. "The Indigenous Churches in Latin America." *Practical Anthropology* 8 (May-June 1961): 97-105.

————. "Mariology in Latin America." *Practical Anthropology* 4, No. 3 (May-June 1957): 69-82; reprinted in Supplement, 1960, pp. 1-15.

————. "The Relationship of Social Structure to the Problem of Evangelism in Latin America." *Practical Anthropology* 5 (May-June 1958): 101-23.

"Notes Evangelical Appeal to Chile." *Christian Century,* 17 October 1956, p. 1205.

Ogawa, Matthew S., and Rossman, Vern. "Evangelism Through the Mass Media and Audio Visual Materials." *International Review of Missions* 50 (October 1961): 417-29.

Ogletree, Thomas W. "The Secular City as a Theological Norm." *Religion in Life* 36 (Summer 1967): 202-15.

Olaya, Noel. "Unidad Cristiana y Lucha de Clases." *Cristianismo y Sociedad* 8, Nos. 3 and 4 (1970): 61-68.

Padilla, C. René. "A Steep Climb Ahead for Theology in Latin America." *Evangelical Missions Quarterly* 7 (Winter 1971): 99-106.

Paradise, Scott I. "A Tale of Two Cities: The Industrial Missions in Sheffield and Detroit." *Religion in Life* 31 (Winter 1961-62): 33-40.

Parsons, Anne. "The Pentecostal Immigrants: A Study of an Ethnic Central City Church." *Practical Anthropology* 14 (November-December 1967): 249-66.

Perkins, Roger D. "Sufficient Attention to the Masses." *Church Growth Bulletin,* September 1967, p. 8.

Pieters, Albertus. "The Final Cause of World Missions." *Church Herald,* 26 February 1965, pp. 12-13, 28.

Plaza, Galo. "Next Decade Better for Latin America." *The News,* Mexico City, 17 December 1969, p. 34.

————. "Opening to the Future." *America,* 31 January 1970, pp. 96-98.

Poethig, Richard P. "Background of the Committee on Industrial Life and Vocations, the United Church of Christ in the Philippines." Committee on Industrial Life and Vocations, Manila, Philippines, n.d. (Mimeographed.)

————. "An Outline of Strategy for City and Town Churches." Committee on Industrial Life and Vocations, Manila, Philippines, n.d. (Mimeographed.)

Poulson, E. N. "Every Thirteen Story Building a Parish." *Church Growth Bulletin,* January 1970, pp. 45-46.

Program and Project Management. Mexico City: Alfa Omega Publicidad, S.A., n.d. Brochure, 14 pp.

Ratz, Calvin C. "American Affluence Redirected." *World Vision Magazine,* May 1970, p. 5.

Read, William, and Bennett, Charles. "Urban Explosions: The Challenge in Latin America." *World Vision Magazine,* June 1969, pp. 5-11.

Rembao, Alberto. "Latin-American Variations on the Protestant Theme." *Religion in Life* 18 (Spring 1949): 199-210.

————. "The Reformation Comes to Hispanic America." *Religion in Life* 27 (Winter 1957-58): 45-53.

Roeda, Jack H. *Mass Communication Center.* Grand Rapids: Christian Reformed Board of Foreign Missions, 1970. Brochure, 4 pp.

Sabanes, Carlos. "Urbanization in Latin America." *International Review of Missions* 55 (July 1966): 307-12.

Santa Ana, Julio de. "Los Cristianos, Las Iglesias y El Desarrollo." *Cristianismo y Sociedad* 7, No. 4 (1969); 51-72.

―――. "Notas para una Etica de la Liberacion (A Partir de la Biblia)." *Cristianismo y Sociedad* 8, Nos. 3 and 4 (1970): 43-60.

Savage, Peter. "A Bold Move for More Realistic Theological Training." *Evangelical Missions Quarterly,* Winter 1969, pp. 65-73.

―――. "Protestantism in Latin America Today." *Christian Heritage,* November 1968, pp. 26-29.

Schemper, Chester. *The Birth of a Church: Only God Could Do It.* Grand Rapids: Board of Foreign Missions of the Christian Reformed Church, 1971. (Promotional material.)

Scherer, James A. "The Service of Theology to World Mission Today." *Occasional Bulletin* from the Missionary Research Library, February 1963, pp. 1-11.

Schippey, Frederick A. "The Changing Fortunes of Urban Protestantism." *Religion in Life* 18 (Autumn 1949): 523-32.

Schoonenberg, Piet. "The Tasks of Theology Faced with Secularization." *Lumen Vitae* 24, No. 2 (1969): 252-60.

Schroeder, W. W. "The Secular City: A Critique." *Religion in Life* 35, (Autumn 1966): 504-12.

Schut, James. "New Horizons for Smaller Congregations." *Church Herald,* 23 January 1970, pp. 12-13, 22-23.

Schuurman, L. "Priesters van de Derde Wereld—II." *Gereformeerd Weekblad,* 14 May 1971, pp. 315-16.

Shaull, Richard. "La Forma de la Iglesia en la Nueva Diáspora." *Cristianismo y Sociedad* 2, No. 6 (1964): 3-17.

―――. "Protestantism in Latin America: Brazil." *Religion in Life* 27 (Winter 1957-58): 5-14.

Shepherd, Norman. "What Church Does Dr. Van Til Belong To?" *Presbyterian Guardian,* May 1971, pp. 70-72.

Smedes, Lewis B. "The Theology of the Secular City." *Reformed Journal,* April 1966, pp. 3-4.

Smith, Don K. "No Magic in the Media." *World Vision Magazine,* May 1970, pp. 8-10.

Stafford, Russell; Conn, Howard; and Villaume, William J. "Church and City: The Challenge of the Modern Urban Congregation." *Religion in Life* 24 (Autumn 1955): 483-515.

Stockwell, B. Foster. "Lights and Shades in Latin-American Missions." *Religion in Life* 19 (Winter 1949-50): 61-129.

―――. "Protestantism in Latin America: Argentina and Uruguay." *Religion in Life* 27 (Winter 1957-58): 15-23.

Strachan, R. Kenneth. "A Further Comment." *International Review of Missions* 53 (April 1964): 209-15.

————. "Call to Witness." *International Review of Missions* 53 (April 1964): 191-200.
Strimple, Robert B. "Theology for Revolution." *Presbyterian Journal,* 5 May 1971, pp. 9-10.

Thiessen, Abe. "Using the Media: An Imperative for the Church." *World Vision Magazine,* May 1970, pp. 11-13.
Thiessen, Lois. "We Can Bring Christ's Love to These Neglected Children." *Latin America Evangelist,* March-April 1970, pp. 9-11.
Thompson, Cecil. "Industrial Evangelism." *Religion in Life* 21 (Summer 1952): 356-66.
Tippett, A. R. "The Components of Missionary Theory." *Church Growth Bulletin,* September 1969, pp. 1-3.
Troutman, Charles H. "Evangelicals and the Middle Classes in Latin America." *Evangelical Missions Quarterly* 7 (Winter 1971): 79-91.
Tyson, Reuel. "Urban Renewal in the Holy City." *Anglican Theological Review* 48 (1966): 78-88.

Van Katwyk, Peter L. "The Sense of Displacement." *Calvinist Contact,* 19 February 1970, p. 1.

Wagner, C. Peter. "Reshaping Missions." *World Vision Magazine,* May 1967, pp. 13-15.
Warren, Max. "Church Growth Day After Tomorrow." *Church Growth Bulletin,* May 1965, pp. 1-3.
Webber, George W. "Training for Urban Mission." *International Review of Missions* 56 (April 1967): 173-79.
White, Herb. "Community Action Training Program Begins in Seoul." *Notes on Urban-Industrial Mission,* Institute on Church in Urban-Industrial Society, March 1970, pp. 4-5.
Wickham, E. R. "Guest Editorial." *International Review of Missions* 55 (July 1966): 269-72.
Winter, Ralph. "A Revolution Goes into Orbit." *World Vision Magazine,* November 1970, pp. 14-16.
————. "Jesuits Yes, Presbyterians No!" *Church Growth Bulletin,* May 1970, pp. 61-66.
Wonderly, William L. "Pagan and Christian Concepts in a Mexican Indian Culture." *Practical Anthropology* 5 (July-August 1958): 197-202.
————. "Social Science Research and the Church in Latin America." *Practical Anthropology* 14 (July-August 1967): 161-73.
————. "The Indigenous Background of Religion in Latin America." *Practical Anthropology* 14 (November-December 1967): 241-48.
————. "Urbanization: The Challenge of Latin America in Transition." *Practical Anthropology* 7 (September-October 1960): 205-9.

Yoshioka, Shigeru. "The Goal of Missions." *International Reformed Bulletin,* No. 35, October 1968, pp. 13-19.

Young, John M. L. "Theology of Missions, Covenant-centered." *Christianity Today,* 22 November 1968, pp. 10-13.

Interviews

Converts to Evangelical Christianity. Forty-eight interviews with persons converted in the decade between 1960 and 1970, Mexico City, 1968-1970.

Currola, M. M. Pastor, First Baptist Church, Chihuahua, Mexico, Ciudad Juarez, 3 June 1969.

Gaxiola, Manuel J. Meeting of Church Growth Study Committee, Mexico City, 20 November 1969.

—————. Telephone conversation, Mexico City, 9 June 1971.

Haro, Efren Robles. Personal interview, Mexico City, June 1971.

Industrial Workers and Their Families. Personal Interviews, Colonia Isidro Fabela, Mexico City, 1969-1970.

Isais, Juan M. Personal interview, Mexico City, 9 June 1971.

López, Moisés M. Private interviews, Mexico City, 7 February 1968, and June 1971.

Luz del Mundo (Light of the World Movement). Interview with eight members, Colonia Provincia, Guadalajara, 17 April 1970.

Manual Laborers. Personal interviews, Mexico City, 1960-1970.

Martínez, Samuel. Methodist pastor. Private interview, Ciudad Juárez, Chihuahua, Mexico, 3 June 1969.

Mohrlang, Roger. Wycliffe Bible translator; Nigeria. Personal interview, Ft. Worth, Tex., 24 May 1971.

Pastors and Church Committees. Personal interviews and questionnaires completed by interviewers on twenty churches, Mexico City, 1969-1971.

Rozales, José. Baptist minister. Private interview, Ciudad Juárez, Chihuahua, Mexico, 3 June 1969.

Schemper, Chester. Personal interview, Ft. Worth, Tex., 17 May 1971.

Shack-builders. Personal interviews with four shack-builders, Colonial Arenal, Mexico City, May 1970.

Stewart, Donald. Wycliffe Bible translator; Mexico. Personal interview Ft. Worth, Tex., 24 May 1971.

Tetsch, Fredrich. Interview, 12 May 1968, Airmail from God Mission. Cuautla, Morelos, Mexico.

Miscellaneous and Unpublished Materials

Baltodano, Rafael. "Informe Especial sobre las Asambleas Familiares Católicas en Colombia." *En Marcha Internacional,* San José, Costa Rica. (Mimeographed.)

Bridges, Julian Curtis. "A Study of the Number, Distribution, and Growth of the Protestant Population in Mexico." Unpublished M.A. thesis, University of Florida, 1969.

Chicago Area Group on Latin America. "Communique to the Press by Priests Taking Part in a Work Meeting Concerning 'Participation of Christians in Building of Socialism.'" *CAGLA,* June 1971. (Mimeographed.)

Church Growth Seminar, Winona Lake, Indiana. "Problems Related to Church Growth and Possible Solutions in the Hispanic World." Findings of the Area Discussion Groups. Winona Lake, Ind., 1967. (Mimeographed.)

Committee on Industrial Life and Vocations. *The Church Serves a Changing Philippines.* Report of the committee. Manila, Philippines: United Church of Christ in the Philippines, 1965.

Eudaly, Nathan Hoyt. "A Critical Evaluation of Leadership for Baptist Churches in Spanish America." Unpublished DRE dissertation, Southwestern Baptist Theological Seminary, Ft. Worth, Tex., 1959.

The Evangelical Alliance Mission. "Chugg-Larson Report to TEAM's 1970 Conference on Their Church Planting Study Trip to Central America." San Cristobal, Venezuela, 1970. (Mimeographed.)

Frankfurt Declaration on the Fundamental Crisis in Christian Mission. Issued by the Theological Convention, 4 March 1970, Frankfurt, West Germany.

Frett, Calvin F. "Discipling Urban Populations." Paper prepared for the Inter-Mission Conference, Taejon, Korea, 21-25 June 1971. (Mimeographed.)

Gammage, Albert W., Jr. "Contemporary Views of Revolution and the Church in Historical Perspective." Fort Worth, Tex., 1971. (Mimeographed.)

Greenway, Roger S. Personal notebook. Mexico City Missions, 1968-1970.

Hoogshagen, Searle. "Notes on the Indigenous Church." (Mimeographed.)

————. Personal letter, 12 April 1970.

————. Personal letter, December 1970.

Huegel, Frederick J. "Thirty Years with the Firemen." Typewritten account of evangelism among Mexico City firemen.

Huegel, John E. "A Bridge into Mexico." Report of Evangelical Churches in Ciudad Juarez, prepared for Disciples of Christ, El Paso, Tex., 1963. (Mimeographed.)

————. Personal letter, 12 March 1971.

Larson, Kenneth W., and Chugg, Norman. Letter, 27 December 1970. (Letter is on stationery of Instituto Biblico Ebenezer, San Cristóbal, Tachira, Venezuela. Larson's signature appears above both their names.)

Loffler, Paul. "Promesa y Desafio de la Evangelización Urbana-Industrial." Undated. (Mimeographed.)

Lores, Ruben. "Algunas Reflexiones en Torno a Los Fundamentos Teológicos de Evangelismo a Fondo." 9 pp. (Mimeographed.)

McGavran, Donald A. Personal letter, 30 May 1968.

Macin, Raul A. Personal letter describing the work of ISAL (Iglesia y Sociedad en la América Latina) in Mexico, 20 May 1971.

Marcus, Abraham. Personal letter, 24 January 1971.

Murphy, Eduard F. "La Influencia de la Cultura en el Crecimiento de las Iglesias." Bogotá, Colombia, n.d. (Mimeographed.)

Penton, Marvin James. "Mexico's Reformation: A History of Mexican Protestantism from Its Inception to the Present." Unpublished Ph.D. dissertation, State University of Iowa, 1965.

Poethig, Richard P. *Guidelines for an Urban-Industrial Ministry.* Manila: Committee on Industrial Life and Vocations, 1966.

———. *Learning Through Participation.* Manila: Committee on Industrial Life and Vocations, 1967.

———. Personal letter, 29 March 1971.

———. *Teaching Material for Urban-Industrial Training.* Supplement to the United Church Letter. Manila: Committee on Industrial Life and Vocations, 1967.

———. "Urban Mission in Southeast Asia." Report of the Committee on Industrial Life and Vocations, East Asia Christian Council. [Manila]: 1 July 1970. (Mimeographed.)

"Proyecto del Presbiterio Azteca." Mexico City, 1970. (Mimeographed.)

Roberts, Larry. Circular letter, 27 January 1971.

———. Personal letter, 2 February 1971.

Roberts, W. Dayton. "La Teología del Evangelismo y de 'Evangelismo a Fondo.' " 13 pp. (Mimeographed.)

Roeda, Jack. Personal letter, 24 January 1971.

———. Personal letter, 15 March 1971.

Symanowski, Horst. "El Domingo en una Mision Industrial." Monterrey, Mexico, n.d. (Mimeographed.)

United Nations Economic Commission for Latin America. *Population Trends and Policy Alternatives in Latin America.* Conference Document. Fourth Session, Santiago, Chile, 28 April-8 May 1971. United Nations, N.Y., 1971.

Werning, Waldo J. "The Theological Task Today for the Church's Mission to Win the World for Christ." Presented to the Illinois and Wisconsin All-Lutheran Campus Pastors' Conference at Milwaukee, Wis., 27 November 1969, and at the Convocation at Concordia Seminary, Springfield, Ill., 22 November 1969. 18 pp. (Mimeographed.)

Zapata, Rene. Personal letter, 28 April 1970.

Zylstra, Bernard. "The Kingdom of God." Paper presented at the Christian Reformed Ministers' Institute, Grand Rapids, 1-3 June 1971, and at the Pre-Synodic Conference for Reformed Presbyterian Ministers and Elders, Beaver Falls, Pa., 10-12 June 1971. 18 pp. (Mimeographed.)

———. "The Place of Christianity in Our Times." University of Toronto, 21 March 1970. (Mimeographed.)

INDEX

275

DATE DUE

OCT 26 '78			
MAR 7 '84			
APR 4 '84			
MAY 2 '84			
FEB 26 '86			
MAR 26 '86			
FEB 4 '87			